Truth is not necessarily stranger than fiction. But sometimes, it can be a good deal more gruesome. And much, much, scarier . . .

The killings that commenced in February 1926 were of a frighteningly different order from the gangland carnage of the day. The victims were ordinary women—most of them middle-aged but some significantly younger—who were savagely slain in their homes. Often, their strangled and outraged corpses were discovered in bizarre hiding places—shoved into steamer trunks, thrust under beds, crammed behind basement furnaces.

The American public had never known anything like it. . . .

BESTIAL

Praise for the true-crime masterpieces of HAROLD SCHECHTER

THE A–Z ENCYCLOPEDIA OF SERIAL KILLERS

by Harold Schechter and David Everitt

"This grisly tome will tell you all you ever wanted to know (and more) about everything from 'Axe Murderers' to 'Zombies'. . . . Schechter knows his subject matter. . . ."
—Mark Graham, *Rocky Mountain News* (Denver)

"The ultimate reference on this fascinating phenomenon."
—*PI Magazine*

DEPRAVED
The Shocking True Story of America's First Serial Killer

"A meticulously researched, brilliantly detailed and above all riveting account of Dr. H. H. Holmes, a nineteenth-century serial killer who embodies the ferociously dark side of America's seemingly timeless preoccupations with ambition, money and power. Schechter has done his usual sterling job in resurrecting this amazing tale."

—Caleb Carr, bestselling author of *The Alienist*

"An astonishing piece of popular history. I unhesitatingly recommend [it] . . . to round out your understanding of the true depth, meaning and perversity on the uniquely American brand of mayhem."

—*The Boston Book Review*

"This is *must* reading for crime buffs. *Depraved* demonstrates that sadistic psychopaths are not a modern-day phenomenon. . . . Gruesome, awesome, compelling reporting."

—Ann Rule

"Destined to be a true-crime classic. . . . As chilling as *The Silence of the Lambs* and as bloodcurdling as the best Stephen King novel. . . . It will deprive you of sleep, and take your attention away from everything else on your schedule until you finish it."

—David Forsmark, *Flint* (MI) *Journal*

BESTIAL

The Savage Trail of a
True American Monster

HAROLD SCHECHTER

POCKET STAR BOOKS
New York   London   Toronto   Sydney   Tokyo   Singapore

An *Original* Publication of POCKET BOOKS

A Pocket Star published by
POCKET BOOKS, a division of Simon & Schuster Inc.
1230 Avenue of the Americas, New York, NY 10020

ISBN: 0671-73219-6

First Pocket Books printing October 1998

10 9 8 7 6 5 4 3 2 1

POCKET and colophon are registered trademarks of
Simon & Schuster Inc.

Front cover photo courtesy of AP/Wide World Photos

Printed in the U.S.A.

This book is lovingly dedicated
(at long last) to my niece,
Ilene Schlanger

The ape, vilest of beasts, how like to us.

Cicero, *De Natura Deorum*

BESTIAL

PROLOGUE

✝

We tend to think of serial murder as a symptom of our own alarmingly violent age—and there's some truth to this perception.

To be sure, homicidal maniacs have existed in all times and places. Historians of crime can cite a host of premodern monsters—human predators whose atrocities easily match (and often surpass) those of Jeffrey Dahmer, John Wayne Gacy, and Richard "The Night Stalker" Rodriguez. The anonymous madman known as Jack the Ripper, for example, may be the most celebrated sex-murderer of the nineteenth century, but he was certainly not the only one. His Gallic counterpart, Joseph Vacher, dubbed "The French Ripper," butchered a dozen victims before his arrest in 1897; while in our own country, the "Archfiend," Dr. H. H. Holmes, committed an indeterminate number of homicides during the same period. (He confessed to twenty-seven.) In the post–World War I era, the German sociopath Fritz Haarmann, the notorious "Vampire of Hanover," perpetrated some of the most unspeakable crimes of the century, including the mutilation-murder of at least fifty young boys.

Clearly, in the realm of sexual homicide, as in all other areas of human experience, there is no new thing under the sun.

Still, it is only in recent years that the problem has become so severe that certain writers on the subject bandy words like plague and epidemic. While this language smacks of hyperbole (not to say hysteria), it remains true that these crimes have increased at an unsettling rate. As much as any movie star or media celeb, the serial killer—the psychopathic monster masquerading behind a façade of bland normality—has become one of the defining symbols of our day.

A chart put together by criminologist Ron Holmes, which lists every American serial killer of the twentieth century, confirms the point. The list contains only 18 names for the first four decades of the century. By contrast, in the years since 1970 alone, there are over 120—and that doesn't count the ones who haven't been caught.

Indeed, the term "serial killer" wasn't even coined until the mid-1970s (by FBI criminologist Robert K. Ressler. Before then, serial murder was so rare that it wasn't perceived as a separate category of crime. Before then, in fact, it was so rare that, when one of these lust-killers went on a spree, the police often couldn't tell what they were dealing with.

That was certainly the case in the 1920s. In the latter years of that decade, the country was shocked by a string of killings that seemed almost inconceivably brutal. This is not to say that Americans of that era were unfamiliar with vicious crimes. On the contrary, it was a time so rife with violence that one historian has dubbed it "The Lawless Decade." But the murders that made the headlines tended to involve tommy guns, bootleggers, and victims with nicknames like Bloody Angelo, Little Mike, and Tony the Gentleman.

The killings that commenced in February 1926 were of a frighteningly different order from the gangland carnage of the day. The victims were ordinary women, most of them middle-aged but some significantly younger, who were savagely slain in their homes. Often, their strangled and outraged corpses were discovered in bizarre hiding places—shoved into steamer trunks, thrust under beds, crammed behind basement furnaces.

The American public had never known anything like it. Other murders may have received more publicity (like the sensational 1922 double slaying of the Reverend Edward Wheeler Hall and his choir-singer mistress, Mrs. Eleanor

Mills, whose corpses were found, amid a scattering of love letters, in a New Jersey orchard). But none provoked greater horror. There seemed to be a monster on the loose. Nowadays, we know what to call such creatures—but back then, the phrase "serial killer" was still fifty years in the future. To the terrified citizens of the time, the unknown maniac—roaming from city to city, selecting his victims at random—seemed like something from a horror story, say, by Edgar Allan Poe.

Indeed, in certain grisly regards, the killer's m.o. bore a chilling resemblance to the horrors in one of Poe's most famous tales, "The Murders in the Rue Morgue." The victims in that story are a pair of Parisian women, a widowed mother and her grown daughter, who are hideously murdered in their apartment. The mysterious assailant, a being of prodigious strength, disposes of the daughter's body by stuffing it feet first up the chimney.

Thanks to the deductive brilliance of Poe's hero, C. Auguste Dupin (the fictional forerunner of Sherlock Holmes), the culprit is ultimately identified. He—or, rather, it—turns out to be an ape: more specifically, a "large, tawny Ourang-Outang" that has escaped from its owner, a French seaman who has brought the creature back from Borneo as a pet.

The true-life horrors that started in the winter of '26 seemed like the frightening realization of these imaginary crimes—women murdered in their homes by a creature of appalling strength and savagery; corpses wedged into tiny spaces in a grotesque effort at concealment. It was as if the homicidal simian dreamed up by Poe had come terrifyingly to life.

Perhaps it was for this reason that an unknown reporter, writing about the killer in a West Coast tabloid, tagged him with an epithet that would send tremors of apprehension from one end of the American continent to the other: the "Gorilla Man."

Eventually the "Gorilla Man" would be captured. But not before he had completed an odyssey that carried him across the country and up into Canada. Along the way, he left a trail of corpses: twenty-two victims, all but one of them female, ranging in age from eight months to sixty-six years.

* * *

They say that truth is stranger than fiction but, in this case, that cliché doesn't stand up. After all, what could be more bizarre than Poe's story of a double murder committed by an Ourang-Outang?

On the other hand, the murderous monkey of Poe's famous fantasy dispatched a total of two victims. By contrast, the true-life "Gorilla Man" did away with nearly two *dozen*—setting a ghastly record that would not be broken until the advent of beings like Ted Bundy, Ottis Toole, and Henry Lee Lucas. It would seem that even an imagination as morbid as Poe's couldn't conceive of the horrors that would become commonplace in our own century.

If there's a lesson to be learned from the appalling life of the "Gorilla Man," it may simply be this: Truth is not necessarily stranger than fiction. But sometimes it can be a good deal more gruesome—and much, *much* scarier.

PART 1

✝

THE NAME
OF THE BEAST

Part 1

The Name of the Beast

1

It was not claimed that Durrant was insane, yet that there was something morally defective in his make-up is apparent. Cases like his do not, most happily, often occur, but their occurrence is frequent enough to show that "man is joined to the beasts of the field by his body," and may become something worse than a beast of prey, when he flings aside conscience, love of humanity and God, and resolves, no matter at the expense of what crimes, to gratify his bestial tendencies.

Matthew Worth Pinkerton,
Murder in All Ages (1898)

To all outward appearances, Theodore Durrant ("Theo" to his friends) was a fine, upstanding specimen of young American manhood. A bright and personable twenty-three-year-old who still lived at home with his parents, he spent his weekdays pursuing his M.D. at San Francisco's Cooper Medical College. When he wasn't engaged in his studies, he could generally be found at the Emanuel Baptist Church on Bartlett Street, where he served as assistant superintendent of the Sunday School, church librarian, and secretary of the Young People's Society. His sense of civic duty seemed as strong as his Christian devotion. In addition to his other activities, he was a member of the California militia signal corps.

He was good-looking to boot: tall, trim, and athletic, with

7

an erect carriage and fine, almost feminine, features—high cheekbones, full mouth, big, blue eyes. True, some of his acquaintances found the cast of those eyes slightly disconcerting. In certain lights, they seemed pale to the point of glassiness, "fishlike" (in the words of one contemporary).

Still, Theodore Durrant cut a handsome, even dashing, figure. Women tended to find him deeply attractive. To a striking degree, he had a good deal in common with another clean-favored psychopath, born fifty years later, with whom he shared a name: Theodore Bundy.

To be sure, even before Durrant's monstrous nature was revealed to the world, a few of his intimates had caught glimpses of his dark side. To one companion, he bragged of his visits to the brothels of Carson City. To another, he described the time when he and three acquaintances, a trio of hard-drinking railroad workers, had assaulted an Indian woman.

Still, his friends weren't especially troubled by these confessions. Even a paragon like Theo needed to sow his wild oats. And the rape victim, after all, had only been a squaw.

Among the respectable young women who were irresistibly drawn to Theo Durrant was an eighteen-year-old named Blanche Lamont. A student at the Powell Street Normal School, where she was training for a career as a teacher, Lamont—a striking blonde with an eye-catching figure—was a relative newcomer to San Francisco, having arrived from Montana in 1894. She had moved into the home of her elderly aunt, a widow named Noble. Sometime shortly after settling into her new life, Blanche Lamont met and became enamored of the charming young medical student, Theo Durrant.

On the afternoon of April 3, 1895, following a full day in the classroom, Blanche emerged from the Powell Street school to find Durrant waiting for her on the sidewalk. Witnesses saw the couple board a trolley, then disembark in the neighborhood of the Emanuel Baptist Church. An elderly woman who lived directly across from the red, wooden church observed the handsome young pair enter the building at precisely 4:00 P.M.

It was the last time Blanche Lamont was seen alive.

When her niece failed to return home that evening, Mrs.

Noble contacted the police. The next day, having learned of Blanche's friendship with Durrant, several officers showed up at his home to question him. Durrant's response to the girl's disappearance was slightly peculiar—he seemed notably indifferent, casually suggesting that she might have been shanghaied by a gang of white slavers.

Still, the officers had no reason to suspect the estimable young man. The newspapers ran a few stories on the case, while the police fruitlessly pursued their investigation. Theo Durrant made a personal visit to Mrs. Noble to offer his own singular brand of reassurance. There was no doubt in his mind, he declared, that Blanche was still alive, though probably imprisoned in a house of prostitution. He would do everything in his power, he vowed, to rescue the poor girl from bondage.

In the meantime, Durrant turned his attentions to another lady friend. She was a petite, twenty-one-year-old brunette named Minnie Williams, who had come to know and love Theo through their shared involvement in the church.

On Good Friday, April 12, 1895—nine days after Blanche Lamont's disappearance—Minnie Williams left her boardinghouse at around 7:00 P.M., informing the landlady that she was going off to attend a meeting of the Young People's Society at the home of its supervisor, Dr. Vogel. She never made it to the gathering. Not far from the Emanuel Baptist Church, she met Theo Durrant. Escorting her to the darkened building, he unlocked the front door with his personal key and led her to the seclusion of the library.

Later that evening, at around 9:30 P.M., Theo showed up by himself at Dr. Vogel's house. The young man's normally pallid complexion was even whiter than usual, his hair was dishevelled, his brow beaded with sweat. Explaining that he had been stricken with a sudden bout of dyspepsia, Durrant hurried to the bathroom. When he emerged a while later, he appeared completely recovered.

The rest of the evening passed so pleasantly that Theo was sorry to see it end. Still, it had been a tiring day and he needed some sleep—particularly since he was scheduled to leave town early the next morning on an outing with the signal corps. They were heading for Mount Diablo, fifty miles from the city.

Durrant and his fellow volunteers had already reached their destination when several middle-aged ladies arrived at the Emanuel Baptist Church the following day, April 13, 1895, to decorate it for Easter. After completing their task, they repaired to the church library and immediately spotted a reddish-brown trail that led to a closed-off storage room. One of the women pulled open the door, let out a shriek, and fainted. Others ran into the street, crying for the police.

The sight that had sent them screaming from the church was Minnie Williams' mutilated corpse, sprawled on the floor of the storage room.

The young woman had been subjected to a monstrous assault. The condition of her body was vividly described in a contemporary account.

> Her clothing was torn and disheveled. She had been gagged, and that in a manner indicative of a fiend rather than a man. A portion of her underclothing had been thrust down her throat with a stick, her tongue being terribly lacerated by the operation. A cut across her wrist had severed both arteries and tendons. She had been stabbed in each breast, and directly over her heart was a deep cut in which a portion of a broken knife remained. This was an ordinary silver table-knife, one of those used in the church at entertainments where refreshments were served. It was round at the end, and so dull that great force must have been used to inflict the fearful wounds; indeed, it appeared that the cold-blooded wretch had deliberately unfastened his victim's dress that the knife might penetrate her flesh. The little room was covered with blood.

Later, after examining the young woman's remains, the coroner concluded that Minnie Williams had been raped after death.

This time suspicion fell immediately on Theo Durrant. That suspicion was confirmed when, searching Durrant's bedroom, investigators discovered Minnie Williams' purse stuffed inside the pocket of the suit jacket he had worn to Dr. Vogel's gathering the evening before.

By Sunday morning, the *San Francisco Chronicle* was

openly naming Durrant as the killer, not only of Minnie Williams but of Blanche Lamont as well—even though there was no definitive proof that the latter had been murdered.

But that situation was about to change.

That same morning—Easter Sunday, April 14, 1895—a party of police officers arrived at Emanuel Baptist Church to conduct a search. They had little hope of success. After all, the Lamont girl had been missing for eleven days, and it seemed highly unlikely that a decomposing corpse could have been stashed on the premises without attracting any notice, particularly during the busy week preceding Easter. Still, they wanted to cover every possibility.

After making a thorough, fruitless search of the main part of the building, they ascended to the steeple. Overlooking Bartlett Street, the steeple had a strictly ornamental function, since it housed no bell. In fact, it was completely boarded up from inside. Few members of the church had ever entered it.

As they pushed open the steeple door, however, the investigators were immediately assaulted by a putrid stench. One of the officers struck a match, and its flickering light revealed the source of the fetor.

"Upon the floor of the lower room of the tower, just inside the door," wrote one reporter, "lay the outraged, nude, and bloated remains of what had once been a beautiful and cultivated girl, Blanche Lamont. A glance told the experienced searchers how the unfortunate young lady had met her death. About her neck were blue streaks, the marks of the strong, cruel fingers that had been imbedded in her tender flesh, choking out her young life. The face was fearfully distorted, the mouth being open, exposing the pearly teeth, and attesting the terrible death the poor girl had died."

That the outrage was the work of a medical student seemed confirmed by the singular position of the corpse. Its head "had been raised by placing a piece of wood under it, or 'blocked,' in the parlance of medical students, who so arrange cadavers on the dissection table." As with Minnie Williams, the autopsy revealed that Blanche Lamont had been the victim of a necrophiliac assault.

News of the discovery quickly spread thoroughout the Bay

Area. By noon on that glorious April day, it seemed, one contemporary has recorded, as though "the entire city had poured into the streets. Thousands crowded around the church, while the streets in front of the newspaper offices were packed with masses of humanity, all struggling to get a view of the bulletin boards."

Telegraphs were dispatched to every sheriff's office in the vicinity of Mount Diablo. At 5:00 P.M., the San Francisco police received a message from one of their own, a detective named Anthoney, who had set out from the city as soon as Blanche Lamont's corpse was found. He had tracked down and apprehended Durrant at a place called Walnut Creek, not far from Mount Diablo.

By the time Anthoney and his captive were headed back to San Francisco, the city was in an uproar. An enormous mob assembled at the ferryhouse to await their arrival from Oakland. Only the presence of a large police contingent prevented a lynching.

Durrant's trial, which commenced in September 1895, was a nationwide sensation. For the three weeks of its duration, the courtroom was packed to overflowing, mostly with young women who couldn't seem to get enough of the accused. One pretty, blonde-haired fan—dubbed "The Sweet-Pea Girl" by the press—presented him daily with a bouquet of the flowers.

Much to the dismay of his female admirers—and the disappointment of his lawyers, who did their best to cast suspicion on the church's pastor, the Rev. John George Gibson—it took the jury only five minutes to convict Durrant. He was sentenced to die without delay.

His attorneys, however, managed to postpone his execution for three years. Finally, on January 7, 1898, Durrant was led to the gallows. He died insisting that he was "an innocent boy."

The psychological specialists who examined him, however, had formed a very different opinion, declaring him a "moral idiot." Those who sought explanations for this deficiency in his family background were tantalized by his parents' behavior on the day of his execution.

Immediately after the hanging, the prisoner's corpse was

placed in an open coffin and carried into a waiting room. Durrant's formerly handsome face was a ghastly sight—skin blackened, eyes bulging, tongue jutting grotesquely from his gaping lips.

When his parents arrived to claim the body, a prison official, as a gesture of courtesy, asked if they might not care for some tea. Mr. and Mrs. Durrant leapt at the offer whereupon a tray, loaded not only with tea but with a complete roast-beef-and-potato dinner, was brought into the room.

Then, with their dead child's body stretched out only a few feet away, Theo's parents sat down to enjoy their midday repast. Even the convict who had carried in the tray shook his head in disgust when he overheard Mrs. Durrant ask her husband for a second helping of beef.

Fortified by their meal, Durrant's parents were now faced with a dilemma: how to dispose of their son's corpse. Public detestation of Durrant was so intense that no cemetery would accept him. His parents were finally forced to transport the remains to Los Angeles for cremation.

"The Durrant murders and the shocking disclosures that followed stirred the people of the Pacific coast as nothing did before," wrote one of his contemporaries, "and the rejoicing at his death was almost universal."

Indeed, the people of the Pacific coast had gone to extraordinary lengths to expunge every trace of Durrant's existence. Nothing, not even his corpse, was suffered to remain. By refusing him even a burial plot, the citizenry of San Francisco were sending a message—that creatures like Theo Durrant would never be allowed to defile their fair city.

It's a grim irony then that, even before it had purged itself of one monster, San Francisco had already become the birthplace of another.

He was born there on May 12, 1897, while Durrant's lawyers were mounting a last, desperate effort to save their client from the gallows. Like Durrant he would grow up to take a lively interest in religion (though he would never be mistaken for a choirboy). Their sexual proclivities were similar, too, since they shared a taste for postmortem rape.

There was, however, a major difference between the criminal lives of the two men. Appalling as it was, Durrant's violent career was mercifully brief. It lasted only nine days, the time between his first and final atrocities.

Earle Leonard Nelson would also savage two women—one in San Francisco, one in San Jose—during a nine-day period.

In his case, however, that was only the beginning.

2

The early home life of many serial killers is often one in
which a stable, nurturing atmosphere is sorely lacking.

Donald J. Sears, *To Kill Again*

Earle Leonard Nelson wasn't the kind of child people
cooed over. His only known baby picture—according to one
observer, a writer named Douthwaite—showed "a loose-
mouthed degenerate infant with the abstracted vacancy of
expression which is one of the hallmarks of degeneracy."

Of course, Douthwaite's description owed a great deal to
hindsight. At the time it was written, Nelson had already
grown up to be a monster—a killer so terrifying that, to his
Jazz Age contemporaries, he seemed like a creature of myth.
Homely as it was, Nelson's infant face couldn't possibly have
foretold his future pathology.

Still, there is no doubt that, from a very early age, little
Earle had a deeply unsettling effect upon people. He was
the sort of youngster that parents warn their own children
to stay away from. Not that his peers required such admoni-
tions. They could sense his abnormality all by themselves.

He was only nine and a half months old when his young
mother, Frances, died of syphilis. His father, James, followed
her to the grave seven months later, a victim of the same
disease.

The tiny orphan was taken in by his mother's family and
grew up in the home of his maternal grandmother, Mrs.

Jennie Nelson, a widow in her mid-forties. There were two other youngsters in the household—Mrs. Nelson's surviving children, Willis and Lillian, who were twelve and ten respectively when their older sister, Earle's mother, died.

Little is known about Mrs. Nelson. She appears to have been a hard-pressed, unimaginative woman who sought solace from the burdens of her life in a particularly zealous brand of Protestantism. She instilled in her young charge a lifelong fascination with Scripture, particularly with the apocalyptic visions of the Book of Revelation. If asked, she would have insisted that she felt an unqualified devotion for little Earle. Certainly, she failed to perceive the full extent of his disturbance, though whether her blindness was a function of love or intellectual limitation is impossible to say.

This is not to suggest that she was oblivious to his peculiarities. They were, after all, impossible to miss. From his earliest years, Earle was strikingly different from other children. Often possessed of a manic energy, he would, at other times, slip into a profound melancholy, withdrawing into his darkened room for days. He would sit for hours in a kitchen chair staring blankly into space or roam about the house with his head cocked in a listening attitude, as though attending to voices audible only to himself.

In spite of Mrs. Nelson's efforts to make him presentable, Earle's personal habits bordered on the bizarre. His slovenliness far exceeded the normal negligence of boyhood. On various occasions, he would set out for school wearing freshly laundered garments and return in a different and dreadfully bedraggled outfit, as though he had traded clothes with a street urchin. In the winter, his grandmother would dress him in warm woolen underwear. By the time he reached home, he had somehow contrived to lose it.

His dietary habits were equally eccentric. At dinner, he would drench his food in olive oil, put his face to the plate, and slurp up his meal like a caged beast at feeding time— much to the disgust of his little tablemates, his Uncle Willis and Aunt Lillian. They began referring to their nephew as "The Wild Man of Borneo," the name of a famous freakshow attraction of the time.

Their taunt had no effect on his etiquette, though it seemed to confirm some deep, inner sense of worthlessness.

From his earliest years, Earle would sink into abject moods of self-loathing, an especially disconcerting phenomenon in a child so young. "I am not good for anything," the little boy would sob. "I will never be good for anything. Nobody wants me. I would be better off out of this world."

His grandmother attributed his "morbid disposition" to his early misfortunes. After all, Earle's syphilitic parents had not only left him an orphan but bequeathed him a legacy of degradation and disease. It would have taken a person of far greater insight and sophistication than Mrs. Nelson to see little Earle's peculiarities—his stupors, strange habits, social isolation, and impaired sense of self—for what they were, the signs of an incipient psychosis.

His conduct became even more troubling as he grew older. By the age of seven, he had already been expelled from Agassiz primary school for his uncontrollable behavior. Though he was often passive and withdrawn—avoiding the standard rough-and-tumble squabbles of boyhood—he was subject at other times to wild fits of rage, lashing out violently at his schoolmates, girls as well as boys. He took to stealing small items from neighborhood shops. Before he reached the age of ten, he had acquired a neighborhood reputation as a serious troublemaker, a young boy destined for reform school—or worse.

Mrs. Nelson grew increasingly desperate in her efforts to deal with her grandson. She resorted to physical punishment, though this expedient grew less practical by the year as Earle matured into a deep-chested, broad-shouldered youth with powerful arms and improbably large hands. Knowing his obsession with Scripture, she attempted to appeal to his religious sensibilities, warning that the Lord would surely punish him for his transgressions.

Nothing seemed to work. In her desperation, she took to reminding him that he was living in her home only through her good graces, and that her patience was not without limits. Unless he began to behave more normally, she would cast him into the streets and let him fend for himself.

It is no wonder, then, that Nelson grew up feeling like a perennial outsider. His grandmother's home often seemed less like a loving refuge than a lodging house, a place where he resided not as a cherished family member but as a temporary, barely tolerated guest.

On April 18, 1906, one month before Nelson turned nine, San Francisco was rocked by a massive earthquake measuring 8.25 on the Richter scale. In less than a minute, the awesome tremor, its energy "greater than all the explosives used in World War II" (according to one historian), toppled buildings, buckled streets, and ruptured virtually every water main in the city, leaving the hydrants dry and the firefighters helpless. In the three ensuing days, the city was devastated by a great conflagration. By the time the fire had run its course, almost 500 city blocks lay in ruins, 25,000 buildings were in ashes, and more than 450 lives had been lost.

To the mind of little Earle, steeped as it was in Scripture, the cataclysm seemed like a biblical story, the fall of Jericho or the Lord's vengeance on Sodom and Gomorrah. The sights and sounds and smell of destruction filled him with a strange exhilaration. Like everyone else who lived through the great San Francisco earthquake, he would remember it for the rest of his days, though his imagination tended to linger on one particular facet of the event.

At the height of the catastrophe, the city was swept by rumors of armed marauders who were reportedly outraging women at gunpoint. Earle always would enjoy recalling the fearful look on the faces of his Grandma Jennie and Aunt Lillian, a pretty young woman of nineteen at the time, as they cowered behind the locked door of their house, barricaded against the shadowy prowlers outside.

One year later, while trying to impress some older boys with his daring, Earle raced across the tracks of an oncoming trolley on a beat-up two-wheeler he had inherited from his Uncle Willis. The trolley caught the rear wheel of the bike, and Earle, sent flying, landed headfirst on the cobblestones.

He was carried back home unconscious. His grandmother nearly collapsed when she saw the ghastly wound on his right temple. For nearly a week, the boy slipped in and out of consciousness, raving wildly when he was awake.

Finally, on the evening of the sixth day, his delirium subsided. The family physician, an elderly gentleman named

Monin, peered into Earle's eyes, palpated his wound, and put a few questions to the boy. Then, reaching for Mrs. Nelson's hand, he gave it a comforting squeeze. He assured the anxious woman that she had nothing to worry about. The crisis had passed.

Little Earle, he declared—in what must surely rank as one of the least prescient prognoses in the annals of medicine—would be "just fine."

It would be another ten days before Earle was back on his feet. During his recuperation, his grandmother would sometimes sit at his bedside for hours and read the Bible to him. He especially liked the part in Revelation about the coming of the great beast:

> And I stood upon the sand of the sea, and saw a beast rise up out of the sea, having seven heads and ten horns, and upon his horns ten crowns, and upon his heads the name of blasphemy. And the beast which I saw was like unto a leopard, and his feet were as the feet of a bear, and his mouth as the mouth of a lion: and the dragon gave him his power, and his seat, and great authority. . . . And he causeth all, both small and great, rich and poor, free and bond, to receive a mark in their right hand, or in their foreheads, and that no man might buy or sell, save he that hath the mark, or the name of the beast, or the number of his name.

Before he reached adolescence, Earle had committed this passage to memory. He often mulled over its meaning, trying to puzzle out the identity of the beast. In his deepening mania, he came to believe that this biblical abomination was afoot in the modern world.

Interestingly, there is one connection he seems never to have made. It had to do with his own name. In the history books—books with titles like *Chronicle of Crime, Crimes of the Twentieth Century,* and *A Criminal History of Mankind*—the notorious "Gorilla Murderer" of the 1920s is invariably listed under the name "Earle Leonard Nelson." But "Nelson" was his mother's name, the name he was given when his grandmother took him in. His father's name, the

one Earle was actually born with, was different. It was
Ferral.

Of course, a name is not destiny, though there have always been some who believe otherwise (one of the messianic
delusions of Charles Manson, for example, was that his last
name was actually an anagram of "Son of Man"). Still, it is
a striking coincidence that the little boy who would grow up
to be the dreaded creature known as the "Gorilla Man"
was born with a name so close in spelling, and identical in
pronunciation, to the word *feral.* The dictionary definition
of *feral* is "of or characteristic of a wild animal; brutal." It
derives from the Latin *fera,* meaning "wild beast."

As Earle grew older, he came to identify the great beast
of Revelation first with Pope Benedict XV and later, after
World War I broke out, with Kaiser Wilhelm II.

It seems never to have occurred to him that it was he,
not the pope or the kaiser, who was born with the name of
the beast.

3

✝

He was just like a child, and we considered him like a child,
and of course, we would never go too far with him, because
there was always the fear of him.

Lillian Fabian

Of the members of his grandmother's household, it was
Nelson's Aunt Lillian who cared for him most. She was only
ten when the tiny orphan came to live with her family, and
from the very start, she lavished a sisterly love on the boy.
To the end of his days she stuck by him, even when the rest
of the world proclaimed him a monster. She had a simple
answer for those who expressed wonder at her steady devotion. Earle, she would say, was her "own flesh and blood."

It is a mark of her fidelity that when her mother died in
1908, one year after Earle's near-fatal bike accident, Lillian
assumed the burden of his upbringing. By then, she was
married to a man named Henry Fabian and living in her
own house at 3573 20th Street. For the next seven years—
though Earle would spend stretches of time apart from the
Fabians, either staying with his Uncle Willis or disappearing
to places unknown—he was essentially a member of his
Aunt Lillian's household.

By the age of fourteen he had dropped out of school and
launched into a succession of menial jobs—so many that
even he quickly lost count of them. He worked as a jeweler's
clerk, hash-house cook, window washer, **hotel** porter, car-

penter's assistant, bricklayer, upholsterer, and common laborer, rarely keeping a job for more than a few weeks, often for only a day or two. Though he tended to make a favorable first impression on his employers—he could be polite and well spoken, and his physical strength was evident from the spread of his shoulders and the breadth of his chest—his underlying disturbance never kept itself hidden for long.

A foreman might assign him a simple task, only to discover, twenty minutes later, that Nelson had passed the time staring fixedly skyward, as though riveted by a vision in the air. Or perhaps the peculiar young man, prompted by the secret voices that chattered inside his skull, might simply lay down his tools in the midst of a job and wander off from the worksite, never to return again.

At his best, there was an endearing, puppy-dog quality about Earle—at least in the eyes of his aunt. Protective of him since birth, she perceived him as an overgrown baby. Certainly, there was something infantile in the way he swilled his food at mealtimes, as well as in his fashion sense. Now that he was earning his own money, it was harder than ever to keep him presentable. He might set out for work in clean, decent clothes, only to return later in the day dressed in frayed yellow pants, a baggy red sweater, leather leggings, and a cowboy hat. What he didn't throw away on such outlandish garments, he would squander on trinkets—gaudy dime-store rings, stickpins with paste "diamonds," and cheap, oversized sunglasses.

His bouts of wild enthusiasm, which alternated with periods of sullen withdrawal, could also be as unrealistic as a child's. When his aunt informed him that her brother Willis was planning to construct a three-story apartment house, Earle—who was fifteen at the time—exclaimed, "Why doesn't Uncle Will let *me* build that house? I could do it all myself, do all the plumbing and everything. He would save so much money!" Lillian just smiled and said nothing. She had a clear recollection of the time, one year earlier, when Earle had volunteered to paint the interior of her own house. After working furiously at the job for a day or two, he had disappeared from home and was gone for three weeks.

For all her tenderness of feeling, Earle's freakish behavior could be a source of deep distress to his long-suffering aunt. (How Henry Fabian felt about acquiring—along with a wife—her bizarre, hulking nephew, history does not record.) Lillian found it especially trying when Earle "acted up" around her friends. On several occasions, for example, when company was over for dinner, Earle suddenly looked up from his plate and began spewing obscenities. When Lillian reproached him, he just gave a mischievous grin, then went back to slurping up his food which, as usual, he had soaked in several cups of olive oil.

At other times, Earle would stroll into the kitchen—where Lillian was enjoying a cup of coffee with a female friend—and, without speaking a word, stare at the visitor in such an unsettling way that, after a few minutes, the woman would grab her belongings and hurry away, stammering an excuse to her embarrassed hostess. Or Earle might come walking into the room on his hands, feet flailing in the air, and position himself in front of the startled guest like a circus acrobat. Or he might step behind an empty chair, bend over and clamp his mouth around the wooden backrest, then lift up the chair with his teeth.

It wasn't long before Lillian's acquaintances began making excuses every time she invited them over to the house.

Still, she could not help feeling sorry for Earle. He seemed so vulnerable and friendless—a lost soul. As far as she could tell, he had no companions his own age. Even as he grew into late adolescence—a barrel-chested youth, not especially tall but powerfully built—he sought out the company of much younger children, like little Arthur West who lived two doors down from the Fabian house.

Arthur, nine years old when Earle was fifteen, was in awe of the older boy, who would impress his young admirer by bragging of his exploits in the Barbary Coast or showing off the spoils of his shoplifting. It wasn't long, however, before Arthur's father forbade him, on pain of a hiding, from associating with Earle. The Nelson boy was "deranged," Mr. West declared. Everyone in the neighborhood knew it.

Shut up inside his room for hours on end, Earle would spend much of the time poring over his favorite reading matter. Though his formal education had ended after seventh grade, he grew up to be a voracious consumer of dime detective novels, tabloid newspapers, and the tracts of various occult and pseudoscientific beliefs—phrenology, astronomy, palmistry, spiritualism. And always, of course, the Bible.

Passing by his locked room, Lillian could hear the muffled drone of Earle's voice as he chanted from the Book of Revelation.

> So he carried me away in the spirit into the wilderness: and I saw a woman sit upon a scarlet-colored beast, full of names of blasphemy, having seven heads and ten horns. And the woman was arrayed in purple and scarlet color, and decked with gold and precious stones and pearls, having a gold cup in her hand full of abominations and filthiness of her fornication: and upon her forehead was a name written, MYSTERY, BABYLON THE GREAT, THE MOTHER OF HARLOTS AND ABOMINATIONS OF THE EARTH. And I saw the woman drunken with the blood of the saints, and with the blood of the martyrs of Jesus.

Even as an adolescent, however, Earle had a secret life that Lillian knew nothing about. Possessed of a furious sexual hunger that even his compulsive masturbation could not allay, he was frequenting the brothels of the Barbary Coast by the time he was fifteen. He had also begun drinking heavily. His periodic disappearances—those times when he would vanish from home and return days or even weeks later, claiming he had been out searching for work—were, in reality, given over to drunken debauches, binges of whoring and boozing and brawling.

Though he was a sight when he returned home—his face battered and puffy, his clothes as bedraggled as a derelict's—his aunt never questioned him closely. He was already beyond her control. She had long ago given up any effort to discipline or improve him. With her deep sense of family loyalty, she simply put up with him, though she had good reason by then to wish that Earle would simply go away—move out of her house and never return.

She had two good reasons, actually, named Henry Jr. and Rose. They were Lillian's son and daughter, already in grade school by the time Earle was sixteen. How the children felt about their uncle no one can say. Certainly Earle, in his freakish way, could be generous with them. Sometimes he would empty his pockets after a day's work and, in spite of Lillian's protests, hand out his entire salary, five or six dollars, to the children.

Still, it must have been disturbing to the little ones to see their uncle when he slipped into one of his "moods" and began holding animated conversations with invisible beings, or spouting profanities at the dinner table, or staggering around the house on his hands.

Lillian, of course, was used to Earle's peculiarities. But with two little ones in the house, even her feelings underwent a change. Not that she would ever dream of casting him out of her home. He was her kith and kin, and she would always feel responsible for him. But by seventeen Earle was not just an encumbrance but a threatening presence. And for the first time since he came to live in her household, Lillian was afraid.

4

✝

Well, I have a stronger tendency to seek higher ideals and
sensible things than I used to.

Earle Nelson, interview,
Napa State Hospital, May 1918

Given her nephew's wildly erratic work habits, Lillian
must have wondered where he got his spending money.
Though he rarely managed to hang onto even the most menial job for more than a few weeks, he continued to throw
cash around on his usual indulgences—outlandish clothing,
flashy gimcracks, and a wide assortment of printed trash,
from lurid exposés of white slavery to such pseudoscientific
tomes as Professor William Windsor's *Phrenology Made
Easy*. He was also hitting the bottle harder than ever, returning home some evenings so redolent of booze that he
seemed to have splashed it on like cheap cologne.

Since the logical conclusion was hard to avoid—that her
nephew was deriving his income from an illicit source—it
seems likely that Lillian simply preferred to ignore the truth.
Stubbornly loyal to her "flesh and kin," she did not want
to know the worst about Earle. From the day he was born,
she had helped raise him; he was almost like one of her own
children. A cynic might also surmise that she was motivated
at least partly by another, less selfless motive. After all,
Earle was contributing to his upkeep, and whatever cash
he didn't squander on himself generally ended up in the
household coffers.

As he grew into manhood, moreover, he was becoming increasingly unpredictable and hard to control. Lillian had good reason to fear that her bizarre, brooding nephew might not take kindly to prying. All in all, it was best to leave well enough alone.

Sooner or later, however, the truth was bound to come to light. It happened in the spring of 1915. Just a month or so before, Earle had been hit with one of his periodic spells of wanderlust and had disappeared from home—much to the relief of both Lillian and her husband, who always welcomed these respites from Earle's discomforting presence. Making his way northwards, he supported himself by picking up odd jobs on construction sites and ranches. He was also supplementing his income, as he'd been doing for a while, through petty thievery, shoplifting, and the occasional ransacking of a conveniently untended house.

While passing through Plumas County, a rugged, sparsely populated area in the northeast corner of the state, Earle broke into an isolated cabin and was absconding with some booty just as the owner returned. Earle, who was travelling on foot, took flight into the forest but was apprehended by a posse before he made it across the county line. Two days later, Lillian's self-willed ignorance about Earle's criminal activities ended abruptly when she received a telegraph from the Plumas authorities, notifying her of her nephew's arrest.

At his trial, Lillian testified on his behalf. Her nephew was a "poor, unfortunate boy," she tearfully declared, "orphaned when just a baby." But her plea was unavailing. Deep-chested, thick-muscled, with a prematurely hardened air, Earle didn't seem much like a boy. Besides, he had been caught red-handed.

In the late summer of 1915, just a few months after his eighteenth birthday, Earle Leonard Nelson entered San Quentin prison to begin a two-year sentence for burglarly.

One year earlier, in the Bosnian city of Sarajevo, a nineteen-year-old Serbian nationalist named Gavrilo Princip gunned down a visiting dignitary, the Archduke Franz Ferdinand, heir to the Hapsburg throne, and plunged the Western world into chaos. Less than two months after the assassination, Europe was at war.

The United States declared its neutrality, but during the years of Earle's imprisonment the country was drawn inexorably closer to the maelstrom. In May 1915—the very month of Earle's arrest—a German U-boat torpedoed the British ocean liner *Lusitania* off the southern coast of Ireland, killing nearly 1,200 passengers, including 128 Americans. This "act of piracy" (as former President Theodore Roosevelt branded it) provoked a widespread clamor for war.

President Woodrow Wilson, however, managed to resist the outcry, and in June 1916—just weeks before Earle's first anniversary behind bars—he was renominated by the Democrats under the slogan, "He Kept Us Out of War." By then, however, even Wilson had begun to acknowledge that the United States could not remain "an ostrich with its head in the sand" forever.

The turning point came in February 1917, when Germany launched a ruthless campaign of unrestricted submarine warfare against all shipping, including American merchant vessels. On the third of the month, President Wilson broke diplomatic relations with Germany. Around the same time, the British Secret Service intercepted a coded telegram from the German foreign minister, Dr. Alfred von Zimmermann, to his ambassador in Mexico. Zimmermann, who clearly foresaw America's impending involvement, wanted Mexico to enter the war on Germany's side. In return, the kaiser's government would reward its new ally not only with "generous financial support" but with the reacquisition of Mexico's "conquered" territories—Texas, New Mexico, and Arizona—once the United States suffered its inevitable defeat.

The outrage provoked by the "Zimmermann telegram"—which was blazoned on front pages from coast to coast—proved to be (in the words of one historian) the final nail "in the coffin of American neutrality." Clearly there were no limits to German perfidy. On April 2, 1917, President Wilson, proclaiming that "the world must be made safe for democracy," asked Congress for a declaration of war.

When Earle Leonard Nelson emerged from San Quentin just a few weeks later, George M. Cohan's rousing ditty seemed to be on everyone's lips:

> Over there—over there—
> Send the word, send the word
> Over there—
> That the Yanks are coming,
> The Yanks are coming,
> The drums rum-tumming ev'rywhere!

Like millions of his contemporaries, Earle was infused with patriotic fervor. No sooner was he released from prison than—using his birthname, Ferral—he enlisted as a private in the U.S. Army and was sent to a training camp in northern California.

It would seem, however, that Earle was not cut out for the rigors of military life. Across the sea, millions of young men were enduring the terrors of humanity's first mechanized war—the hell of the trenches, where soldiers wallowed in foul slime while rats gorged on the flesh of the unburied dead; the horror of mustard gas, which left its victims drowning in the bloody fluid that inundated their lungs; the unspeakable mutilations caused by machine-gun fire and artillery shells. As one medical orderly wrote, recalling the aftermath of a typical engagement, "It was difficult to select the most urgent cases. Men had lost arms and legs, brains oozed out of shattered skulls, and lungs protruded from riven chests; many had lost their faces and were, I should think, unrecognizable to their friends. . . . One poor chap had lost his nose and most of his face, and we were obliged to take off an arm, the opposite hand, and extract two bullets like shark's teeth from his thigh, besides minor operations."

For Earle Leonard Ferral, on the other hand, even the most minimal demands of army life proved too onerous. After just six weeks in uniform, he went AWOL because he was forced to stand guard duty one night in the cold.

Among the various religious works Earle had read during his stint in San Quentin was a life of Joseph Smith. Following his desertion, he made his way to Salt Lake City. His interest in Mormonism came to nothing, but—for unknown reasons—he decided to give the military another shot. Enlisting as a cook in the navy, he soon found himself back in his hometown stationed at San Francisco's Mare Island Naval Base.

This second fling at military life, however, turned out to be no more successful nor long-lasting than his first. Once again, he deserted after a few weeks because of chores he regarded as too oppressive.

Less than two months later, however—in July 1917, not long after the first American troops arrived in France—Earle enlisted once again, this time as a private in the Medical Corps. He lasted six weeks, deserting because (as he would later explain to military psychologists) he was bothered by "burning about his anus" from his hemorrhoids.

He was back in the navy in March 1918—around the time that the German army launched a massive assault on the Western Front, where American doughboys were fighting shoulder to shoulder with their French and British allies. This time Earle did not desert; he simply refused to work, preferring to pass his days reading the Bible and spouting apocalyptic prattle about the coming of the Great Beast whose number is 666. Earle found himself shunned by his shipmates and assailed by his superior officers. Nothing, not even a tortuous, two-day confinement inside a stifling coke oven, could force him to fulfill his duties.

On April 24, 1918, after complaining bitterly of headaches and refusing to leave his cot, he was placed in the Mare Island Naval Hospital. After three weeks of observation by a hospital psychologist named Ogden, Ferral was committed to the Napa State Mental Hospital, arriving on May 21, 1918, just nine days after his twenty-first birthday.

In the papers he forwarded to Napa, Ogden summed up his reasons for recommending commitment. The subject, he wrote, "continually reads his testament or gazes fixedly into space; answers questions slowly; takes no interest in what is going on about him; shows some mental deterioration. Due to refusing to work, he was put in coke oven for two days but still would not work. His reason for not working is that he did not want to serve the adversaries of the Lord. He believes the beast spoken of in Revelation as being #666 is either the pope or the kaiser. He does not think he is crazy." Ogden's conclusive diagnosis was "Constitutional Psychopathic State."

* * *

Immediately after his arrival at Napa, Earle was examined by Dr. J. B. Rogers, who would oversee his treatment for the next thirteen months. Physically there seemed to be nothing anomalous about the robust, well-nourished young man except for one ocular peculiarity: his right pupil was notably larger than the left. His teeth were also (as Rogers wrote in his report) "remarkable" in their perfection, so strikingly square and even that they would have been the envy of a matinee idol.

From interviewing Earle, Dr. Rogers learned that the young man had contracted both syphilis and gonorrhea in early adolescence. (Subsequent blood tests confirmed the presence of both diseases.) Earle confessed that he had masturbated daily between the ages of thirteen and eighteen but "not since then." He also claimed to have overcome his "addiction to liquor," swearing that he had not had a drink for seven months. He described his childhood life as "pleasant," insisted that "his mind is all right," and declared that he was perfectly capable of "making his way in the world." He had, he said, no "history of trauma or previous mental attacks."

After putting various pointed questions to the young man for about ten minutes, Rogers concluded that Earle was not disoriented, paranoid, or abnormally depressed. The patient (Rogers wrote in his report) was "correct for place, month, and year—did not think anyone was trying to harm him—was not despondent, nervous, or apprehensive and did not think he should have been sent here. Denied illusions or hallucinations. Cheerful at time of examination. Denies being irritable. Says he approves of sociability very much and enjoys himself to a reasonable extent. Could take an interest in an occupation—is very fond of his family and is so fond of them that he feels bad to be away from home."

"Would you say you've noticed any changes in yourself since joining the navy?" Rogers asked, to which the young man replied, "Well, I have a stronger tendency to seek higher ideals and sensible things than I used to."

Next, Earle was subjected to a battery of intelligence tests, most of which he performed well on. "Test of Memory Pictures in General good," reads Rogers' report. "Memory of Ideas in Series good. Knowledge of Arithmetic excellent.

General Knowledge correct except for the name of the Governor of California and rate of interest a bank usually pays. Memory of Recent Past good. No Disturbance of Idea Association. Orientation good."

When Rogers related the fable about the wolf who disguises himself as a shepherd but gives himself away when he opens his mouth to speak, Earle offered a reasonable summary of the moral: "It shows that when a person is not always truthful they suffer for it."

Earle insisted "that it was not difficult for him to think." When Rogers asked if he "experienced any peculiar thoughts," Earle replied, "Well, not exactly—not any more than a first-class intelligent person would."

"Do you believe you've done anything wrong?" asked Rogers.

"Yes," said Earle. "I blame myself for enlisting in the navy."

Rogers then asked if the young man was afraid of anything.

"Only God," Earle answered. Then, fixing Rogers with a meaningful stare, he said, "If you don't serve Him, you should be afraid, too."

Exactly whose God Earle believed in at the moment is somewhat ambiguous. For unknown reasons, his commitment papers record his affiliation as Jewish. It is possible that Earle, who was always flirting with different religions, was going through a brief Judaic phase. It may also be the case that Dr. Rogers assumed (in the casually racist manner of his day) that Earle must be Jewish because of his swarthy complexion and broad nose. If so, this is not the only mistake Rogers recorded on his written report.

The other, far more serious, error appears just a few lines down from the misstated religion, where the psychologist concluded that Earle Leonard Ferral was "not violent; homicidal; or destructive."

Several weeks after his transfer to Napa, Earle received a visit from his Aunt Lillian and Uncle Willis. We do not know what words passed between them, though Lillian would later testify that her nephew, who was dressed in his sailor's uniform, was unhappy with his treatment. Exactly what that treatment consisted of is also undocumented. The record shows, however, that on June 13, 1918, Earle managed to escape.

He was tracked down and returned to Napa on July 11. Six weeks later, on August 25, he escaped again. This time, he remained at large for over three months. When he was brought back to Napa on December 3, his obvious gifts as a breakout artist earned him the ultimate tribute from his fellow inmates. They began calling him "Houdini."

As soon as the United States entered the war, the great "escapologist" himself had registered for the draft. But at age forty-three, Harry Houdini was too old for military service. Determined to do his part, Houdini immediately declared that he would cancel his vaudeville bookings and devote himself to patriotic causes. For the duration of the war, he staged a string of highly publicized benefits for the Red Cross, the Army Athletic Fund, the widows of the young men who had died aboard the torpedoed troopship, *Antilles,* and more. At one point, he put his talents to a novel use, teaching soldiers how to escape from German handcuffs should they ever be captured by the enemy.

Breaking out of handcuffs, of course, was child's play to the world-famous "self-liberator," who could work himself free of the most fiendish restraints human ingenuity could devise—sealed and buried coffins, padlocked milkcans filled with beer, tightly nailed wooden crates submerged in rivers. During one public demonstration in the nation's capital, an enormous crowd—the "biggest ever assembled except for the inauguration of a president" (according to the *Washington Times*)—watched him wiggle out of a straightjacket while, hooked to a rope, he dangled from his heels 100 feet above the sidewalk.

After enjoying one of his performances, Woodrow Wilson paid a call on Houdini. "I envy your ability to escape from tight places," remarked the president. "Sometimes, I wish I were able to do the same."

In spite of his new nickname, Earle's feats were, of course, on an infinitely smaller scale than Houdini's. Still, they were impressive in their way. The very day after his return to

Napa, he escaped yet again. Hauled back a few months later, he managed one final "elopement" (in the language of his official records). Altogether he pulled off no fewer than four escapes during his thirteen-month incarceration.

By the time of his final breakout in May 1919, the war had been over for six months. The Paris Peace Conference was underway at Versailles and millions of veterans were struggling to readjust to civilian life. For ten million other young men, life's struggles were over.

This time, the navy, which had been paying for Earle's treatment at Napa, did not even bother pursuing him. He was simply written off, formally discharged from the service on May 17, 1919.

On his hospital record, his supervising physician, Dr. Rogers, made a final entry as wildly mistaken as his earlier observation about Earle's harmlessness. Describing the patient's condition upon his discharge from service, Dr. Rogers noted simply that Earle Leonard Ferral was "improved."

5

✝

She's almost like a mother to him, you know, as she's twice his age. Often he would leave her flat, and she wouldn't hear from him for months at a time. But she understands him, and he is much better off married to her than to a flapper.

Lillian Fabian, referring to Mrs. Mary Fuller,
her niece by marriage

He returned to his Aunt Lillian's home and within days found work as a janitor at St. Mary's Hospital. At that point, before the navy decided to cut its losses by simply discharging him, Earle was still a fugitive. As a precaution, he took the job under a pseudonym, the first of many he would assume in the coming years: Evan Louis Fuller.

The work was strictly menial. What redeemed it from absolute drudgery was the presence of a congenial co-worker, a cleaning lady in the maternity ward, who cast a spell of enchantment over Earle.

To other eyes, her charms were not quite as evident as they were to his. Even she was bewildered by the young man's regard. No one else in her life had ever lavished such attention on her, and she had already lived a considerable span.

Her name was Mary Teresa Martin. She was a pinched and gray-haired spinster who resided in a boardinghouse a short trolley-ride away from the hospital. In the spring of

1919, she had just turned fifty-eight and looked every day of it.

Her other co-workers regarded Mary as a sweet, if mousy, old maid. Painfully shy, she could be tongue-tied to the point of incoherence around other adults. Addressed by her supervisor, Mary would cast her eyes downwards, wring her hands nervously, and stammer a barely audible response.

Earle was the single exception to this rule, the only other adult she seemed fully at ease with. Of course, having just turned twenty-two, he was a child by comparison to the aged Mary. He often acted like a child, too—a big, irrepressible boy full of puppyish enthusiasm. At the same time, there was a worldliness about him, the air of someone who had already seen and done things that the timorous spinster had never so much as dreamed of, let alone experienced.

The details of their early relationship—how Mary and Earle first came to speak, the course of their friendship, the blossoming of their love—are largely unknown. To the diffident old maid, the young man must have seemed deeply compelling, a fascinating mix of worldly experience and childlike exuberance. Besides, he was clearly a serious individual who was always musing on religious matters and citing Scripture by heart, traits that must certainly have made an impression on the pious Mary.

And there was something else about him that quickly became evident, a raw emotional neediness that brought out powerfully maternal feelings in the elderly woman. Something about the nearly sixty-year-old Mary Martin also stimulated powerful feelings, though of a significantly different nature, in Earle Ferral.

Just a few weeks after they met, Earle broached the subject of marriage. Mary, who had waited her whole life for a proposal, seemed ready to accept. There was, however, an obstacle. She was Irish Catholic; Earle was a Protestant. Always open to varieties of religious experience, he had no objection to a wedding conducted according to the rituals of the Roman Catholic church.

And so on Tuesday, August 5, 1919, at St. Agnes' Rectory, Mary Teresa Martin married a man young enough to be not just her son but her grandson. And Earle Leonard Ferral took a wizened bride, the first in a string of elderly women who would become the objects of his increasingly deadly obsession.

The newlyweds rented a few cramped rooms in a dilapidated house on Masonic Avenue and Eighth Street. Sheltered as she was, Mary Fuller understood, of course, that matrimony required patience, even fortitude. After all, the vows she had taken spoke directly of its vicissitudes: "for better or worse, for richer or poorer, in sickness and in health." Even so, she wasn't prepared for life with Earle Leonard Ferral. Who could have been? As she herself would later testify, in her primly understated way, her brief time with the man she knew as Evan Fuller was a "trying experience."

His personal habits were an early source of mortification to the fastidious Mary. It quickly became clear that her husband's standards of hygiene were not much higher than a hobo's. He rarely bathed, a problem that acquired a special urgency in their claustrophobic living quarters. Mary was immediately cast into the role she would play throughout their marriage, the long-suffering mother to Earle's feckless son.

One evening, before they were about to go out and visit her family, Mary finally put her foot down and insisted that he bathe. With a relenting shrug, Earle disappeared into the bathroom and emerged moments later carrying a glass of water. Then, seating himself on the edge of their mattress, he removed his shoes and socks and poured the contents of the glass over his feet.

"That is your bath?" Mary exclaimed.

Earle nodded. "My toes are nice and clean. That's what counts." With that, he slipped his shoes and socks back on and made ready to leave.

His public behavior also made her squirm with discomfort. Just a few blocks from their house was a down-at-the-heels little eatery called the Blossom Restaurant where the food, if not especially palatable, was plentiful and cheap. For prices ranging from ten cents to two bits, a diner could eat his or her fill of pigs' feet and kraut, meatballs and beans, oxtail goulash, lamb stew, or Yankee pot roast—coffee, tea, or buttermilk included.

Every now and then, when their finances allowed it, Earle and Mary would treat themselves to dinner at the Blossom. But the experience invariably proved a trial for poor Mary. To begin with, her husband's diet was highly eccentric. He would take forever to study the menu, then order something like a bowl of stewed prunes or a dish of boiled spinach. Mary (who, in spite of her scrawny physique, could pack away a corned-beef-and-cabbage dinner with gusto) was always disconcerted by Earle's peculiar choices.

But watching him eat was far worse. Seated with his hat pulled so low on his head that it half-covered his ears, he would raise the dish to his face and consume its contents as though he were feeding at a trough. The patrons of the Blossom weren't sticklers when it came to etiquette. It was the kind of place where the men shovelled up their black-eyed peas with their knife blades. But at least they ate with utensils. Even in that greasy spoon, Earle's table manners drew ugly stares.

His freakish fashion sense, unmodified since childhood, was also a source of constant mortification to Mary. He would leave home in the morning dressed in decent clothes, then show up later that day in a completely different outfit, garments so tattered that a tramp would have scorned them. Or he might appear in some outlandish getup, purchased for a pittance from one of the secondhand shops in the Tenderloin—a sailor's suit, golfing apparel, or the uniform of a Stanford University student. At other times, he would come home in a weird, color-coordinated ensemble, arrayed from head to foot in white or yellow or green.

Like another elderly woman who had been burdened with him—his grandmother, Jennie, who resembled Earle's new wife in more ways than one—Mary did what she could to keep him presentable. But her efforts were unavailing. Early in their marriage, she used some of her savings, painfully amassed over many years, to buy him a new overcoat. The following day, Earle went off wearing her gift. When he returned that evening, the coat was gone. So were the rest of his clothes, which had been replaced with a suit of rags. He had also managed to lose his underwear, a habit of his since childhood.

The self-abasing Mary did not reproach her husband,

though she never bought him clothing again. She did not even chide him when she came home one evening and discovered that he had removed her best brown-cloth skirt from her trunk, cut it up, and fashioned it into a pair of trousers for himself. Dressed in one of his baggy, thrift-shop shirts and the crudely stitched pants, he looked like a shipwreck survivor. But what use was there in upbraiding him? By then, Mary Fuller had already concluded (as she would later testify) that her husband "was not reponsible for his acts."

She continued to stick by him in spite of his increasingly bizarre behavior. There were the times when he would spring out of bed, throw on his clothes, and announce that he was going out to look for a job—at three o'clock in the morning. There were his crackpot schemes, undertaken with such intense (if short-lived) zeal—like the time he put a small deposit on a vacant lot and set about constructing a house, a project he abandoned after erecting a wall approximately one foot high.

Earle, in fact, was always promising Mary a house of their own, a pledge that led to one of the most humiliating experiences of her married life. One Saturday, he suggested that the two of them travel to Oakland to look at houses. They found a real-estate agent who spent several hours showing them some modest cottages outside of town. One of the places struck Earle and Mary as ideal. "This is the one," Earle declared.

By then, however, the agent had evidently become a little dubious about Earle—a feeling confirmed when he asked if the young man could afford the down payment. Digging a hand into his pants pocket, Earle fished out his entire fund of cash. "Is this enough?" he asked, holding out two dollars. Mary thought she would perish from embarrassment.

Even worse, however, was Earle's jealousy. At first, Mary found it quaint, even endearing. No one had ever felt that way about her before, and it seemed sweet (if slightly odd) to be treated as such a desirable woman at her age.

It wasn't long, however, before Earle's possessiveness lost its charm. Mary found it impossible to have anything to do with another human being without sending her husband into a jealous fit. He would berate her if she so much as chatted with a trolley conductor or stopped a stranger on the street to ask the time. Even her female friends became the objects of his resentment. He would accuse her bitterly of caring more for them than she did about him. It reached the point where Mary was afraid to talk to her own brother in front of Earle.

Mary rarely let herself get angry at her husband. But there was one occasion when his crazy jealousy drove her into a rage.

Among her most cherished possessions was a framed, inscribed photo of Mr. John Dillon, a member of the House of Commons, who was a personal friend of her uncle. Mary had stowed the photograph in her trunk for safekeeping. One day, not long after she and Earle moved into their little place on Masonic, she decided to brighten up the dingy living room by displaying the photo on a shelf. When she opened her trunk, however, she discovered that the frame was empty.

Confused and distressed, she sought out Earle, but he professed ignorance. Not long afterwards, however, while she was getting ready to do the laundry, she emptied his pants pocket and found the photograph, mangled and torn beyond salvaging. When his outraged wife confronted him with the ruined picture, Earle explained that he had thought it a memento from a male admirer and destroyed it in a jealous fit of pique.

In spite of his violent moods, his wild suspicions and angry accusations, Mary never felt threatened by Earle. Not, at any rate, in the beginning of their marriage. There was something so hapless and childlike about him. Children, in fact, were the only human beings he seemed fully at ease with. Whenever she and Earle would visit his aunt, he would spend the whole time playing games with his little cousins—hide-and-seek and ring-a-levio and tag. Even at home he would play silly games. Sometimes, when Mary asked him to perform a simple household chore, he would run off and hide like a mischievous toddler, concealing himself behind the window curtains or squeezing behind the sofa. To Mary, living with Earle often seemed less like marriage than motherhood.

In another way, however, their relationship was all too

much like marriage for her tastes. Though she was willing, up to a point, to submit to Earle's carnal demands—accepting the whole distasteful business as part of her conjugal duties—she was unprepared for his nightly importunities. On those nights when she rebuffed his advances, he would lie beside her on the mattress and abuse himself repeatedly, forcing her to flee the bedroom in disgust.

There was no respite from his lust. In February 1920, six months after they married, Mary was taken ill and rushed to St. Mary's Hospital. At first Earle behaved solicitously, visiting daily and bringing her trifles like flowers and candy. His presence, however, quickly became oppressive. He would sit at her bedside hour after hour, staring blankly into space or glowering at her doctor, whom he regarded as a rival for Mary's affections. The very day she was discharged, Earle brought her home, helped her change into her nightclothes, and put her to bed. Then he climbed in beside her and forced himself on the enfeebled woman.

For the first time, she began to wonder if her brother, Frank, was right. For months, he had been urging her to leave Earle. His sister, he believed, had been driven by her own desperate loneliness into a disastrous union.

Visiting Mary in the hospital one day, Frank found his brother-in-law seated on a chair at her bedside, staring unblinkingly upward. "Hello there, Earle," Frank said amiably. But if the peculiar young man was aware of the greeting, he gave no indication. He continued to gape at the ceiling, his lips working ceaselessly as he chattered silently to himself. "That fellow is crazy," Frank whispered to his sister, who simply chewed on her bottom lip and blinked back her tears.

As soon as Mary was discharged, Frank begged her to break off with Earle. Mary, however, was not only a devout Roman Catholic but also, as she put it, an "Irish woman of the old type." Divorce was out of the question. She had vowed to stick by her husband in sickness as well as in health. And he *was* sick, mentally sick—the "worst kind of sickness you could have," she believed.

He became even worse after the accident. Right from the start of their marriage, Earle had been afflicted with savage, recurrent headaches. When they struck, his face became haggard and pinched, his skin turned ashen white, and his eyes seemed to darken until they looked like two black, fathomless holes. Mary would try to soothe him by applying witch hazel to his brow but nothing seemed to help. One day, while working for a landscape gardener, he fell from the upper branches of a tree and landed on his head. He was admitted to a hospital with a serious concussion but fled after two days, showing up at home with his head so heavily bandaged that his eyes were barely visible beneath the thick turban of gauze.

Afterwards, his headaches grew more frequent. And his behavior became even more erratic. And scarier. More and more often, she would find him sitting silently in the kitchen staring intently at nothing. When she asked what he was doing, he would point wildly at the blank, flaking wall.

"The faces!" he would cry. "Don't you see them?"

His religious preoccupation grew more extreme, too, burgeoning into a kind of mania. He took to wearing a rosary. One evening, when he and Mary were out for a walk, they passed a store that sold religious articles. In the display window was a painting of a beatific Christ, his soft eyes gazing heavenward.

Earle grew strangely excited. "See! See!" he exclaimed, jabbing a finger at the picture.

"See what?" asked Mary.

"There! Don't I look like Christ?"

Mary stared at her husband. Far from looking beatific, there was a coarse, hulking quality to Earle. If anything, his thick, sensual features were the very opposite of the sublime face in the picture. A saying she had once heard flashed into her mind. "For where God built a church, there the Devil would also build a chapel. Thus is the Devil ever God's ape."

Not long afterwards, Mary went to see her priest. Tearfully, she explained her predicament and asked his advice. He told her that "kindness can cure insanity." She should "do her best" and "bear with it." Mary was heartened by this counsel. Perhaps Father O'Connell was right and, with a little kindness and patience, Earle's condition would improve over time.

For a while, they moved in with his Aunt Lillian. During

this period, Earle would sometimes disappear for weeks at a time without telling anyone where he was going. Even Lillian could not understand why Mary would tolerate such behavior in a husband. Still, she was grateful that her nephew had found such a loyal woman.

When Earle returned from one of these mysterious sojourns in the spring of 1921, Mary decided that a change of scenery might be good for them. That April, they moved to Palo Alto and rented a little bungalow. Within days, both of them had found work at a private school for girls—Mary as a cleaning woman, Earle as a handyman. It wasn't long, however, before Earle began making life miserable for her again.

One morning, not long after they began their new jobs, the school's headmistress, Miss Harker, asked Mary to bring in the laundry. As Mary was plucking the clothes from the line, an elderly man named Patrick, who doubled as gardener and watchman, strolled up and began making small talk. Seconds later, Earle burst from the schoolhouse, his eyes (as Mary would later describe them) "all black and angry and fierylike." While Mary stood there trembling and speechless, Earle stormed up to the old man, shook a fist in his face, and began shouting threats. "What do you think you are doing? She's my wife! I'd better not see you talking to her again. If I do, why, I'll—"

At that point, Miss Harker herself, alarmed by the commotion, came bustling out, demanding an explanation. The two livid men simply glowered at each other. It was left for Mary to stammer an apology and promise that there would be no such scenes in the future.

That night, back at home, Earle went wild, accusing Mary of deliberately going out to the school's backyard to flirt with other men. He worked himself into such a state that Mary, fearing for her safety, fled the house.

In spite of Mary's promise to Miss Harker, Earle continued to make mortifying scenes in public, sometimes in front of the students. On one occasion, he confronted his wife in the dining hall and, florid with rage, accused her of having a boyfriend. As the horrified children looked on, he grabbed her left hand and tore off her wedding ring, bloodying her finger.

Mary managed to break free of his grasp and ran sobbing to Miss Harker's office while Earle stormed out of the school.

Inside her office, the headmistress urged Mary to leave Earle before he did serious harm to her. "That man is absolutely insane," warned Miss Harker.

By the time she arrived home that evening, Mary had made up her mind. She found Earle pacing back and forth in the kitchen. "Pack up your bags," he commanded. "We're leaving this place. They're all against me, every one of them."

Steeling herself, Mary told him her decision. She was staying. She liked Palo Alto. And she was happy at the school. But she wanted Earle to go. She could not live with him anymore.

Earle said nothing. But the look on his face was so terrifying that Mary turned and bolted, taking refuge at a neighbor's. When she returned in the morning, Earle was gone.

That afternoon, however, he came back. Mary was at work at Miss Harker's, sweeping out the kitchen, when Earle suddenly appeared, looking as if he'd spent the night in a gutter. There was something in his face that rattled Mary so badly that she dropped her broom and ran. Earle gave chase, cornering her in the pantry.

Clutching his hands like a supplicant, he implored her to take him back. When Mary refused, his eyes took on a startling look, the pupils contracting so completely that there seemed to be nothing but white.

"It's him, ain't it?" he snarled.

In her terror, Mary could barely croak out a reply. "Who?"

"*Him.* The one who's keeping you from me."

"There is no one, Earle," she managed to say.

"I'll get you back," he said with an emphatic nod. Taking a step towards her, he raised his curled hands as though he meant to throttle her.

Letting out a scream, Mary ducked beneath his outstretched arms, scrambled out of the pantry, and made for the nearest office. It belonged to Caroline Wellman, the matron of the school. "He's after me!" Mary shouted as she burst into the room.

The startled matron snatched up her phone and called the Palo Alto police. Just then, Earle appeared at the threshold. Panting, hands clenching spasmodically, he stood there looking wildly from Mary to Miss Wellman, who was talking excitedly into the phone.

It was a cloudless day in late spring, and the school windows stood wide open. Backing toward the hallway window directly behind him, Earle climbed halfway through and fixed his wife with a baleful look. "I'll get you!" he shouted. "I'll get you yet!"

Then, hurling a final curse at the ashen-faced woman, he slipped out the window, dropped to the grass, and was gone.

6

✝

If you'd seen the look on her pale mug when she shriveled away with her hands over her eyes to shut out the sight of him! Sure, 'twas as if she'd seen a great hairy ape escaped from the zoo!

Eugene O'Neill, *The Hairy Ape*

After the lapse of so many years, it's impossible to know the particulars of the incident that occurred on May 19, 1921. The only existing record is a brief article from the following day's *San Francisco Chronicle,* and the information it contains is very sparse. It doesn't say, for example, how Earle Leonard Ferral came to choose the house at 1519 Pacific Avenue, or what his motives were for bluffing his way inside.

Only these facts are known: sometime during that Wednesday afternoon, Ferral appeared unexpectedly at the threshold of Mr. Charles Summers' modest home. The door was opened by Summers' twenty-four-year-old son, Charles Junior. Claiming to be a plumber who had come to repair a leaky gas pipe, Ferral gained admittance to the house and immediately descended into the cellar where twelve-year-old Mary Summers was playing with her dolls.

Moments later, Charles Junior heard his sister scream.

Though the news account supplies no physical details about little Mary Summers, she must have been a strapping girl. Earle himself was no flyweight but a burly twenty-four-year-old who had done manual labor throughout his adult life. But when Earle suddenly set down the tools he was carrying and fell upon the child, she put up a ferocious struggle. Screeching, kicking, tearing at his face, she was able to fend him off until her brother heard her frantic cries.

Rushing down to the basement, Summers threw himself on the attacker. The two young men grappled fiercely until Earle managed to break loose and flee the house. Summers chased him into the street and tackled him. They battled again, Summers knocking Earle down at least three times. Finally, Earle landed a punch that staggered his opponent and took to his heels. After checking to see that his sister was unhurt, Summers hurried to the nearest precinct house and reported the crime.

Two hours later Earl Ferral was arrested on a Polk Street trolley car by Traffic Policeman Elmer Esteranz, who had been supplied with a detailed description of the suspect. Earle was taken to the city jail and booked on an assault charge. In his mug shot, he looks more like the victim than the perpetrator. Hair wildly dishevelled, face battered and clawed, he gazes at the camera through hurt, hooded eyes. There is a strange mix of coarseness and sensitivity to his face. He looks like a thug who might burst into tears at any second.

In Palo Alto the next morning, Mary Fuller received a double shock. Less than a week had passed since her last, frightening confrontation with Evan (as she still believed he was called). Early Thursday morning, not long after she arrived at work, two policemen showed up at the school to inform her that a man claiming to be her husband had been arrested for attacking a young woman in San Francisco. Mary had to sit down to keep from swooning. Her distress was compounded when the officers told her the prisoner's name, Earle Leonard Ferral. For the first time, Mary Fuller discovered that her husband had married her under a false identity.

In spite of all he had put her through, Mary continued to feel responsible for Earle, as she would until the end of his life. She promptly made arrangements to take several days off from work and visit him in jail. By the time she arrived in San Francisco, however, he had already been transferred to the city Detention Hospital at Ivy Avenue and Polk

Street. From the moment of his arrest, he had acted bizarrely—babbling about voices, staring intently at the empty air, threatening suicide. During his first night in jail, he had somehow managed to pluck out his eyebrows with his fingernails.

In his cell at the Detention Hospital, Mary found her husband bound in a straitjacket and strapped to a cot. Though he gaped at her with his crazed, browless eyes, he did not seem to recognize her. He kept ranting about the leering faces on the wall. When Mary insisted that there *were* no faces, he clamped his eyes shut for a full minute, then popped them open, stared at the wall, and let out a cry. *"There! There!* Can't you *see* them?"

That same afternoon, Mary called on Lillian Fabian, who told her about Earle's previous stint in Napa. It was the first Mary had heard of it. Suddenly, she was faced with many disturbing discoveries about her husband: his true identity and his recent history as a mental patient in a state institution, as well as another piece of information the police had uncovered and conveyed to her, namely, Earle's ignominious record as a military deserter.

In an effort to keep him out of prison on the assault charge, the two women decided to institute insanity proceedings against Earle. On June 10, 1921, an Affidavit of Insanity was filed in superior court before Judge John J. Van Nostrand. Earle was ordered to appear for a hearing in three days.

The hearing took place as scheduled at precisely 11:00 A.M. on June 13, 1921. Mary was there to testify, as were two medical examiners, Doctors D. D. Lustig and Arthur Beardslee, who had interviewed the prisoner in his cell at the Detention Hospital two days earlier. Their conclusions were summarized in an official "Statement of Facts"—essentially a two-page, fill-in-the-blanks questionnaire—that became part of Earle's file.

There is a distinctly perfunctory quality to the answers on this form. In response to question #4, "What is alleged insane person's natural disposition, temperament, and mental capacity?," the medical examiners typed, "Eccentric, not industrious, could not concentrate." Question #10 asked, "Is alleged insane person noisy, restless, violent, dangerous, destructive, incendiary, excited or depressed?" Instead of supplying an answer in the space provided, the examiners simply crossed out the words they regarded as inapplicable (*noisy, destructive, incendiary*), underlined the relevant ones (*restless, violent, dangerous, excited, depressed*), and inserted one small emendation, typing "to wife and self" above the word *dangerous*.

The only answer that runs more than a few words is the response to question #14, which asks about "other facts indicating insanity." Here the two examiners wrote the following: "Brought to D.H. [Detention Hospital] order Judge Superior Court Dept. 11, charged with attacking girl—at D.H. patient apathetic—difficult to elicit information—hears voices and spirits and sees them—threatened suicide. People about him say that he is crazy—will not associate with him—claims to have lapses of memory."

The cursory quality of this document leaves little doubt that Drs. Lustig and Beardslee did not subject the prisoner to a particularly probing psychological examination. Even so, they came to a reasonable conclusion, finding Earle Ferral "so far disordered in his mind as to endanger health and person."

The Hon. John J. Van Nostrand declared that "by reason of insanity" Earle was "dangerous to be at large." A commitment order was filed that same afternoon. On June 16, 1921, Earle Leonard Ferral, who had escaped from Napa State Hospital exactly two years earlier, found himself back inside its walls.

Once again he was put under the supervision of Dr. J. B. Rogers, though it was another staff member, a psychiatrist named William Pritchard, who conducted Earle's preliminary interview. "This patient shows to good advantage on superficial examination," Pritchard wrote in his report. "To bring out his defects, it is necessary to recount his life's story."

Pritchard's brief synopsis of Earle's dismal past touched on all the salient points, beginning with the early death of both his parents from syphilis. It noted Earle's rudimentary formal education, which ended when he was fourteen—the same year he himself contracted a venereal disease that left him with a urethral stricture and a chancre in the perianal region.

Questioned further about his sexual habits, Earle replied that he had "masturbated several times a day" from the ages of fourteen to eighteen. He confessed that his sex drive remained undiminished. Since his marriage to his fifty-nine-year-old wife, whom he described as his "soul mate," he had engaged in "excessive intercourse" as well as in "occasional periods of excessive masturbation." Otherwise, Pritchard noted, he "denied further sexual perversions."

Earle did admit to two vices: using tobacco "excessively" and indulging in "alcoholic sprees at irregular intervals of a week to a year since puberty." He had apparently experienced some fearsome d.t.'s as a result of these binges. "After dissipations," Pritchard reported, "he sometimes sees snakes." Earle complained that he had not been physically well since puberty, "considering himself suffering from his stricture (which he was ashamed to seek medical relief for), from fleeting pains in various parts of the body, and from occipital headaches. He has also fainted a few times and infrequently felt dizzy."

After summarizing the patient's sorry work history and even sorrier military record, the report went on to speak of Earle's previous stint in Napa, explaining that he had been committed "for refusing to work in the navy and doing nothing but read the Bible and expound his religious views."

Earle continued to hold all sorts of "views" derived from a dizzying array of religious, occult, and pseudoscientific sources. "In his conversation," Pritchard reported, "the patient uses the lingos of various cults and 'isms,' and says he has studied Phrenology, Psychology, Anatomy, Palmistry, Occultism, Christian Science, Plain and Solid Geometry." At one point, Earle asked the psychiatrist to touch a spot on his skull. "Feel that cranial depression?" he said as Pritchard put a finger on the place. "There's a brain lesion under that."

As the interview progressed, the psychological "defects" that Pritchard had detected earlier became increasingly evident. Earle began to speak of his hallucinations, delusions, and dark, destructive moods. "He has seen faces," Pritchard recounted, "heard music, and at times believed people were poisoning him. Voices sometimes whisper to him to kill himself. Says that if he were kept in jail, he would get something sharp and cut the veins in his wrists."

Still, the interview ended on an upbeat note. When Pritchard asked Earle how he felt about his future, the young man's expression grew thoughtful. "I feel I can do much better now," he replied after a moment. "I am ready to lead a more evolved life."

The very next afternoon, according to the hospital records, Earle made a "desperate attempt" to escape. He was thwarted by two husky orderlies, who managed to subdue him and wrestle him back into his cell. For the next several weeks, he was never allowed outside his cell unless he was locked in restraints.

On July 5, 1921, three weeks after Earle was committed to Napa, the supervising psychiatrist, Dr. J. B. Rogers, recorded his formal diagnosis of the patient: "Constitutional psychopath with outbreaks of psychosis."

The surviving record of the next two and a half years is extremely sparse, consisting of just seventeen entries by Dr. Rogers, most of them no longer than a few curt sentences. The first of these "progress notes" (as they are labelled) is dated July 13, 1921, when Earle began receiving intramuscular injections of the arsenic-based, antisyphilitic drug, Salvarsan (also known as "606," the number of experiments that its inventor, Dr. Paul Ehrlich, conducted during his researches).

The very next day, July 14, Earle attempted to escape again, this time from the infirmary where he'd been taken for his injection.

There are no further notes until November 1. For the remainder of Earle's first year at Napa, Dr. Rogers made only one brief entry per month. After that, the entries become even more infrequent. Perfunctory as they are, however, these notes provide a revealing glimpse of Earle's "progress" during his incarceration:

> Nov. 1, 1921: Patient has a dose of Salvarsan this morning, feels nauseous. Has been well behaved most of the time but made a desperate attempt to escape from the hospital last June. About three weeks ago,

was seen to have a piece of wire fashioned as a screwdriver. Was in a plot with Gary, Hutchinson, Sessions, Stark and Reynolds to escape.

Dec. 19, 1921: Patient is quiet and well behaved on the ward—rational in ordinary conversation. Says he feels well; is much better, as though he has a "blessing upon him" since he had treatment. Nothing bothers him except his past troubles; he hopes to get over them.

Jan. 14, 1922: Well behaved on ward. Causes no trouble. Excellent physical condition.

Feb. 14, 1922: Patient talks rationally. Is out of restraint. Quiet and well behaved.

March 8, 1922: Patient has been confined to bed for several days since he had marked reaction from dose of Salvarsan. Is now feeling better. Quiet and well behaved.

April 12, 1922: Patient is quiet and well behaved. Talks rationally. Helps about the ward. No longer wears restraints when out of doors.

May 3, 1922: Patient is quiet and well behaved. Appears to have improved as a result of treatment. Eats and sleeps well.

June 1, 1922: Patient is well behaved and appears to be cooperating in every way in what is done for him.

July 1, 1922: Doing well. Well behaved. In excellent physical condition. In hospital one year.

For the most part, as these records show, Earle was a model inmate—cooperative, uncomplaining—during his first year in Napa. Having been foiled in his early escape attempts, he seems to have bowed to circumstances, even experiencing something like a religious conversion around Christmastime when he felt he had been visited by a regenerative "blessing."

However, by the time of the next entry, recorded in early October, 1922, something had changed. Earle was clearly growing disgruntled again, if not yet openly rebellious. Increasingly, the word *quiet*, which appears so frequently in the preceding entries, is supplanted by the more ominous word *restless*.

Oct. 2, 1922: Patient remains about the same, has been taking treatment for some time. Seems to be a little excited at times, helps some with work, reads a great deal. Well behaved, except has made several attempts to escape. Was caught with a saw a short time ago.

Jan. 12, 1923: Patient remains the same. Is quiet and well behaved. Occasionally seems to get a little melancholy and wants to get outside, says he could get along all right. Helps some with work. Reads a great deal. A little restless at night.

April 2, 1923: Restless, says he will try to escape again soon, that he is not insane. Helps some with work. Bad record—ran away four times. Sleeps restlessly.

July 23, 1923: Patient has been dissatisfied for the last couple of months. Has been asking for front yard privileges and several other favors. Has threatened to stop working on the ward if he is not granted more consideration. Refuses to take any more 606 treatments, stating he is well. Has a bad reputation. No delusions manifested at present. Sleeps little.

Oct. 5, 1923: Patient about the same.

There is only one more entry in this series, made a month later, on November 2, 1923. Given the tenor of the notes leading up to it, it does not come as a surprise. The entire entry consists of a single word: *Escaped*.

Lillian Fabian and her family were moving to a new, larger house. On the afternoon of November 2, the day of Earle's escape, she and her husband had been over to the new places getting it ready for the move, which was scheduled for the following morning.

It was already dark by the time Lillian returned home. Her husband wasn't with her. He had stayed behind to take care of a few last-minute tasks. As Lillian stepped into her darkened kitchen and reached for the light switch, a funny feeling came over her—one of those strange, unsettling sensations, as though she were being watched. She turned to look behind her. Earle was standing right outside the back door, his face pressed to the glass panes.

Later Lillian would recall the incident in a tense, breathless style that captured the terror of that moment:

He had his face right against the glass with a horrible crazy hat on, and I let out one terrible scream because he looked so awfully insane. His eyes were just black, glaring in at me, and the children rushed up to me, and of course, I opened the door because he was my own flesh and kin, and I loved him, and I opened the door, and he came in, and he acted so queer in the house, and I was scared to death of him because of the condition he was in. His legs were all bleeding with no stockings on at all and old ragged shoes that he must have picked up on the ground when he tried to escape there. And I hurriedly gave him a suit of my husband's clothes and a cap and stockings, and had him clean himself up, and I said, "For goodness' sake, Earle, get out of here as quick as you can." I was scared to death of him, and I gave him some food to take and money. I said, "Get away from here and don't come back," because my husband wasn't home that night, I was alone. And I rang up Napa State Asylum and told them who I was, and that Earle was there and that I was scared to pieces of him. They said they would look for him, and Earle went away.

He had been gone for several hours when two police detectives arrived at the Fabian house looking for the escapee.

"He was here earlier," Lillian told them.

"And where is he now?" one of the men asked.

Lillian shook her head. "I don't know," she said. And that was the truth.

The detectives thanked her and left. Two days later, Earle was apprehended in San Francisco and returned to Napa.

And that, more or less, is where the official record of this period in the life of Earle Leonard Ferral runs out. He would remain locked up in Napa for another sixteen months. But for unexplained reasons, there would be no more monthly "progress notes" entered into his files. The only record that remains of this period is the testimony of his wife, Mary Fuller, who visited him in Napa sometime in the fall of 1924. But even these recollections are extremely sketchy. Mary would describe the west ward of the asylum where her husband was confined—how it looked like a hospital ward, "very clean" with "little cells" lining the walls. She would recall the unsettling sights she had witnessed there—the patient who had cut out his own tongue because he imagined that his "father and mother despised him"; another who had "been a prominent attorney" and was declaiming to the other inmates as though addressing a jury.

She found Earle looking very melancholy, staring off into space, muttering that he had nothing to live for. The world was against him, he cried. "I'll cut my wrists if I get the chance. Damned if I won't."

And that is all the documentation that exists for this epoch in Earle Leonard Ferral's life—except for one final, terse notation, just three words long, entered into his file on March 10, 1925: "Discharged as improved."

Three months later, the matter of Mary Summers' assault was officially laid to rest in the superior court of California. Because of the statute of limitations, the outstanding indictment against Earle Ferral was dismissed on June 13, 1925, four years having elapsed since he was charged with assaulting the child in the basement of her San Francisco home.

7

✝

We are all born mad. Some remain so.
Samuel Beckett, *Waiting for Godot*

When Earle was discharged from the Napa asylum in March 1925, he was about to turn twenty-eight. Except for two limited stretches of freedom, he had spent the past ten years in lockup, behind bars in San Quentin or immured in a mental institution.

Momentous events had transpired during that decade, from the Great War to the Russian Revolution. In our own country a different kind of revolution had taken place, a social revolution so sweeping that nothing like it would be seen again until the heyday of the sixties counterculture.

The Roaring Twenties had gotten underway with all its now-familiar features—the flappers and flaming youth, speakeasies and bootleggers, petting parties and hip flasks, sax music, sex talk and sleek, high-speed automobiles. F. Scott Fitzgerald's *Tales of the Jazz Age* had given the era a name, and Ernest Hemingway's *Sun Also Rises* had defined the disillusioned ethos of his "lost generation" contemporaries. During that time, the country was rocked by sensational events—the Red Scare, the Sacco and Vanzetti trial, the Teapot Dome scandal. The Red Sox sold Babe Ruth to the Yankees, while the "Black Sox" sold out the whole country. For diversion, the public had the Little Tramp on the big screen, "Yes, We Have No Bananas" on the radio, and, on the newsstands, a brand-new spate of lurid tabloids and true-confession magazines.

Altogether, the changes in manners, morals, styles, and daily living were so radical and complete that, for someone like Earle Leonard Ferral—buried alive for the bulk of that era—reemerging into the world must have been akin to the experience of Rip Van Winkle, who awakens to find his sleepy, pre-Revolutionary village transformed into a bustling part of a new, independent nation.

There was another way in which Earle resembled Washington Irving's mythic sleeper. Though Rip awakens after twenty years to find himself gray-bearded and arthritic, he is essentially the same man—older but in no way wiser or more mature. Something similar was true of Earle Leonard Ferral. Though a decade had passed since his first incarceration, he was, in every meaningful way, unchanged. Dr. Roger's assessment of his patient as "improved" was not just wrong. As events would soon prove, it was dangerously wrong.

The paper trail documenting Earle's public life during the year following his discharge from Napa is very sparse. We know from her testimony that he spent some of this time helping his Aunt Lillian paint the interior of her new house. He wasn't staying with her, however, but rooming at an unknown place. Even she wasn't sure where he was living. He would show up in the morning, work for as long as he liked, then abruptly disappear, usually returning the next morning but sometimes staying away for days at a time.

Some months later, at the tail end of 1925, he left San Francisco and returned to Palo Alto, where—after making a tearful appeal to his long-suffering wife—he finally persuaded her to take him back.

For several months, they lived together in relative serenity. Then, on a warm day in mid-February, he abruptly announced that he had decided to go to Halfmoon Bay in search of work. Mary didn't see him again until June 25, when he showed up unexpectedly at her door. Less than two months later, he took off again, headed—so he said—for Redwood City.

Mary didn't raise any objections. Though he no longer

threatened her with violence, he was still a burden to have around. Besides, she knew that the poor man was possessed by forces beyond his control. The doctors at the mental hospital had explained to her that, among his other disorders, Earle suffered from "nomadic dementia," an irresistible urge to wander.

The only eyewitness accounts of Earle's activities from this particular period of his life are those of Frank J. Arnold—the sales manager for a printing company called the Walter Brunt Press—and one of Arnold's acquaintances, a Mrs. L. J. Casey of Los Angeles. Sometime in the spring of 1926, Earle found work with Arnold, who needed a handyman, gardener, and groundskeeper for his premises at 1927 Alma Street in Palo Alto.

Though Earle's habits were, as always, highly erratic, he could work hard when he wanted to. Arnold seems to have felt some patronizing affection for his oddball employee, perceiving him as a "simple fool" and even deriving amusement from Earle's peculiarities. Several years later, when Arnold was asked to describe those peculiarities, he recalled the way Earle would "repeatedly go to work with his tools in one hand and a Bible in the other and, laying down the Bible, proceed to work with his tools for a short time, when he would suddenly cease, stand fixed as a statue, gaze upward at the sky and remain in that posture." Interrupting his work to stare at "nothing in particular" was, in fact, a habitual practice of the eccentric handyman.

Arnold recalled another instance when Earle shaved his head "in such a way that the hair was not altogether taken off in one place and the head completely denuded in another." Earle had saved his shaven hair, offering it to Mrs. Arnold as pillow stuffing.

One occasion stood out with particular force in Arnold's recollections—the time that Earle "took a wheelbarrow and slowly walked around the road for a distance of about five miles, picking up small pebbles." After wheeling his load back to Arnold's workshed, Earle painted the pebbles with whitewash, then proceeded to lay them out in strange, seemingly random trails around the property. Arnold also remembered a time when Earle "left an automobile he was driving on the road without explanation and did not return for it."

In spite of all this weirdness, Arnold regarded Earle as a strong, willing laborer with a "kindly tractable manner" who readily followed instructions, "never demurring or hesitating." As far as Arnold was concerned, his handyman was "altogether harmless."

Others who encountered Earle during this period, however, weren't so sure. One of these was Mrs. L. J. Casey, Jr., a friend of the Arnolds', who spent a week with them at their Palo Alto home in 1926. To Mrs. Casey's eyes, there was something deeply unsettling about the young handyman, who was always "laughing and talking to himself" (as she would later testify). On one stormy afternoon during her visit, she saw Earle sitting coatless in the drenching rain, gazing with a weird intensity at the dismal sky.

"I would not have that man around," she remarked later that day to Frank Arnold. "He is surely crazy." But Arnold just laughed and said that there was no harm in the handyman. He was just a "simple fool."

Increasingly, however, Arnold's wife, Rhoda, came to share the opinion of her friend. As Arnold would later explain, his wife eventually grew "anxious and fearful of having [Earle] around our home and children, a man of such peculiar traits and tendencies, and she requested that I send him away, for the reason that he was not mentally sound and right."

Though Arnold continued to believe that his wife's fears were exaggerated, he finally gave in to her urgings and let Earle go.

As it turned out, the intuitions of the two women, Mrs. Casey and Mrs. Arnold, were even keener than they knew. No other facts about Earle's life from this period can be ascertained with any precision—except for one: By the time Frank Arnold fired him, Earle Leonard Ferral had already begun to kill.

PART 2

✝

STRANGLER

8

†

The truth is that the United States is approaching a condition somewhat resembling anarchy, and that unless something practical is done pretty soon, it may be too late.

St. Paul Pioneer Press, August 1925

In a nation where cultural change occurs at a head-spinning pace, seventy years is an aeon. From the perspective of the present moment, the 1920s seem like a period full of quaint and curious customs, from the mah-jongg fad to the Charleston craze to the popularity of Dr. Emile Coué's surefire panacea (a twelve-word formula guaranteed to bring contentment if recited regularly: "Day by day in every way I am getting better and better"). For all its wildness and sophistication, the Jazz Age seems like a time of sweet simplicity compared to the 1990s—the era of "My Blue Heaven" instead of "Murder Was the Case," *Son of the Sheik* instead of *Terminator II, Our Dancing Daughters* instead of *Teenage Bondage Sluts.*

There is one respect, however, in which a time traveller from the present, journeying back seventy years, would feel surprisingly at home. Opening a newspaper in any city of the land, such a sojourner would quickly discover that, in 1926 as in 1996, the paramount concern of most Americans was the frightening increase in violent crime.

Concern is really an understatement. At its height in the mid-1920s, the mood that gripped the country was more like mass hysteria, stoked by the crime-frenzied news media. The 1924 murder of little Bobby Franks seemed to confirm the worst fears of the older generation about the evils of the "Younger Set." The fourteen-year-old Chicago boy was kidnapped and killed by two older acquaintances, Nathan Leopold and Richard Loeb, a pair of pampered collegians who committed the outrage to prove that they could pull off the "perfect crime."

But the Leopold and Loeb case, however sensational, was only one of countless crime stories that dominated the news. Every day, from coast to coast, the papers were packed with tales of murder and rape, arson and assault, burglary, banditry, and blackmail. On a single day in 1925, every column on the first two pages of the *Chicago Tribune* was devoted to crime. During an average week in the summer of that same year, San Franciscans would have encountered the following headlines in the pages of the *Chronicle:* CASHIER SLAIN AT DESK AS WIFE MOURNS HER DEAD SON, BODY FOUND IN GAS-FILLED ROOM LINKED TO GIRL SLAYING, MODESTO WIFE MAKES CHARGE OF TORTURE, HIKERS FIND BODY OF MAN ON BEACH, MADMAN SETS OFF NITRO BOMB IN BANK, GIRL'S DEATH IN "LOVE PILL" CASE INVOLVES OHIO STUDENT, SHOTS FIRED INTO CHURCH KILL PASTOR AND WOMAN, ASYLUM ESCAPEE ADMITS MURDERS, "DIAMOND GIRL" SHOT IN DUAL TRAGEDY, "ACID BRIDE" BEGINS 14-YEAR TERM IN SAN QUENTIN, FIFTH MAN SLAIN IN LIQUOR WAR, FATHER FACES GALLOWS IN SLAYING OF DAUGHTER.

In one editorial cartoon after another, the crisis was depicted in dark, dramatic imagery: Uncle Sam being held up at gunpoint by a thug named "Crime." The figure of Liberty choking on poison from a bottle labelled "Crime." A map of America inundated with a great, black wave titled "Crime."

In the view of certain pundits, the phrase "crime wave" was a slight misnomer. The problem, they argued, was less like a sudden, overwhelming wave than "a steadily rising tide." But whichever aquatic metaphor they preferred, most observers agreed that, in the words of a special report issued by the American Bar Association, "the criminal situation in the United States so far as crimes of violence are concerned is worse than in any other civilized country." The statistical evidence was shocking. During the ten-year period ending in 1923 (according to the ABA report), 100,000 Americans "perished by poison, pistol, knife, or other unlawful and deadly injury." In 1923 alone there were 10,000 homicides in the United States. The following year, the figure topped 11,000. A single major city, St. Louis, had more murders during 1924 than England and Wales combined.

As for lesser crimes, the figures were equally staggering. In 1919, Chicago had 2,000 more burglaries than London. That same year, there were close to 1,100 cases of armed robbery in St. Louis, as opposed to 29 in all of France. Thieves made off with 2,327 automobiles in Cleveland during 1924. In Liverpool, a city one and a half times the size of Cleveland, the total number of stolen cars for that year was 10. And so on.

From the perspective of the 1990s, there is something perversely reassuring about these figures, since they suggest that the moral fabric of our nation may not be degenerating as dramatically as the doomsayers claim. But back in the 1920s, they were only a cause for alarm. To Americans of that era, particularly the older generation, the burgeoning crime rate was terrifying proof that the country, unloosed from its moorings in the Victorian code of the pre-War era, was plunging into moral chaos.

The popular magazines of the period were full of ruminations on the "crime problem." From *The American Mercury* to *The Atlantic Monthly*, *Scribner's* to *The Saturday Evening Post*, *Collier's* to *Current History*, the periodicals of the day were packed with articles like "Crime and Punishment," "Crime and Society," "The Crime Complex," "Poverty and Crime," "What Makes a Criminal," "Inside the Criminal Mind," "Combating Crime," "The Scientific Treatment of Crime," "The Persistence of Crime," and many more.

Encountering these articles now, a reader is struck by how contemporary they sound. Remove their references to "bootleg brigands," Leopold and Loeb, and the Sacco-Vanzetti trial, and they might have been published in yesterday's *Washington Post*. Virtually all the writers agreed, for example, that a primary cause of the 1920s crime explosion was the frightening proliferation of handguns. "Americans carry more revolvers than all the people of Europe, Asia, and Africa combined," one writer noted in the *Boston Globe*. "This one fact alone causes more violent crime than all other factors put together." A Chicago judge painted an even more hair-raising picture of the problem. "It is almost armed insurrection that confronts the nation," he declared.

Another alarming aspect of the 1920s crime epidemic was the shocking rise in youthful offenders. "Within the last fifteen years," according to a columnist for the *Indianapolis News,* "the average age of persons committing crimes of violence has decreased ten years. In former times, most of the burglars, safe robbers, and hold-up men were hardened criminals. Today, the worst offenders are young men. Not infrequently, mere boys begin a career of crime as hold-up men." What was behind this disconcerting phenomenon? "Only one conclusion is inevitable," the columnist wrote. "Children are not being instructed, trained and disciplined as they ought to be."

As for remedies, the proposals put forth sounded much like today's. Many believed that handguns should be subject to strict state and federal regulations that would make "the sale of fire-arms as difficult as that of opium." "The pistol, made only to kill people, must go!" proclaimed an editorial in the *Atlanta Constitution*. "The indiscriminate carrying of pistols is the greatest menace to human life and law and order, and the most distressing instrument of homicide known to our civilization."

Others insisted that the only cure for the crime plague was a revival of traditional family values. "There must be a return to good old-fashioned virtues that were practiced in the home," declared the *Troy Record*. "There is less crime in England than in America because over there all children are brought up with an inherent respect for the law."

Then there were those who advocated harsher penalties for criminals. "The only way to stop crime is to punish the guilty and do it quickly, firmly and severely," wrote an editorialist in the *Boston Globe*.

The trouble at present is that we are spending millions of dollars and valuable time in providing ways to "reform" criminals and make it easier for persons who ought to be in jail to escape the law. A whole army of criminal experts, probation officers, and publicity-seeking judges are trying to educate the public to the idea that no crime deserves real punishment. They are full of theories for coddling criminals and excuses for bandits, thugs, and the lawless generally. And they are spending good money to this end.

There is no new way to deal with criminals. The experience of centuries has shown that tolerance is fatal. No lawbreaker fears anything but swift and certain punishment. He can't be turned from his evil ways by appeals to his "better nature." He needs but one lesson—stern justice.

Let citizens, juries, and judges do their duty fearlessly and strictly. Put the criminals where they belong. Stop this nonsense of coddling lawbreakers. Get back to sane justice. That's the only medicine for the disease.

While all this sounds remarkably familiar, there is one area where things have changed dramatically, and for the better, since the mid-1920s. In considering the reasons for America's egregious "crime record," many commentators pointed to the appalling performance of the nation's police. The record seemed to speak for itself. For the 2,825 serious crimes reported in Baltimore during the first six months of 1923, for example, only 724 arrests were made and fewer than 500 people indicted. The following year, St. Louis had a total of 13,444 reported felonies, 964 arrests, and just 624 indictments—less than one indictment for every twenty crimes. "The deterrence of penal treatment can have little effect," one writer noted dryly, "if a prospective criminal believes that, even if his crime is discovered, there is less than one chance in twenty of his being brought to trial."

Incompetence and corruption were only part of the problem. Another was the primitive state of police science in this country. Compared to the law-enforcement systems of the major European nations, America's police departments seemed to be operating in the Dark Ages. Various specialists, among them George W. Kirchwey—former warden of Sing Sing and dean of Columbia Law School—pointed to the great technical sophistication of European investigators who were "trained to examine with a high degree of skill every detail connected with a crime and to rely on scientific experts at every turn. Nothing is too minute for examination and study. The investigating officer therefore spares no pains to seek for the slightest clue—even a single hair caught on the hands of the victim, lodged upon some piece of clothing, or fallen on the ground nearby. Thus, in a recorded case in Austria, a man was gravely wounded by an unknown person on a very dark night. The criminal dropped his cap in his flight, and inside the cap two hairs were found. After a careful examination, the expert microscopist was able to describe the wearer as a 'man of middle age, of robust constitution, inclined to obesity; black hair intermingled with gray, recently cut; commencing to grow bald.' "

By way of comparison, Kirchwey described the treatment of one of the key pieces of evidence in the Sacco-Vanzetti case—a cap, allegedly belonging to Nicola Sacco, found at the murder scene in South Braintree, Massachusetts. "Upon the identification of its wearer hung an issue of nation-wide concern," Kirchwey observed. And how did the Braintree police handle it? Chief Jerome Gallivan stuck the cap under the front seat of his automobile, where it lay for nearly two weeks, then ripped open the lining with his bare hands in the hope of finding some kind of identification mark.

If there was one bright spot in this dismal picture of Keystone Kops forensics, it could be found in California, which boasted the nation's oldest State Bureau of Criminal Identification and Investigation. Established in 1917, this centralized agency kept voluminous files—including fingerprints, mug shots, physical descriptions, and arrest records—on thousands of criminals. In addition, it maintained a highly trained staff of specialists in microscopy, handwriting, chemistry, photography, ballistics, fingerprinting, etc. In every area, the bureau had proven its worth. In 1927, for example, maintenance of the bureau cost the taxpayers $37,776, as against $1,253,205 of stolen property recovered and returned to its rightful owners.

Its success in dealing with "migratory criminals," felons who eluded the law by moving from city to city and state to state, had been especially striking. During the first decade of its existence, more than 7,000 men picked up on minor charges by various small-town police departments had been identified by the bureau as fugitives from other states—murderers, escaped convicts, bank robbers, and bunko men—and returned for imprisonment.

Writing in the monthly magazine *Current History,* Superintendent C. S. Morrill gave a vivid illustration of his bureau's achievements. On the evening of July 29, 1926, while magician Charles Joseph Carter—known as "Carter the Great"—was mystifying a San Francisco audience with his world-famous vanishing act, $14,000 worth of jewelry vanished from his apartment. Within forty-eight hours, the State Criminal Identification Bureau had ascertained that the stolen jewelry was being peddled in Nevada. Travelling to Nevada, city detectives were able to recover most of the loot and arrest four "well-known migratory criminals," the burglar and three accomplices.

"The recovery of the jewels and apprehension of the criminals were possible because California has broken down the barrier of isolation that surrounds the police of many states," Morrill wrote with quiet pride. "California's centralized crime bureau reaches out from city to city and state to state to gather information for her otherwise isolated police units and to coordinate their efforts in apprehending migratory criminals."

Ironically, at the very moment that the California crime bureau was helping to crack the Carter jewelry heist, it was faced with another, far more frightening case involving a "migratory criminal." Already, he had thrown several cities into a panic. Assisted by the bureau, police throughout the state were doing everything possible to identify this shadowy figure. Their failure would make Superintendent Morrill's boasts about California's system seem painfully hollow, though the bureau's forensic experts couldn't really be blamed.

When it came to burglars, robbers, check forgers, even run-of-the-mill murderers, the bureau had an impressive record of success. But the crimes that commenced in early 1926 represented a phenomenon so unparalled that, even in the nation that Morrill called "the most crime-infested society on earth," nothing quite like them had ever been seen.

9

✝

This house is to be let for life or years;
Her rent is sorrow, and her income tears.
Francis Quarles, "Emblems"

Sixty-year-old Clara Newman was a person of means, a shrewd, tough-minded woman who had managed to turn a small inheritance into a considerable fortune by her canny investments in real estate. In 1926, she owned property in several states, including two houses in San Francisco and a big spread in Pennsylvania.

From her manner of living, a stranger would never have guessed at her wealth. Parsimonious by nature, the "aged spinster" (as the newspapers would soon be describing her) dressed simply, subsisted on a meager diet, and inhabited a few sparsely furnished rooms on the ground floor of her house at 2037 Pierce Street. Though her mind was keen as ever, Miss Newman was physically frail and required help in managing her affairs. She received it from her nephew, Merton Newman, Sr., who also lived in the Pierce Street house, occupying two second-story rooms with his wife and nineteen-year-old son.

The top floor of the house was divided into two modest apartments. One of these was tenanted by a couple named Brown. The other had been vacant since the start of the New Year. For nearly two months, Miss Newman had been trying to rent it, displaying a hand-lettered "Room to Let" sign in the big bay window fronting Pierce Street.

On the morning of Saturday, February 20, 1926, Merton Newman was alone in his second-floor apartment, his wife and son having gone out on an errand. Shortly before noon, he heard the doorbell chime. Glancing up from his newspaper, Newman could make out some muffled sounds from below—his aunt going to the front door and exchanging a few words with the caller. Then Merton returned to his reading.

About fifteen minutes later, he laid down his paper. It was chilly in the apartment. The temperature outside was hovering at around forty-eight, but the radiators were stone-cold. He decided to go down to the basement and check the furnace, which had been acting up lately.

The stairs to the cellar ran down from a door in the kitchen. Crossing the kitchen, Merton noticed a half-cooked sausage in a frying pan on the stove. The burner beneath the pan was off. Apparently the caller had caught his aunt in the middle of preparing her lunch, and she had turned off the gas before answering the door.

Merton spent about fifteen minutes in the cellar, tinkering with the furnace, before heading back up to the first floor. As he left the kitchen and stepped into the central hallway, he spotted something—a strange figure walking briskly towards the back door. Merton called out to the man, who paused with a hand on the doorknob and glanced over his shoulder. In the shadowy corridor, Merton couldn't see much of the stranger's face. The man was rather oddly dressed, in dark, baggy trousers and a drab, military shirt. In spite of the chilly weather, he was coatless. Merton, who judged the man's age at around thirty, could see that he was powerfully built, not especially tall but deep-chested and stocky.

"Can I be of assistance?" Merton asked.

"Tell the landlady I will return in an hour," the stranger replied. "I would like to rent that empty apartment." With that, he pulled open the door and strode away.

Walking to the back door, Merton looked down the street, but the stranger had already disappeared around the corner. Before returning to his rooms, Merton engaged in a brief conversation with two workmen who were doing repairs on the roof of a neighboring house. Merton called up to them, asking them to stop by and see him once they were done with their job; his aunt's roof needed some patching. "All right," one of the men shouted back. "We will drop by before going home."

Shutting the back door, Merton returned to his second-floor apartment and, within moments, had become absorbed in some bookkeeping.

It was almost 2:00 P.M. when he laid down his ledger book and went downstairs in search of his aunt, intending to discuss the possibility of replacing the antiquated furnace. As he passed through the kitchen again, Merton noticed something strange. The frying pan with the unheated sausage was still on the stove.

He walked to his aunt's bedroom. The door was open, and Merton could see at a glance that his aunt was not inside. He checked the other rooms on the first floor, but she was nowhere to be found.

Puzzled, he ascended to the third floor and knocked on the door of the Browns' apartment. Charles Brown answered. Yes, he confirmed, both he and his wife had heard Miss Newman up there a few hours ago, talking with someone. The Browns had assumed that the landlady was showing the vacant apartment to a prospective tenant.

Stepping across the hallway, Merton tried the knob of the vacant apartment and found that it was locked. That was peculiar. He pounded on the door. Silence. For some reason, his heart was seized with alarm. Taking a step back, he raised one foot and delivered a powerful kick that sent the door crashing open.

The attic apartment consisted of a single, cramped bedroom and a tiny kitchen, just big enough to accommodate a stove, an icebox, and a sink. Small as she was, Clara Newman's body covered most of the kitchen floor. She was curled on her left side, naked from the waist down, her housedress having been yanked above her waist. The wooden beads from her old-fashioned necklace lay scattered on the floor.

Shouting for Brown to call the police, Merton dropped to his knees beside his aunt. He shook her by a shoulder as if to rouse her from a nap, though from her ghastly stillness and the grotesque look on her face, he already knew that the old woman was dead.

The autopsy took place that evening. Police Surgeon Selby R. Strange concluded that the bruises on the victim's neck had been made by powerful fingers. Miss Newman's death, he told reporters, "looked like murder by strangulation." Three officers—Lieutenant Charles Dullea, along with Detective-Sergeants Allan McGinn and Charles Iredale— were assigned to the case. Fingerprints found on the inside knob of the attic door were photographed by Police Photographer George Blum and sent to the Bureau of Criminal Identification in the hope of finding a match.

A hard-looking vagrant was picked up in Oakland within twenty-four hours of the killing but, after viewing the man, Miss Newman's nephew declared that the suspect was "blameless." The two workmen who had been repairing the neighboring roof at the time of the murder were questioned as witnesses, but neither man had gotten a good look at the suspect.

The story of Miss Newman's death—headlined FIEND MURDER OF SPINSTER in the *San Francisco Chronicle*—made the front page. But at a time when every day brought news of another stabbing, shooting, bombing, or poisoning, it quickly faded from the papers. The old lady's murder was shocking but not nearly sensational enough to cause widespread consternation.

The public's reaction might have been different if Dr. Strange had revealed one appalling detail. Though the surgeon had confirmed that the old lady had been raped— or, as the newspapers put it, "criminally attacked"—he had withheld one fact from the public. The "criminal attack" had been postmortem.

The unknown fiend who had gained entrance to Miss Newman's house in the guise of a renter had committed a double outrage on the sixty-year-old spinster. First, he had throttled her to death. Then he had raped her corpse.

10

✝

Earle Nelson was of the type of human wolf who, once having tasted blood, becomes possessed with a lust for killing which cannot be gainsaid.

L. C. Douthwaite, *Mass Murder*

Though officially retired from the real-estate business, Harvey J. Beal kept an office in downtown San Jose where he spent a few hours each week overseeing his investments. At approximately 1:00 P.M. on Tuesday, March 2, 1926, he kissed his wife, Laura, goodbye and left their ground-floor residence in the Deer Park Apartments, a four-story building in a fashionable residential district of town.

The building itself, at 521 East Santa Clara Street, was actually owned by Mrs. Beal. At that time, all the apartments were occupied except one, a recently vacated, furnished one-bedroom on the third floor. Mrs. Beal, who managed the property, had hung out a "Room to Let" sign just a few days earlier.

In addition to her duties as landlady, Laura Beal was active in church work and as the leader of the local branch of the Women's Christian Temperance Union. By all accounts, she was a sweet-tempered soul. The photograph of her that would run in the following day's *Chronicle* shows a woman whose strong, slightly mannish features are softened almost to loveliness by her gentle expression. The picture highlights something else, too: Mrs. Beal's one, truly elegant feature—her long, lovely neck, as graceful as a flower stem.

When Harvey Beal returned home shortly before 6:00 P.M., the door to his apartment was open. He called to his wife as he entered the front hallway, but, surprisingly, she wasn't home. Inside the living room, he found his wife's reading glasses lying atop the afternoon newspaper at the foot of her favorite easy chair. Assuming that she had gone over to a neighbor's and would return momentarily, he went into the kitchen and fixed himself a sandwich.

Mr. Beal was not a worrier, but when an hour passed with no sign of his wife, he began to grow concerned. He checked with the other residents of the building, but none of them had seen his wife all day. One of the tenants, however—a woman named Florence Turner—had noticed the door of the Beals' apartment standing open as early as 4:00 P.M.

When he heard this information, Mr. Beal's emotions quickly passed from concern to alarm. Enlisting the aid of his tenants, he began a search of the entire neighborhood, but Laura Beal was nowhere to be found.

By ten, the frantic man was at a loss. There was only one place left to look—the vacant, third-floor apartment. Mr. Beal had already tried the door earlier that evening but had found it locked. Now, fetching the spare key from his wife's bureau, he hurried back up to the apartment, opened the door, and stepped inside.

He found his wife's body sprawled across the mattress in the bedroom. From the condition of the room, and the dreadful bruises on her face, he could see that there had been a violent struggle. She had been strangled with the silken cord from her dressing gown, which had been twisted so savagely around her neck that it was embedded in her flesh. Her garments were hiked to her waist. It was clear that the sixty-five-year-old woman had been sexually assaulted, though it wasn't until the autopsy that Coroner Amos Williams determined she had been raped after death.

The page-one story in the next day's *San Francisco Chronicle,* headlined FIEND MURDERER STRANGLES WOMAN IN SAN JOSE HOME, sent shock waves throughout the area. As the story noted, the appalling murder of Mrs. Beal appeared to be the work of the "same fiend who two weeks ago strangled a woman in similar circumstances in San Francisco."

That conjecture was confirmed late Wednesday afternoon by Mr. H. S. Bailey, proprietor of an ice cream parlor directly across the street from the Beals' apartment building. Questioned by police, Bailey recalled that he had spotted a sallow-faced man hurrying from the building at around 4:30 P.M., the approximate time of the murder according to the findings of Coroner Williams. Bailey's description matched the one provided by Merton Newman, nephew of the fiend's previous victim, who had travelled to San Jose to assist with the investigation. Bailey was immediately taken to the Bureau of Criminal Identification and Investigation where, as the papers reported, he was shown photographs of "every degenerate known to police" in the hope that he would be able to identify the culprit.

In the meantime, the San Jose police turned for advice to a specialist in abnormal psychology, Dr. L. E. Stocking, head of a local mental hospital, who declared authoritatively that the killer was unquestionably "a maniac possessing extreme criminal cunning."

The news that a homicidal maniac was at large in San Jose set off a full-blown panic, particularly among the city's female population. The police were inundated with phone calls from women reporting close encounters with the fiend. Some of these callers were landladies, like Mrs. F. C. Rochester of the Melrose apartments, who claimed that, the previous Friday, a "suspicious character" had appeared at her door to apply for a job as a handyman. Something about his appearance made Mrs. Rochester so nervous that, excusing herself, she ran to a neighbor's for help. By the time she and the neighbor returned, however, the mysterious stranger had fled. Unfortunately, the detailed physical description she gave to police did not tally at all with the strangler's known attributes.

Like Mrs. Rochester's story, most of the ostensible "leads" that flooded police headquarters in the days following Laura Beal's murder were utterly useless, either facts that had no bearing on the case or sheer, overwrought fantasy. In spite of their dubious quality, however, at least two of these tales were taken seriously. One came from a woman named Mrs. D. L. Currier of 33 Hester Avenue, who reported that, on Friday afternoon, while napping in her bedroom with her four-year-old son, she became aware of a strange noise and opened her eyes to see "an unkempt man standing over her."

Screaming in terror, she leapt from her bed and fled the room "with the fiend in close pursuit." He managed to seize the hem of her nightdress, ripping off a strip of the garment as she bolted for the front door. She had just pulled open the door when the maniac overtook her. Gripping her in his powerful arms, he stuffed a pocket handkerchief into her mouth to stifle her cries, then wound the torn strip of nightdress around her neck, preparing to strangle her. Struggling wildly, Mrs. Currier managed to wrest herself out of his grasp but, in doing so, fell across the threshold, struck her head on the doorframe, and—as she explained to the police—was "rendered unconscious." When she awoke sometime later, the fiend, apparently fearing "that passersby might be attracted should he attempt to carry out his nefarious purpose in public view," had fled.

Later that same afternoon, Miss Ethel Ehlert was alone in her father's plumbing shop at 1060 Alameda when, in her words, a "tall man of uncouth appearance, with several days' growth of beard on his face" entered the store. When Miss Ehlert asked what he wanted, he stepped up to the counter, looked at her with "an evil leer," and responded, "Nothing."

Suddenly, he lunged across the counter, seized her wrists, and tried to drag her into his arms. Yanking herself free of his grasp, she dashed to the end of the counter towards the rear door "with the fiend in pursuit." Bursting into the alley, Miss Ehlert, according to her account, sped around to the front of the building, ran back into the store, slammed and locked the door, then raced to the back door and threw the latch— just as the fiend, who had chased her all around the building, came rushing up. Pressing his "ugly face" to the door pane, he "stood there leering" at her until he saw her snatch up the telephone to summon the police, at which point he "took to his heels and fled."

The wild-eyed accounts of Mrs. Currier and Miss Ehlert, blazoned as unvarnished truth on the front page of Saturday's *Chronicle,* plunged the citizens of San Jose into a state of near hysteria. "San Jose homes were in the grip of terror," the paper reported. "Women are keeping behind locked doors.

Children are not being permitted to leave the house alone. Men are secretly arming themselves."

Given this frenzied state of affairs, the whole city must have heaved a sigh of relief when Sunday's edition hit the stands. STRANGLER MANIAC SUSPECT JAILED BY SAN JOSE POLICE read the headline.

A police detective named Thomas Short made the arrest late Saturday afternoon. The suspect was a thirty-three-year-old Austrian immigrant named Joe Kesesek whose description tallied closely with that of the "strangler maniac"—dark hair, olive complexion, barrel chest, unusually long arms. When Short spotted him "acting suspiciously" on Market Street, Kesesek was dressed in a drab army shirt, the same kind of garment that the strangler was wearing when he fled Clara Newman's house in San Francisco.

Taken into custody, Kesesek (as Short later explained to reporters) began talking "in a rambling manner, all of his talk being about women." At times, his speech was so garbled that the detective couldn't begin to understand it—a sure sign, as far as Short was concerned, that the man was dangerously unbalanced.

While the suspect was being booked, two other detectives proceeded to 53 Market Street, a dingy little fleabag that Kesesek had given as his address. But if the cops hoped to discover evidence that would link the Austrian to either murder, they came away disappointed. All they managed to turn up in Kesesek's room were five dollars in cash, a key, and a letter—written in German—to a woman named Mary Ritter.

Back in the stationhouse, Kesesek, whose babbling clearly had less to do with his presumed mental pathology than with sheer terror at being collared as the strangler suspect, had calmed down sufficiently to give a perfectly lucid account of his recent history to Police Chief John Black. According to Kesesek, he had been working as a handyman in the Veterans' Home near Sawtelle until two weeks earlier, when he decided to go to San Francisco to seek treatment for his asthma. Along the way, he had stopped off at a hospital in San Luis Obispo, where a doctor had given him some medicine for his condition. The medicine bottle had, in fact, been found in Kesesek's possession at the time of his arrest.

Continuing his journey northward, Kesesek had encountered a traffic officer outside Salinas. At that point, Kesesek—who had been travelling by foot when he couldn't thumb a ride—was flat broke. He appealed to the policeman, who gave him five dollars out of his own pocket for a room. Kesesek arrived in San Jose early Saturday morning and immediately rented a bed in the Market Street flophouse. After settling into his squalid quarters, he had gone out for a stroll and was promptly identified as the "strangler maniac" by Detective Short, although—as Kesesek now insisted—he was nowhere near San Jose on the previous Tuesday when Laura Beal's murder had occurred.

The day after Kesesek related this story, Monday, March 8, 1926, several witnesses came forward who confirmed every portion of his alibi. The Austrian was back on the street before noon.

By the time of his release, rumors had begun circulating that the *real* "strangler maniac" had been seen leaving the city on the afternoon of the murder with an unknown companion. According to witnesses, the two men had been hiking southward over Monterrey Boulevard.

It was alarming, of course, to think that the fiend had escaped, but at least San Jose was rid of him—a comforting thought to the citizenry.

As the days and weeks passed without further incidents, San Franciscans began breathing easier, too. Though the vicious killer of two elderly landladies remained at large, it seemed clear that he had left the Bay Area.

But he hadn't left. He was only taking a respite—and it wouldn't last long.

11

✝

Thus speaks the red judge, "Why did this criminal murder? He wanted to rob." But I say unto you: his soul wanted blood, not robbery.

Friedrich Nietzsche, Thus Spake Zarathustra

Every afternoon around 2:00 P.M. Mrs. Lillian St. Mary put on her hat and coat and went out to do her daily shopping. The sixty-three-year-old San Francisco woman, who had been separated from her husband for a dozen years, lived at 1073 Dolores Street with her adult son, James, a secretary for an official of the Southern Pacific Railroad. To bring in extra income, Mrs. St. Mary rented the spare rooms in her large, private house. Two of them were vacant in the summer of 1926. The others were occupied by boarders, a couple named Van der Zee and Mr. R. C. Brian, who worked in a local printing shop.

One of Mrs. St. Mary's duties was preparing dinner for her lodgers. Early each afternoon, she would make the rounds of the neighborhood shops, picking up provisions for the evening meal.

On this particular day—Thursday, June 10, 1926—Mrs. St. Mary was just about to head out on her daily expedition. Her coat and hat were already on, her purse was in her hands.

At that moment, the doorbell sounded. Walking to the front door, the elderly woman pulled it open and found

80

herself facing a swarthy, heavyset young man, neatly dressed in a blue pinstriped suit. He was looking for a place to stay, he explained, and had seen the "Room for Rent" sign in her front window.

Mrs. St. Mary invited him inside. "Lucky you came when you did," she said. "I was just about to walk out the door."

Leading the way up to the second floor, she opened the door to the furnished room and stepped inside. The stranger entered behind her. As soon as he crossed the threshold, he carefully closed the door and threw the lock. Hearing the metallic click, Mrs. St. Mary turned. Police later speculated that she may have tried to scream. But she never had a chance. Before she could utter a sound, his hands were on her throat.

It was one of the boarders, R. C. Brian, who found the old lady's body. Returning from work around 5:00 P.M., Brian was surprised to find the kitchen empty. Normally, Mrs. St. Mary could be found working at the counter or standing by the stove, busily preparing dinner.

Climbing the stairs to the second floor, Brian noticed that the door to the unoccupied room was ajar. He paused at the doorway and glanced inside. And froze.

The landlady was stretched atop the bed, her mouth agape, her glazed eyes bulging behind her thick-lensed spectacles. Her steel-gray hair, normally pinned back into a tidy bun, was in wild disarray, and her clothes were badly dishevelled, the cotton dress shoved almost to her waist, exposing her splayed, spindly legs.

Even from the doorway, Brian could see that she was dead. Turning on his heels, he half-ran, half-stumbled down the stairway and ran into the parlor to telephone the police.

First on the scene was Sergeant F. P. Suttman, who made a brief examination of the room. After noting several significant details, including a still-damp urine stain on the rug, Suttman contacted the Bureau of Criminal Identification and Investigation. Then he posted himself at the doorway and stood guard until a team of detectives showed up.

From the evidence of the urine stain, apparently produced when the victim had voided her bladder, the investigators concluded that Mrs. St. Mary had had been attacked in the center of the room. The ugly fingermarks on her throat showed how savagely she had been throttled. So did the nine broken ribs Police Surgeon Selby Strange discovered during the autopsy. Evidently, the killer had knelt with the full weight of his body on the frail old lady's chest while strangling her.

The fact that her eyeglasses were still on her face suggested that she had not put up a struggle. The attack had been too swift. The killer had gotten his hands around her throat before she could even utter a cry. Mrs. Herman Van der Zee, a boarder who lived directly beneath the murder room, had been at home the entire day and never heard a sound.

Before fleeing the room, the killer—for reasons known only to himself—had taken care to arrange Mrs. St. Mary's body on the bed, setting her hat on the mattress beside her and placing her folded topcoat underneath her feet. Though the landlady's purse (reportedly containing five dollars in cash) was missing, she was still wearing the pearl necklace and jeweled earrings she had put on in preparation for leaving the house.

Clearly, the motive for the attack wasn't robbery. It was criminal depravity. Dr. Strange's autopsy, conducted later that evening, confirmed that, like the previous victims, the sixty-three-year-old landlady had been sexually assaulted after death.

Though Mrs. St. Mary's estranged husband, Joseph, was brought down to police headquarters for routine questioning, it seemed clear that the killer was the same maniac who had already taken two lives in the Peninsula area, the one that the papers were now calling "the Dark Strangler." The testimony of a streetcar conductor named Al Wolf bolstered that assumption.

Appearing at headquarters first thing Friday morning, Wolf told police that, at approximately 2:40 P.M. the previous afternoon, a swarthy, heavyset man, roughly forty years old, had boarded the Number 11 trolley at Twenty-third and Dolores streets. Though there were plenty of empty seats, the man stood near the front of the car, fidgeting so badly that Wolf kept shooting him curious glances. Then, after riding only one block, the strange, jittery man had leapt from the car and fled down Dolores Street.

Speaking to reporters on Friday afternoon, Captain of Detectives Duncan Matheson confirmed that "this description and other circumstances leave no doubt in my mind that the so-called Dark Strangler is the man we want for the slaying of Mrs. St. Mary. He gained admission to Mrs. St. Mary's home through the same pretense of renting a room, and the method of strangulation in each instance was similar."

Matheson announced that he had put every member of the city's homicide and robbery squads, ten detectives in all, on the case. With so much manpower concentrating on the investigation, he felt confident that it was only a matter of time before the strangler was apprehended.

In the meantime, he urged that all women in the region, particularly every landlady and rooming-house proprietress, follow special precautions. Under no circumstances should they enter a vacant room with a strange man, or even admit one to their premises unless a third party was present. He advised that, whenever possible, all negotiations with a stranger should be conducted through a speaking tube or over the house telephone. "Such precautions are essential," Matheson warned, "to prevent further depredations by the strangler."

The public response to this latest depredation was an exact replay of the reaction to the Beal murder three weeks earlier—mass hysteria, fantastic reports of hair-raising attacks, followed by short-lived relief at the news that police had arrested a suspect.

FIEND DARKENS HOUSE, THEN SURPRISES VICTIM IN BED blared the headline of Monday's *Chronicle*. According to a fifty-five-year-old woman named Alice Wilberg, she and her husband Edward had taken an automobile ride to the beach early Sunday afternoon. When Mrs. Wilberg, who had only recently been discharged from the hospital following a successful gallbladder operation, began feeling ill, her husband drove her back to their house at 414 Duboce Avenue. As soon as they got home, Mrs. Wilberg retired to their bedroom to rest. Edward stayed around for a few minutes, then went out to visit friends, leaving his dozing wife alone.

About an hour later, shortly after 3:00 P.M., Mrs. Wilberg was roused from her nap by a strange noise in her bedroom. Opening her eyes, she was horrified to see a tall, shadowy figure looming over the bed. Though the shades were drawn and the room was shrouded in darkness, she could tell that the intruder was in a state of partial undress.

Screaming, the sickly woman tried to rise from the bed, but the stranger was too fast for her. Grabbing her by the shoulders, he struck her across the face, then dragged her from the mattress and administered several more savage blows. Then he wrapped his hands around her neck.

Fighting with a desperate strength, Mrs. Wilberg managed to loosen his choke hold long enough to plead for mercy. She told him all about her gallbladder operation and warned that her husband would be home at any minute.

At that very instant, just as his fingers were starting to tighten on her throat, the intruder was stopped by a noise from the street, a sound like that of an automobile coming to a halt. Thinking that Mrs. Wilberg's husband had arrived, the stranger gave the kneeling woman a final blow to the face, then turned and fled the room. Swooning, Mrs. Wilberg lay in a semiconscious state until 11:00 P.M., when her husband returned and found her collapsed on the floor.

Though Mrs. Wilberg's account was nearly identical to the equally thrilling (and improbable) tale related by Mrs. D. L. Currier three weeks earlier, the San Francisco police chose to regard it as authentic. Three detectives—John Sturm, John Dolan, and William Johnson—were assigned to her case. Unfortunately, Mrs. Wilberg wasn't much help to the investigators. Though she was absolutely clear about one detail, that the man in her bedroom was partly unclothed, she claimed she could not see his face because the room was too dark. All she knew was that he was tall.

Meanwhile, the San Francisco police continued to pursue every lead. At least fifty ostensible tips were phoned in to headquarters on Monday. Investigators followed through on every one of them; all of them proved groundless.

"We are not overlooking even the wildest and most unpromising tips," Detective Lieutenant Charles Dullea of the homicide squad told reporters late Monday afternoon. "And despite the fact that it means many wild goose chases, we encourage the public to cooperate in good faith with us, for this is the only hope we have of catching the dangerous criminal."

Asked what advice he had for the citizens of San Francisco, Dullea replied that he would "personally advise elderly women who have furnished rooms to rent to take every precaution in admitting strangers to their homes and to telephone the police whenever they have something to be suspicious of."

In making this recommendation, Dullea realized that he was opening the door to practical jokers who might be tempted to have some fun by calling in phony information. But all Dullea could do was appeal to the public's good sense and follow up with a warning. "This is far too serious a matter for a hoax, and anyone caught playing a practical joke on the police will be dealt with severely."

Still, the phony tips and dead-end leads continued to pour in. In spite of Dullea's warning, some of these were deliberate hoaxes. Others were either the product of hysterical delusion or desperate, attention-getting ploys. One or two may have been based on actual incidents—though, given their particulars, it seems doubtful that even these cases involved the "Dark Strangler."

Late Monday afternoon, for example, a fifteen-year-old Alameda girl named Helen Lawrence reported that she had been attacked by a strange man who had called at her parents' home to inspect a vacant room. Finding the girl alone, the man had immediately grabbed her. She was saved by the proverbial bell, for at that very instant the telephone rang. Evidently mistaking the sound for the front doorbell, the intruder fled.

At almost the same instant, an elderly San Francisco woman, Mrs. L. O. Quinn, who ran a boardinghouse on Bryant Street, called the police to report that a suspicious-looking man who matched the published descriptions of the strangler had just tried to rent a room from her. A squad of policemen, headed by Captain Goff of the Southern Station, immediately set off in pursuit of the man, tracking him down within the hour. He turned out to be a slightly shady but essentially innocuous character, well-known to some of the officers, who worked for a neighborhood junk peddler.

Tuesday's paper brought welcome news to the tense and fearful residents of the Bay Area: S.F. BUTCHER JAILED AS STRANGLER SUSPECT read the headline.

The suspect was Otto Krueger, a sixty-three-year-old sausage maker whose appearance was an approximate match for that of the strangler, dark-skinned and burly, with large, powerful hands. Though Krueger was considerably older than the man the police were hunting for, his hair had not a trace of gray, and he radiated an air of youthful vigor. He could have passed for forty-five.

He was taken into custody on exceptionally slim evidence. During a boat ride on board the steamer *Admiral Fiske*, which ran between San Francisco and Los Angeles, several passengers noticed that Krueger was acting strangely, pacing on deck and muttering darkly to himself. They alerted ship officers, who contacted the Los Angeles police. On the orders of Captain of Detectives Herman Cline, Krueger was arrested as he stepped off the steamer in Los Angeles.

At first, Krueger's odd behavior in custody encouraged his captors to believe that they had nabbed the right man. He ranted bitterly about his wife, though the two had been estranged for nearly twenty years. He claimed that he worked at a sausage-making shop at 1319 Pacific Street in San Francisco. But when police tried to contact his boss, they discovered that no such shop existed.

Just a short distance away, however, at 1331 Pacific Street, there *was* a sausage factory where Krueger had, in fact, been employed five years earlier. His former boss remembered the suspect as an erratic, unreliable worker who had left because of trouble with a union official.

Investigating Krueger's movements on the day of Mrs. St. Mary's murder, detectives confirmed that he had, in fact, been in San Francisco at the time, having checked into the Curtis Hotel on Valencia Street under an assumed name, "Mr. Gordon." They were also able to ascertain that he had come to San Francisco from San Jose, "the scene" (as the *San Francisco Chronicle* pointedly observed) "of one of the strangler murders."

At least one person, however, refused to believe that

Krueger was guilty of murder. This was Conrad Gabler, president of the local branch of the Sausage Maker's Union, who had known the suspect for more than ten years. Speaking to a reporter on Tuesday afternoon, Gabler acknowledged that Krueger was a "peculiar-acting fellow." But he felt sure that the sixty-three-year-old butcher was "innocent of this strangler business."

His opinion was borne out by Merton Newman—nephew of the strangler's first victim and the only person to have seen the killer face to face—who, after viewing mug shots of the suspect, declared that Krueger was definitely not the man. Less than twenty-four hours after being picked up by the L.A. police, the sausage-maker was set free.

Over the next few days, women throughout the Bay Area continued to report terrifying encounters with sex-crazed intruders in the darkness of their bedrooms. The San Francisco police continued to run down scores of dead-end leads, scour the streets for suspicious-looking panhandlers, and haul in derelicts by the dozen for questioning. But it soon became clear that the elusive killer had gotten away with murder once again.

By Thursday, June 17, the story had disappeared from the front pages. The only article to appear in that day's *Chronicle* was a short, dispirited piece reporting that the strangler investigation had hit "a blank wall, without a trace or clue as to the identity of the man who claimed two lives here and one in San Jose." The article consisted of only a few brief paragraphs on page four. Occupying more than twice as much space on the page was a lengthy piece, complete with captioned photo, about the opera singer, Madame Claire Eugenia Smith, who—having just returned from a tour of the Hawaiian Islands—was eager to promote the immeasurable physical, moral, and social benefits of hula dancing. "If American dancing schools would only teach the hula rather than the Charleston to the young," declared the diva, "the change would be astounding!"

12

✝

Yes, yes, said the Beast, my heart is good, but still I am a monster. Among mankind, says Beauty, there are many that deserve that name more than you.

Madame Leprince de Beaumont,
"Beauty and the Beast"

Just one day later, on Friday, June 18, a week after the discovery of Lillian St. Mary's mangled and ravaged body, the strangler struck again. At least that was the common assumption when the news of Sylvia Gaines' brutal murder first broke.

To be sure, there were notable differences between this latest atrocity and the three that had preceded it. For one thing, the slaying took place not in northern California but in Seattle, Washington. And Sylvia Gaines was not a sixtyish landlady but a vivacious twenty-two-year-old who had graduated from Smith College the previous summer.

Still, the police found logical ways to account for these differences. With every detective on the San Francisco P.D. on the lookout for him, the strangler had evidently migrated northward in search of safer hunting grounds. And his choice of victim simply meant that he preyed on vulnerable females whatever their age or situation.

The details of the case, reported in papers from Seattle to San Francisco, provoked consternation up and down the coast. Sylvia Gaines had been living in Seattle for less than a year. She had come west the previous fall to renew her relationship with her father, Wallace Cloyes Gaines, who went by the nickname "Bob." Her parents had gotten divorced when Sylvia was a child, and she had not so much as seen her father for over sixteen years.

In the interim, Wallace Gaines, invariably described in the papers as a "disabled veteran," had become an alcoholic, having suffered a severe case of shellshock during the Great War. He had been remarried for five years to a woman named Elizabeth, who had also taken to booze because, as she would later explain to reporters, "I always felt that it was much better for me to drink with Bob than to have him drinking alone or with someone else."

Ever since Sylvia's arrival on the scene, there apparently had been a good deal of tension between Wallace and his wife, provoked by the former's allegedly "inappropriate attentions" to his nubile daughter whom he hadn't laid eyes on since she was a kindergartner. So ugly had these quarrels become that, only a few months before Sylvia's murder, Elizabeth had carried a pistol to the basement of their home and attempted to kill herself. After recuperating from her self-inflicted wound, she had, at her husband's suggestion, gone off to stay with a friend in San Francisco. She was still residing there when the murder took place.

On the night of the killing, Sylvia reportedly left the house after supper to take a stroll around Green Lake, slightly less than a mile away. The lake was bordered on three sides by private houses and on the fourth by a forested area called Woodland Park. At approximately 9:30 P.M., a couple named Stokes, who lived in one of the lakefront homes, saw Sylvia walking along the gravel trail that circled the lake. Moments later, they spotted someone else, a husky man dressed in a blue serge suit jacket and dark gray trousers. Except for his prominent nose and strong, square chin, his features were obscured by his low-pulled cap. But he appeared to be in his forties. He was striding rapidly along the trail, as though trying to catch up with the young woman.

That was the last time Sylvia Gaines was seen alive. Her nude, ravaged body was discovered the following morning in a grove of alder trees a few yards from the lake. Her neck bore the marks of powerful fingers, and her skull had been crushed with a rock. Police found the makeshift weapon, dabbled with blood and hair, about fifteen feet away from the corpse.

From various pieces of evidence, including a trail of blood leading from the shore to the alder grove, investigators concluded that, after being attacked by the rock-wielding assailant on the gravel trail, the mortally injured young woman had stumbled into the lake in a desperate effort to escape. Dragging her from the water, the killer had carried her into the alder grove, where he had throttled her to death, then ripped off her clothing and assaulted the body.

Given the brutal particulars of the crime, police initially hypothesized that it was the work of the same shadowy fiend who had been terrorizing the California coast. It wasn't long, however, before they were focussing on another, even more shocking possibility—that the killer was the victim's own father, Wallace, who had been putting on a highly ostentatious show of grief ever since his daughter's death.

Speaking to reporters from his bed, the apparently prostrate man acknowledged that Sylvia had been a source of contention in the household. "It is true my wife and I quarrelled over Sylvia. Perhaps I was too attentive. I don't know." But he tearfully denied having harmed her. "To think that a finger of suspicion has been pointed at me," he sobbed. "I—I who loved my daughter more than anything on earth!" His wife, who had returned from San Francisco to be at his side, stoutly defended his innocence.

In spite of these protestations, however, incriminating evidence against Gaines began piling up as the investigation proceeded. Witnesses who saw him on the night of Sylvia's death reported that he had been dressed differently earlier in the day, as though he had changed clothing sometime during the evening. When police sought to examine the garments he had been wearing at the time of the murder, Gaines could not produce them. Four boys who had been playing by the lakeside at the time of the killing had not heard any unusual sounds. "If Sylvia Gaines had been accosted in a threatening manner by a man she did not know," Sheriff Matt Starwich opined, "she would have screamed, and the boys would have heard it."

And then there was the neighbor who told police that

around 10:00 P.M. on the night Sylvia was killed, Wallace Gaines had shown up at his door in a highly agitated state begging for a drink and muttering something about murder.

After interrogating Gaines at home on Friday, June 25, Sheriff Starwich met with reporters and announced that the case was solved. "The fiend theory is bunk," he scoffed. When one of the reporters asked if Wallace Gaines was now the primary suspect, the sheriff refused to comment. But he didn't have to. He simply stared at the reporter with a look that seemed to say, "What do *you* think?"

So it hardly came as a surprise when, on Tuesday, June 29, Wallace Gaines was arrested for the murder of his twenty-two-year-old daughter. The news was titillating enough to make the front pages as far away as Santa Barbara. But by that time, it seemed almost anticlimactic, a foregone conclusion. Besides, the citizens of Santa Barbara had something more urgent to worry about by then.

Five days earlier, on Thursday, June 24, another woman had been slain, a fifty-three-year-old boardinghouse proprietress named Ollie Russell. And this time the killer really was the "Dark Strangler."

13

✝

That moment she was mine, mine, fair,
  Perfectly pure and good: I found
A thing to do, and all her hair
  In one long yellow string I wound
Three times her little throat around,
And strangled her. . . .
        Robert Browning, "Porphyria's Lover"

It wasn't as though Mrs. Russell was a careless woman or indifferent to the warnings that police had been issuing since Lillian St. Mary's murder two weeks before. On the contrary. If anything, she seemed more apprehensive than most of her neighbors, taking unusual precautions to keep crime at bay.

To deter burglars, she had fixed the windows of her home at 425 Chapala Street so that they could be opened no higher than six inches. And on the fateful day of her murder (as police later reconstructed the crime), she made sure to remove the rings from her fingers, tie them in a kerchief, and conceal them behind some books in her sitting room before answering the door.

So there must have been something about the caller—something about his appearance, behavior, or manner of speech—that disarmed Mrs. Russell's suspicions. The police could only guess at what that something might be. Only one fact was certain: That when the dark, stocky stranger appeared at her door, asking to see the vacant room advertised on a placard in her parlor window, Mrs. Russell let him inside.

It was one of her boarders, a fireman for the Southern Pacific Railroad named William Franey, who discovered the murder—though the story he told the police seemed so peculiar that, for a short time, Franey himself fell under suspicion.

Franey, who worked at night, was asleep in his room on the afternoon of June 24, when he was awakened by a commotion from the adjoining bedroom, which had been vacant for several weeks. Thinking that some new boarders were moving in and banging their luggage on the floor, Franey closed his eyes again. But when the noises continued, he arose from his bed, walked to the door which separated the two rooms and, bending low, peered through the keyhole.

Much to his confusion, he saw a man, with his trousers pulled down to his knees, lying atop a woman, whose features were obscured by the man's body. The banging noise that had awakened Franey was the knocking of the headboard on the wall, the result of the man's vigorous motions.

Embarrassed, Franey moved away from the door and walked over to the bureau to check the time on his pocket watch—3:32 P.M. He stood there for a moment in a state of nervous excitement, then stepped back to the door for a second peek.

Through the keyhole he saw the man rise from the bed, pull up his trousers, and adjust his clothing, a dark gray suit that appeared to be in rather shabby condition. Then the man walked out of Franey's range of vision.

The woman, meanwhile, continued to lie motionless on the mattress, her dress drawn up above her hips, her stockinged legs parted and exposed. The window shades in the bedroom were drawn, and her head was turned so that Franey could not make out her features. But as he squinted through the keyhole, he began to grow convinced that the woman sprawled on the bed was his landlady, Mrs. Russell.

At that moment, the man reappeared. Pulling out a pocket handkerchief, he mopped his brow, then plucked his greasy, gray fedora from the mattress, brushed it off with a jacket sleeve, settled it on his head, and strolled from the room shutting the door behind him.

Flustered and sweaty, Franey left his own room and walked onto the back porch where a washbasin was set on a little table. After splashing some cold water onto his face, he dried himself with a towel then stood there and wondered what, if anything, he should do.

It was obvious that the man in the gray suit was not Mrs. Russell's husband, George, who ran a pool hall and eatery called the Texas Lunch at 622 State Street. Franey found it hard to believe that the fifty-three-year-old landlady would be entertaining gentlemen callers while her husband was away at work. But stranger things had happened, and Franey was not the kind to poke his nose into other people's private affairs.

The bedroom in which the woman lay led directly onto the back porch by way of a glass-panelled door. There was a curtain blocking the glass, but it was so loosely arranged that, by placing his face close to one of the panes, Franey could see inside the room.

The woman was still lying in precisely the same position. But, viewing the bed from a different angle this time, Franey saw something he had not noticed before: dark stains on the mattress. They appeared to be blood.

Hurrying around to the front of the house, he made for State Street and headed for the Texas Lunch.

Halfway there, however, he came to a sudden halt and took a moment to reconsider. Perhaps Mrs. Russell was only sleeping. Perhaps the stains on the mattress *weren't* blood— or, if they were, perhaps they'd been caused by a nosebleed. After all, there had been some pretty strenuous activity taking place on that bed.

He turned around and headed back to the house.

He reasoned that if Mrs. Russell was, in fact, napping, the best tack to take was to rouse her in a discreet, unintrusive way. Standing outside the front door, he put his finger on the doorbell. But though the buzzer sounded insistently, no one answered.

He stepped inside the house. As he proceeded down the

hallway, he noticed something peculiar. The door to Mrs. Russell's bedroom was standing open. Franey had never known her to leave it open before, not even when she was at home. She was too nervous about her own safety. He poked his head inside and called out to her.

Silence. This time Franey felt something stronger than worry—something closer to alarm. Hurrying outside, he jumped into his automobile and drove the few blocks to the Texas Lunch.

Franey still wasn't sure what he'd seen in the next-door bedroom. Hanky-panky? Foul play? He thought he'd better approach the subject cautiously. Spotting George Russell at the back of the pool hall, Franey walked over and asked if he knew where Mrs. Russell was.

"Why, she's at home," Russell replied, surprised at the question. "Unless she's gone over to play cards at Clara Brown's house."

"Has the apartment next to mine been rented?" Franey asked.

"Not as far as I know," Russell said. By this point, his brow was furrowed with concern. When he asked Franey what was going on, the fireman told him about the strange noises coming from the next-door room, though he took care to say nothing about what he had seen. "I think you'd better come home and have a look," Franey advised.

A few minutes later, the two men were back at the boardinghouse. Discovering that the door to the vacant bedroom was locked, they headed around to the rear porch. Peering through the partly obscured pane in the door, Russell could see the woman stretched out on the bed. But he couldn't make out her face.

The two men decided to check with several of Mrs. Russell's friends in the neighborhood, but no one had seen the landlady since 2:45 P.M. when she'd paid a brief visit to her friend, Laura Fields, who had given her a jar of homemade jelly. Shortly after three, Mrs. Fields had received a thank-you call from her friend. That was the last anyone had heard from Ollie Russell.

Returning to his house with Franey, George Russell hunted up a key to the door of the bedroom, opened it, and stepped inside. "My God," he gasped, clutching Franey's arm. Franey stood there for a moment with gaping eyes, then ran to call the police.

Her battered face gruesomely discolored, Ollie Russell lay dead on the mattress. She'd been strangled with a loop of cord pulled tight enough to tear the flesh of her throat. Blood had spattered from her neck onto the mattress, and there were bloody marks on the casing of the door.

William Franey himself was the first to fall under suspicion. After paying a visit to the crime scene, Police Captain S. S. Kelley declared that it would have been "extremely difficult, if not impossible, for Franey to have seen the things he said he saw through a keyhole." It seemed equally unlikely that the fireman could have peered through the backdoor glass pane and "seen blood on the bed where the dead woman lay, as her body was between the glass and the blood spots."

While Franey was detained at police headquarters, his room was thoroughly searched by criminologist J. Clark Sellers, who had been summoned from Los Angeles to assist with the case. Within twenty-four hours, however, District Attorney Clarence Ward ordered Franey released for lack of evidence.

By then, Drs. Frank Nuzum, Kent Wilson, and William Moffat had completed the autopsy on Mrs. Russell's body at the funeral parlor of Charles Holland. The autopsy revealed that, as D.A. Ward disclosed to reporters, the victim had been "attacked by a degenerate" who had violated her body after death. This ghastly finding confirmed what many had already assumed, that the landlady's killer was the same fiend who had already perpetrated three identical atrocities in the Bay Area. "There is no doubt in my mind," Police Chief Lester Desgrandchamp declared, "that the murder was committed by the strangler."

At Desgrandchamp's orders, a telegram was transmitted to every city along the coast, alerting police to be on the lookout for a man matching the description provided by Franey. The next morning, a similar bulletin was featured on the front page of the *Santa Barbara Daily News:*

POLICE ASK ALL AID IN MURDER HUNT

The man who is alleged to have strangled Mrs. Ollie Russell at 425 Chapala Street on Thursday afternoon is described by William J. Franey as:

Age about 35 years.
Height about 5 feet 8 inches.
Medium build.
Rather high cheekbones.
Dark skin, rather thin face.
Long wavy sandy hair.
Looks like a laborer.
Was dressed in a dark grey suit, clothes were not in a very good condition and rather shabby.
Had on a grey fedora hat which may have some grease spots on it.
Broad chest and shoulders.

Communicate with the police department at once if a man answering this description is seen.

From San Francisco to the Mexican border, investigators combed the coastline in search of the strangler. In Santa Barbara itself, police launched the biggest manhunt in city history. Over the next week, they arrested a succession of suspects, only to release each of them within hours.

A drifter named Clark Culer was picked up for no other reason than that he was wearing a greasy, gray fedora. He was let go after Franey failed to identify him. A man decked out in a different type of hat became the object of a brief, citywide search after a streetcar conductor named W. M. Blevans reported that, on the afternoon of the murder, a passenger in a Panama had asked for directions to 425 Chapala. As it happened, this mysterious suspect, who promptly showed up at police headquarters, had a perfectly innocent explanation for his interest in Mrs. Russell's rooming house. He turned out to be a member of the Benevolent and Protective Order of Elks, who had been sitting at the local club alongside his fellow member Coroner E. G. Dodge, when the latter was notified of Mrs. Russell's slaying. Having nothing else to do, the man decided to go check out the crime scene simply out of curiosity.

Other suspects who proved to have airtight alibis included a man named George Boska, who was picked up after telling a friend that police were on his trail; one Theodore Anderson of San Francisco, arrested after threatening the life of a female acquaintance in her hotel room at 168 Eddy Street; and Mrs. Russell's former husband, Charles, a mail-truck driver in Riverside.

Meanwhile, police were applying the latest advances in crime-detection technology in an effort to track down the strangler. Under the supervision of Sergeant Carl Newman, head of the Santa Barbara branch of the Bureau of Criminal Identification and Investigation, a bloody thumbprint found on the door casing of the murder room was photographed by Deputy Sheriff Carl J. Wallace using a sophisticated fingerprint camera borrowed from the Ventura P.D. Afterward, the section of wood imprinted with the bloody mark was removed from the doorframe, carefully packaged, and sent to bureau headquarters in Sacramento for analysis by experts.

Unfortunately, they were unable to come up with a match. The strangler case was rapidly turning into an embarrassment for the bureau whose achievements had been so highly touted in the national press.

14

✝

Brown's story is somewhat incoherent.
San Francisco Chronicle

The week of August 8, 1926, wasn't a time for particularly weighty news. Leafing through their morning papers, readers would have learned about Bishop Adna W. Leonard's anti-Catholic assault on Alfred E. Smith, governor of New York and aspiring presidential candidate. "No Governor can kiss the Papal ring and get within gunshot of the White House!" thundered Leonard, superintendent of the Methodist Episcopal Church and president of the Anti-Saloon League. Bishop Leonard, whose attack formed a part of his Sunday morning sermon, devoted the bulk of his speech to a nationwide call for Anglo-Saxon unity against foreigners, particularly Latins.

In the view of many people, who regarded the bishop's remarks as distinctly un-Christian, two other men of the cloth fulfilled the precepts of their faith in a far more exemplary way. After leaping into the waters off Sidi-Biahr beach near Alexandria, Egypt, to rescue a trio of drowning girls, two American missionaries—the Reverends J. W. Baird and R. G. McGill of the United Presbyterian Church—ran back into the waves to help a struggling countrywoman, Mrs. A. A. Thompson of Pittsburgh. Before they could reach her, Mrs. Thompson had managed to swim out of danger and was floating placidly towards shore when the young missionaries themselves were caught in an undertow and drowned.

Two other swimmers were luckier that week, narrowly escaping death during an attempt to cross the English Channel. Ten hours after setting out from Cape Gris-Nez, France, on Monday, August 9, Ishak Helmy and George Michel noticed that the crew of their accompanying tug, the *Alsace*, was frantically signalling to them. It took a moment for the swimmers to understand what all the commotion was about. An enormous school of sharks—at least twenty in all—was rapidly approaching the swimmers. Helmy and Michel were hauled to safety just as the sharks closed in. "I am not afraid of them," Helmy said to reporters afterward. "But I do not like them."

Sharks weren't the only man-eating creatures in the news that week. According to a report from the Chief Game Warden of the British Colony of Uganda, a unique race of man-eating lions had created a virtual "reign of terror" in the Sanga district of Ankole. "An appalling death toll has resulted in the region," wrote the warden. "One lion alone was responsible for eighty-four deaths and another for more than forty kills before they were destroyed." Unlike the average lion—which has an instinctive fear of people and kills them only under extreme circumstances—the Sanga breed appeared to have an innate preference for human flesh, presumably inherited from man-eating forebears who had been "driven by accident or hunger in a period of starvation" to prey on the local populace.

A pair of notable thefts was also reported in the papers. In Madrid, three famous paintings—a Van Dyck, a Velasquez, and a Titian, whose combined worth was estimated at nearly half a million dollars—were stolen from the home of Señor Isidor Urzaiz, brother of the late Spanish minister of finance. And at the Breakers, the magnificent Newport estate of General Cornelius Vanderbilt, three small boxes belonging to Mrs. Vanderbilt disappeared during a Saturday-evening dinner party. Much to Mrs. Vanderbilt's delight, the missing boxes, which contained priceless jewelry and unset stones, were returned three days later by a gardener's helper named Louis Shantler, who claimed to have discovered them under a bush on the estate of the Vanderbilts' neighbors, Mr. and Mrs. Hamilton Twombly.

The scion of another eminent American family made the

front pages that week, though not in a way that could have brought much pleasure to his relatives. On Tuesday, August 10, a member of the Rockefeller clan, twenty-two-year-old James Sterling Rockefeller, grand-nephew of John D., was collared by customs guard Louis P. Cassidy as the young man disembarked from an ocean liner following a vacation in France. Though the day was sweltering, Rockefeller was swathed in a heavy topcoat that was full of strange bulges. Searching its pockets, Cassidy turned up a motley assortment of stuff—fourteen razors, a pair of binoculars, a meerschaum pipe, and two radiator-cap ornaments—that the young man was attempting to smuggle into the country. Young Rockefeller, however, had no trouble in covering the fine of $476.20, which was paid in cash the following morning by his father's accountant.

The big news from overseas that week emanated from England where members of the British Association for the Advancement of Science had gathered for their yearly convention at Oxford. On Tuesday, Sir Daniel Hall created a sensation by predicting an inevitable worldwide famine unless science found a way to increase food production. Professor Julian Huxley, on the other hand, charmed his listeners with his lecture on animal courtship, a talk that (as the *New York Times* playfully reported) gave vivid proof "that romance blossoms almost in the primal ooze, that even the humble bristleworm woos his mate in the moonlight, and that the male spider brings his inamorata a nice fly neatly wrapped in a silk bouquet."

On the same day as Huxley's speech, an American visitor to England, former Chief Detective Dougherty of the NYPD, made the papers by calling for the restoration of the old British custom of crossroads hangings:

> I believe in the "horrible example system" which was in force in this country a century or so ago, when people were hanged at crossroads. In ninety-five cases out of a hundred today when a hold-up takes place, the resister is killed or wounded. The bandit has a revolver and intends to use it if necessary. Therefore, if he is caught, he should be strung up at once by the friends of the people he has killed.

Diverting though much of this was, none of it was especially earthshaking. But there was one front-page story that seemed momentous enough, at least to the citizens of San Francisco and particularly to those elderly landladies who had been living in terror for the previous five months. The headline appeared in the *Chronicle* on Wednesday, August 11: STRANGLINGS CONFESSED BY SUSPECT HELD IN NEEDLES, PRISONER ADMITS HE THROTTLED SEVERAL WOMEN IN CITIES OF PACIFIC COAST. After nearly half a year, it looked as though the "Dark Strangler" had finally been caught.

His name was Phillip H. Brown. At least that's what he told the police when they picked him up for vagrancy in Needles, California, on Tuesday afternoon. He was a thoroughly seedy-looking tramp of medium height—hollow-chested, lank, and dressed in a shabby, dark-gray suit. His mug shots show a suntanned, unmemorable face, thin-lipped and heavily stubbled. The pupils of his eyes were a pale, frosted blue—his most remarkable and disconcerting feature.

From inside his jail cell, Brown revealed that he'd done time in two state penitentiaries, Colorado and Idaho. Then—in a casual, offhanded way, as though he were acknowledging some minor infraction like jaywalking or shoplifting—he mentioned that he'd recently had some "trouble with about twelve women" on the Pacific Coast and that he had "strangled to death a number of them."

Though Brown's confession was immediately trumpeted in the headlines, few people were prepared to accept it at face value. For one thing, there were some notable inconsistencies in his tale. When Sheriff Walter Shay of San Bernardino County arrived in Needles to interrogate the suspect, he discovered that Brown was rather "vague as to localities." At first, the prisoner admitted having murdered three victims—one in San Francisco, one in San Jose, and one in Los Angeles. The only problem with this statement was that, as far as the authorities knew, no women had been strangled in Los Angeles during the previous six months.

Later that afternoon, Brown revised his story, claiming that he had killed two women in San Francisco, one in San Bernardino, one in Santa Barbara, and one "around Oakland." But again, there were no records of a recent strangling case in Oakland.

One man who greeted the news of Brown's confession with particular caution, if not outright skepticism, was Merton Newman, nephew of the strangler's first known victim. "I don't like to make a statement without seeing the suspect," Newman told reporters. "But if the report that he is five-feet-eight-inches tall is correct, I doubt if he's the man. I am five-feet-seven-inches in height, and I am positive that the man I talked with in the hall of my aunt's house was shorter than I, unless the angle of vision at which I saw him deceived me. He was of stocky build, of very dark complexion, with smooth, glassy skin. He had very black hair, and his features were full and of the general contour of an Oriental, although there was a European cast to his expression. He had a square, muscular torso and was powerfully built, though very short."

Certainly this description did not appear to fit the suspect, who was blue-eyed and raw-boned, with a face that would have seemed common in a British doss house. Arrangements were immediately made to have Brown's mug shots sent to San Francisco so that Newman could view them.

The prisoner's credibility received another blow when authorities turned up some additional facts about his background. It turned out that his name wasn't Phillip H. Brown at all. He was actually a twenty-eight-year-old narcotics addict named Paul Cameron who had grown up in Lincoln, Nebraska, and was regarded as the shame of his otherwise respectable family. "He has been in trouble with authorities on a number of occasions in recent years," his uncle Archibald told reporters, "and we do not care to have anything to do with him."

Not only had Cameron done stints in the two state pens; he had also been a patient at the Southern California State Hospital for the Insane at Patton. He had managed to escape after only six months by prying off the window bars of his cell with an iron rod. According to Cameron's statement, he had an older brother named William, also an inmate at Patton, who was "more daring than myself when not in confinement." Though a check of the files at the mental asylum confirmed that Cameron had been committed there in 1915, there was no record of this alleged older brother.

It was beginning to seem as though Cameron were simply a dope-addled drifter and small-time crook who, out of his own bizarre motives, had decided to confess to the highly publicized crimes. Then something happened which added new weight to his story.

Under the custody of several officials, including District Attorney Clarence Ward and Chief of Police Lester Desgrandchamps, Cameron was transported to San Fernando. There, on Wednesday night, August 11, he was positively identified by William Franey as the man who had strangled Mrs. Russell.

The viewing took place at police headquarters. Cameron was placed inside a closed room, while Franey, led into the adjoining office, was asked to look at the suspect through the keyhole of the connecting door. Dropping to one knee, Franey squinted through the hole for a moment, then straightened up and declared unequivocally that Cameron was the man.

A crowd of reporters was waiting for Cameron as he was escorted from the building twenty minutes later. The gaunt-looking prisoner seemed to enjoy all the attention, grinning broadly and posing for cameramen as their flashlights exploded. However, when reporters began shouting questions—Had he ever attacked women in San Jose? In San Francisco? In Santa Barbara?—he grew visibly uncomfortable and began mumbling unintelligible replies.

Indeed, vagueness and confusion seemed to characterize virtually every statement from Cameron's lips. Interrogated by Police Chief Desgrandchamps on Thursday morning, he claimed that he had been working in San Pedro until late May, when he decided to visit San Francisco. Shortly after arriving there on June 1, he "strangled a woman on Dolores Street," then, according to his story, headed south. After stopping briefly in King City, he went back to San Jose, where he supposedly "attacked a woman in a restaurant." From San Jose, he proceeded to Santa Barbara. On the day of his arrival, he went looking for a bed in a lodginghouse. When the proprietress showed him up to his room, he claimed he "attacked her, beat her, and choked her with a cord," then fled the city.

Unfortunately, Cameron was exceptionally hazy about the particulars of all these events—dates, times, addresses, names. And the few details he did provide were not at all consistent with the known facts. Nevertheless, based on Franey's identification, D.A. Ward felt justified in declaring that there was "no doubt in my mind that Cameron is Mrs. Russell's murderer."

The developments of the following day didn't make matters any less muddied. On the one hand, a report emerged from Piedmont that a man matching Cameron's description had attacked an elderly landlady the previous month. On July 5, when sixty-year-old May E. Kenney answered the doorbell of her rooming house at 37 Sharon Avenue she found herself facing a dark, dishevelled stranger who said he was looking for a room. As soon as he stepped into the house, however, he slammed the door behind him, then grabbed Mrs. Kenney by the throat. Luckily, a plumber had been to the house the previous day and left a length of iron pipe standing in the hallway. Grabbing up this makeshift weapon, Mrs. Kenney had beat her assailant about the head and shoulders until he turned and fled. The elderly woman had been so traumatized by the attack that she had since moved back to her hometown, Carson City, Nevada.

This disclosure certainly seemed to bolster the case against Cameron. But even as Mrs. Kenney was making her way to Santa Barbara to view the suspect, another key witness, Merton Newman, was casting doubt on his guilt. After studying Cameron's mug shots, which had finally arrived from San Bernardino, Newman met with reporters and declared absolutely that the suspect was *not* the Dark Strangler. "This is nothing like the man. The man I saw was very short, heavy, and erect, with somewhat foreign-looking features. This man is just the opposite of that type."

Cameron himself added to the confusion by repudiating the confessions he had been making for the past several days. After being formally charged on Thursday afternoon with the murder of Ollie Russell, he spoke to reporters and insisted that he was not guilty of any crime. "They told me to say those things," he growled before being led back to his cell. Though D.A. Ward scoffed at this accusation, other officials remained openly doubtful of Cameron's guilt. The biggest problem, the papers reported, was the "condition of the prisoner's mind. He will start a recital of his travels and crimes and then switch to unimportant topics. His conversation is ragged and his statements are hazy at times. He apparently is incapable of consecutive thought or narration. The police do not believe that this mental deficiency is assumed."

Over the next few days, the police continued to pour all their efforts into the investigation of Cameron's maddeningly indefinite story, attempting to establish its validity once and for all.

And then, on the afternoon of Monday, August 16, while the suspect remained locked up in the Santa Barbara city jail, the matter was settled with one sudden, brutal stroke.

15

✝

This familiar that I called out of my own soul, and sent
forth alone to do his good pleasure, was a being inherently
malign and villainous; his every act and thought centered on
self; drinking pleasure with bestial avidity from any degree
of torture to another; relentless like a man of stone.

Robert Louis Stevenson,
The Strange Case of Dr. Jekyll and Mr. Hyde

Stephen and Mary Nisbet, both in their early fifties,
owned a small apartment building at 525 Twenty-seventh
Street in Oakland. At around 4:50 P.M. on August 16, Mr.
Nisbet, who also held a job as a school custodian, arrived
home from work. Entering his second-floor flat, he called
out to his wife but received no response. Inside the kitchen,
he found the ingredients for a stew—sliced carrots, chopped
onions, quartered potatoes—heaped on a cutting board, as
though his wife had been interrupted in the midst of her
dinner preparations. He assumed that she had stepped out
on a sudden, unexpected errand—perhaps to borrow a
needed ingredient from a neighbor—and would return
momentarily.

Placing his jacket and hat on the hallway coattree, he
spent a few minutes puttering around the apartment. In the
bedroom, he found his wife's purse sitting on her bureau.
Obviously she couldn't have gone far. Carrying his newspaper into the living room, he settled down in his easy chair

and began to read. The big story of the day was the condition of movie idol Rudolph Valentino, who had been stricken with appendicitis on Saturday afternoon and was in acute danger from spreading peritonitis.

When Nisbet looked up from his paper, it was nearing six and his wife still hadn't returned. Where in the world could she have gone? As far as he knew, there was only one errand she had intended to accomplish that day—to travel downtown to the offices of the *Oakland Tribune* and take out a classified, advertising the vacant flat on the first floor of their building. But she had planned to do that before noon.

He decided to check with the neighbors, but no one had seen Mary Nisbet all afternoon. Margaret Bull—one of the second-floor tenants, who was entertaining a pair of friends when Stephen Nisbet came to her door—suggested that he walk to the corner grocery. Perhaps his wife had needed to make a last-minute purchase.

After taking a peek inside the vacant first-floor flat to make sure that his wife wasn't inside, Nisbet hurried to the grocery. But the proprietor, who was just closing up his store, hadn't seen Mrs. Nisbet all day.

Returning to his apartment, Nisbet sat at the kitchen table and, forcing himself to stay calm, tried to run through all the possibilities. But as 7:30 P.M. came and went, he couldn't sit still any longer.

Fifteen minutes later, he was at the police station. His wife, he reported to the desk sergeant, was missing. The officer listened sympathetically, then tried to allay Nisbet's fears. It was not quite 8:00 P.M., just three hours since Nisbet had arrived home to find the apartment empty. Though Mrs. Nisbet's absence was puzzling, particularly since she had gone off without her purse, it was too soon for alarm. The sergeant advised Mr. Nisbet to return to the apartment and wait another hour. If his wife wasn't back by then, the police would look into the matter.

Back at his building, Nisbet decided to take another look inside the one place he hadn't searched thoroughly, the vacant ground-floor apartment. Opening the unlocked door, he moved quickly through the living room, bedroom, and kitchen, turning on lights as he went. But the flat seemed completely vacant. The only place left to check was the bathroom, though what his wife would be doing in there he couldn't imagine. Still . . .

Crossing to the end of the hallway, he swung open the bathroom door and switched on the light.

Upstairs, Margaret Bull and her two male visitors, Joseph Hill and Rawley DeBaw, were startled by a fearful scream from below. They were just heading to the door to investigate when Stephen Nisbet, ashen-faced and hysterical, came bursting into the flat, crying wildly for help.

When a wife is murdered, suspicion immediately alights on the husband, and so it was in the case of Stephen Nisbet. Still, he seemed like a most unlikely suspect. Everyone who knew the Nisbets—friends and family members, neighbors and tenants—attested to their deep devotion for each other. They were, according to all accounts, a "perfect couple" who basked in each other's company and had never been known to quarrel. And, indeed, the double portrait that ran in Wednesday's paper seemed to offer vivid proof of their closeness. The juxtaposed photographs showed a handsome, middle-aged pair whose faces, through years of loving intimacy, had grown so alike that they might have belonged to siblings.

That Nisbet truly loved his wife seemed confirmed by his reaction to her death. His grief was so violent that he appeared to be on the brink of a nervous collapse. Fearing that he might do physical harm to himself, the police kept him under close surveillance in the hours following his awful discovery.

Of course, even a man less attached to his wife might have been thrown into shock by the horror of what he had seen. Of the five landlady-killings committed to that date, the murder of Mary Nisbet was, in many respects, the most brutal. Her husband had found her sprawled facedown on the tiled floor of the bathroom. She had been garrotted with a kitchen towel, knotted around her throat and pulled with such savage force that the fabric had frayed. The ferocity of the attack had puckered her neck as though it were a tightly squeezed pastry tube. Her blackened face had been slammed against the tiles as the killer knelt on her back. Fragments of her shattered front teeth lay in a bloody pool that seeped from her mouth. Her hair was wildly dishevelled, her clothing badly torn, her lower body naked and bruised.

Though Nisbet was held in custody for almost forty-eight hours while police checked his alibi, there seemed little doubt that the killing was the work of the "Dark Strangler," a supposition that was confirmed when the autopsy revealed evidence of postmortem rape. The press, however, didn't bother to wait for this finding. On Wednesday morning, hours before the autopsy, the *San Francisco Chronicle* had already run the dual portrait of the Nisbets under a headline that declared: STRANGLER BRINGS SORROW WHERE HAPPINESS REIGNED.

Throughout the Bay Area, the news that the "Dark Strangler" had struck once again overshadowed every other story, even the medical status of Rudolph Valentino (who would finally succumb on August 23, setting off a nationwide frenzy among his female devotees that seemed like a large-scale magnification of Stephen Nisbet's suicidal grief). Under the supervision of Chief Drew, Oakland police launched a massive search, focussing on proprietors of boardinghouses and apartment buildings to see if anyone had been approached by a dark, suspicious stranger inquiring after a room.

Their investigation turned up two witnesses who appeared to have set eyes on the suspect. One of these was David Atwood, postman for the Nisbets' neighborhood, who told police that he had seen a strange man loitering outside the Nisbets' apartment building at around 2:00 P.M. on the day of the murder. Atwood described the man as about forty years old, five feet six inches tall, wearing a dark gray suit and a dark fedora hat. Unfortunately, Atwood hadn't gotten a very good look at the man's face, though he had been struck by one, peculiar feature—the stranger's unsettling half-smile.

The same "smiling stranger"—as the tabloids immediately tagged him—had been seen by Miss Charlotte Jaffey, one of the Nisbets' tenants, when she left her apartment to do some shopping at around 2:20 P.M. on Monday. The man, who was standing on the front steps of the building when Miss Jaffey emerged, had muttered something inaudible to her as she passed. Glancing over at him, she had been so unnerved by his weird little smile that she had quickly looked away and hurried down the street.

While a team of detectives tried to track down the "smiling stranger," others pursued the physical leads. At first, the towel seemed like a promising clue. Presuming that it belonged to the killer, investigators believed that they might be able to trace it by its laundry marks. But that hope was dashed when Stephen Nisbet identified the murder weapon as a towel from his own kitchen. Nisbet's information raised a whole new set of questions. Why had his wife been carrying the towel while showing the stranger the vacant flat? Wouldn't she have left it in the kitchen when she went downstairs to answer the door? And if she *hadn't* been carrying it, then how did the strangler get hold of it?

In the meantime—though Mary Nisbet's murder seemed to prove that he'd been lying all along—the self-confessed strangler, Paul Cameron, continued to languish in jail. His claims, already highly suspect, were further eroded when investigators determined that on June 24, the day Mrs. Ollie Russell was strangled in Santa Barbara, Cameron had been in Los Angeles, living and working at Salvation Army headquarters. Nevertheless, having declared so unequivocally that Cameron was guilty, District Attorney Clarence Ward appeared loathe to let him go.

And then, on Thursday, August 19, just three days after Mary Nisbet's murder, another landlady was strangled.

This time, the killing took place in Stockton. The victim was Isabel Gallegos, a seventy-six-year-old widow who rented rooms in her weatherbeaten home on Channel Street, not far from the railroad tracks. She was found by a former tenant named C. C. Parlett, who had dropped by the house to pick up his mail.

As soon as Parlett stepped inside, he saw that something was wrong. The place had been turned upside down—closets ransacked, bureaus emptied, clothes and household objects scattered all over the floors. He found Mrs. Gallegos crumpled in the bedroom, face blue, eyes bulging, a cotton pillowcase twisted tightly around her neck.

The immediate assumption—shared by the police, press, and public alike—was that the murder was the work of the "Dark Strangler," who had been lured by the "Room to

Let" sign in the victim's parlor window. That same afternoon, a Stockton landlady named Sadie Powers reported another attack to the police. According to Mrs. Powers, who managed an apartment building at 100 Union Street, a "dark-complexioned" stranger with "bushy eyebrows" had come to the front door, inquiring about the vacancy sign posted on the front of the building. As soon as they were alone in the flat, the man had grabbed her by the arms, then attempted to wrap his hands around her throat. Mrs. Powers, however, put up such fierce resistance that the assailant—whom she described as approximately twenty-five years old, five feet seven inches tall, and weighing 150 pounds—fled.

Even as police followed up on this lead, however, they were beginning to wonder whether Isabel Gallegos had, in fact, been the victim of the strangler, since the state of the crime scene suggested robbery, not rape-murder, as the main motivation. Mrs. Gallegos' daughter, Mrs. Jack Meaney of Petaluma, reinforced this theory when she revealed that her mother had a local (and totally erroneous) reputation as a woman of wealth, the type of eccentric old lady who stuffs wads of cash inside her mattress. When the autopsy revealed that Mrs. Gallegos had not, in fact, been subjected to a sexual assault, Police Chief C. W. Potter and other members of the Stockton force were even less inclined to attribute her death to the strangler.

Once again, the investigation had hit a dead end. However, on Saturday, August 21, another suspect was identified. John Slivkoff was a Russian immigrant whose squat build, swarthy complexion, and sullen looks matched the widely broadcast descriptions of the strangler. A police detective named John Greenhall had spotted Slivkoff loitering on a Sacramento street corner and, noting his resemblance to the mystery killer, had picked him up for vagrancy.

Greenhall's suspicions seemed confirmed when—after seeing Slivkoff's photograph in the newpapers—two landladies, one in Sacramento, the other in San Francisco, came forward to recount frightening encounters with the suspect. According to Mrs. Mary Kent, Slivkoff had showed up at her rooming house the previous year and, after ascertaining that the sixty-year-old woman was all alone, had "attempted to embrace her." When she fought off his efforts, he threatened her with violence. "Do you know how easily I could choke you to death?" he had growled. The quick-thinking landlady had scared Slivkoff away by persuading him that there were workmen right outside the house.

Mrs. H. Wallis told police that Slivkoff had appeared at the front door of her lodging house at 914 North Street to inquire about a room. He had acted so strangely, however, that she refused to let him inside, slamming and bolting the door while he stood on the stoop shouting imprecations at her.

By Sunday, August 22, plans were afoot to transport the prisoner first to Oakland, then to San Francisco, where he would be viewed by various witnesses, including David Atwood and Charlotte Jaffey—the pair who had seen the "smiling stranger" lurking outside Mary Nisbet's apartment building—and, of course, Merton Newman.

Even before Slivkoff left Sacramento, two other strangler suspects had materialized: an Oakland man named Ralph Olivera, who showed up at police headquarters and confessed to the Nisbet crime, and Raymond Escovar, alias Raymond Abrego, a ranch hand who was held on suspicion when he showed up at the Marysville stationhouse and declared that he had an overpowering desire "to strangle someone."

Wihin twenty-four hours, the statements of both Olivera and Escovar were dismissed as the ravings of cranks. The following day, Tuesday, August 24, efforts to identify John Slivkoff as the strangler fell through when, after viewing the suspect, David Atwood, Charlotte Jaffey, and Merton Newman concurred that the Russian bore no resemblance to the man they had seen. And on Friday, August 27, a Santa Barbara alienist, Dr. N. H. Brush, made official what the rest of the world had already surmised. After examining Paul Cameron, alias Phillip H. Brown, in his Santa Barbara cell, Dr. Brush reported that the prisoner was a lunatic who should be remanded to a psychiatric hospital for immediate treatment.

Precisely six months had passed since the strangler's first murder, and—though four more elderly landladies had met horrible deaths in that time—investigators were no closer to a solution than they had been in February. On Saturday, August 28, the Oakland police publicly admitted their failure, resorting to arboreal metaphors to sum up their predicament—"stumped," "up a tree."

Only one thing seemed certain. Whoever the strangler was, he clearly possessed a Jekyll-Hyde nature. To win his way into the homes of his victims, particularly at a time when the entire Pacific Coast was on the alert for the mysterious strangler, he would have to be a man who made an exceedingly favorable impression: polite, well-spoken, apparently innocuous.

Once alone with his prey in a vacant apartment, however, he underwent a terrifying transformation, instantly turning into a lust-driven monster, a creature who murdered and raped with the fury of a beast.

PART 3

†

PREY

16

✝

Build for yourself a strong box,
Fashion each part with care.
When it is as strong as your hand
   can make it,
Put all your troubles there.
                    Anon., "Then Laugh"

Again and again during his sixteen-month murder spree, the strangler's bloodlust would erupt in a lethal frenzy, then subside for a period lasting anywhere from three to twelve weeks. Nowadays, we recognize this as the classic pattern of serial homicide, officially defined by the FBI as a string of random murders interspersed with "emotional cooling-off periods" of varying duration. But back in 1926, the FBI was still a fledgling organization (J. Edgar Hoover had become its director only two years earlier), and the agent who would coin the phrase "serial murder," Robert K. Ressler of the bureau's Behavioral Science Unit, hadn't even been born.

Not that serial murder was a wholly unknown phenomenon. Before the strangler had throttled his first landlady, two of the most ghastly killers of modern times, Fritz Haarmann and Georg Grossmann, were already at work in Weimar Germany. A vampiric monster who battened on teenage boys, Haarmann slaughtered at least two dozen young drifters in the years following World War I. After luring a victim to his lodgings near the Hanover train station, he would set upon and savage his prey, reaching an orgasmic pitch as he chewed through the boy's throat. Afterwards Haarmann and his lover, a male prostitute named Hans Grans, would dismember the body and peddle the flesh as black-market beef.

Butchering humans for both pleasure and profit was also Grossmann's m.o. Night after night, the brutish street vendor would pick up a prostitute, bring her back to his squalid flat in a Berlin slum, then rape her, kill her, and carve up her body. In the chaotic aftermath of the Great War, Grossmann had no trouble peddling his hideous cutlets to his meat-deprived neighbors, who—believing that they were purchasing pork—were transformed into unwitting cannibals.

In our own country, too, there had already been one celebrated case of serial homicide—that of the nineteenth-century "multimurderer," Dr. H. H. Holmes, who became America's bogeyman when he confessed to twenty-seven killings, most of them committed in the labyrinthine depths of his Chicago "Murder Castle," a Gothic horror house masquerading as a Gilded Age office building. From the moment of his arrest, Holmes (a.k.a. "The Archfiend," "The Murder Demon," "The Chicago Bluebeard") became America's most talked-about criminal, and his 1895 trial became a nationwide sensation, the O.J. Simpson circus of its day.

As notorious as he was at the turn of the century, however, Holmes had all but faded from public memory by the 1920s, while the enormities of the two German lust murderers were largely unknown in this country. As a result, when the "Dark Strangler" first materialized in 1926, police were slow to define the phenomenon they were dealing with, since there was no apparent context in which to comprehend the horror. The only comparable case that people continued to remember (indeed, that had long passed into the imperishable realm of myth) was that of Jack the Ripper—and in the fall of '26, it would finally dawn on one anonymous newspaperman that the monster who was terrorizing the Pacific Coast was a homegrown version of the legendary "Butcher of Whitechapel." But before that happened, four more women would die.

Beginning on Thursday, October 21, 1926, when the story first broke in the *Morning Oregonian*, the city of Portland was transfixed by a spellbinding mystery.

Two days earlier, at around 3:30 P.M. on Tuesday, a fifteen-year-old boy named Charles Withers, a student at the Benson Polytechnic School, had returned to his house at 815 East Lincoln Street and found that his mother was gone. At first the teenager wasn't concerned. His mother, a pretty thirty-two-year-old divorcée named Beata, was often out running errands or visiting with friends when he got home from school. He went about his business, expecting her to show up at any moment.

When she still wasn't home by suppertime, however, he became worried enough to telephone W. R. "Bob" Frentzel, an intimate friend of his mother's, who lived just a few blocks away. As soon as Frentzel arrived, the two made a search of the house and discovered that Mrs. Withers' overcoat was missing along with her hat and pocketbook. Clearly she had gone off somewhere. Frentzel telephoned around to her friends, but none of them had seen or spoken to Beata all day.

That night, young Charles slept alone in the empty house. Early the following morning, he went to the police station and reported that his mother was missing.

He spent that day attending his classes, hoping that his mother would be there waiting for him when he got home. As soon as he stepped through the front door, however, his heart sank—he could *feel* the emptiness of the house even before he confirmed it with a quick tour of the rooms.

Once again he telephoned Frentzel, who showed up this time with another family friend, a gentleman named Cook. Frentzel proposed that the three do a more thorough check of Mrs. Withers' wardrobe to see what garments she might have taken with her besides her topcoat and hat.

The Withers house was a tidy, pleasantly furnished bungalow with two bedrooms, a living room, dining room, kitchen, breakfast nook, and bathroom on the ground floor. The second story consisted of a large, unfinished attic. While Charles searched through his mother's bedroom closet, the two older men ascended to the attic, where Beata Withers stored some of her clothing in a steamer trunk.

That, as everyone later agreed, was the only good thing that could be said about the tragedy—that the boy had not been present when the ghastly discovery was made.

It was Frentzel who opened the trunk, while Cook looked over his shoulder. Lifting the heavy lid, Frentzel carefully removed the partitioned tray and set it on the floorboards. The trunk was crammed with clothing, which appeared to be in a surprising state of disarray. Frentzel, who knew Mrs. Withers to be a fastidious woman, would have expected her to fold and store her clothing in a more orderly fashion.

Reaching into the trunk, he removed a few of the garments—then let out such a startling cry that Cook "just about jumped out of my skin," as he would later put it. As Frentzel staggered backward a step, Cook peered inside the trunk and gave his own little cry as he saw what his companion had uncovered—a pair of naked female legs, half covered by blouses, skirts, and sweaters.

The police were called. By the time they arrived, Frentzel and Cook had pulled most of the clothes from the trunk. Inside, Beata Withers' corpse—naked except for a thin cotton slip bunched up around her armpits—lay curled in the fetal position, one arm shoved between her legs.

While Deputy Coroner Ross examined the body, Detective James M. Tackaberry and two of his subordinates searched the house for clues. It was Tackaberry who made the discovery that would lead to so much controversy in the coming days. He spotted it hanging on a kitchen wall, a framed little print showing a troop of winged fairies swarming out of an open strongbox. Inscribed above the illustration was a bit of versified inspiration entitled "Then Laugh":

> Build for yourself a strong box,
> Fashion each part with care.
> When it is as strong as your hand
>   can make it.
> Put all your troubles there.
> Hide there all thought of your failures
> And each bitter cup that you quaff,
> Lock all your heartaches within it,
> Then sit on the lid and laugh!
>
> Tell no one else its contents,
> Never its secrets share;

When you've dropped in
   your care and worry
Keep them forever there;
Hide them from sight so completely
That the world will never dream half;
Fasten the strong box securely—
Then sit on the lid and laugh!

The moment he laid eyes on this doggerel, Tackaberry gave a little grunt—the sound of a man who has just had a brilliant flash of insight. He called to his subordinates and hurried up to the attic.

By then, Beata Withers' body was already on its way to the city morgue. At Tackaberry's orders, one of his men squeezed inside the trunk, reached out a hand and began piling clothes over himself, then managed to work the partitioned tray over himself and somehow close the lid. It was a feat worthy of Houdini, but it persuaded Detective Tackaberry that the theory he had formed in the kitchen was correct. The mystery was solved, as far as he was concerned.

Beata Withers had suffocated herself by shutting herself inside the trunk, having taken the advice of the anonymous poetaster a little too literally.

Needless to say, Detective Tackaberry's theory, announced to reporters on Wednesday afternoon, was greeted with a good deal of skepticism if not outright scorn. Even Tackaberry had to concede that "trunk suicides are rare." In fact, neither he nor any other member of the Portland P.D. had ever heard of "such a method being used."

Still, the detective held stubbornly to his belief, insisting that the dead woman had gotten the idea from the framed bit of poesy in her kitchen. "Mrs. Withers read that motto and took it too seriously," he declared. "I could not be convinced that it was not murder until I read the poem. Then I tried the trunk to see if a person could do as Mrs. Withers did—enter, arrange the clothing, work the tray in place, and drop the lid. It could be done easily and all suspicion of murder vanished."

Others, however, weren't so sure, particularly after some recent stains that turned out to be a mix of blood and saliva were discovered on the pillow of Mrs. Withers' bed. In spite of Tackaberry's certainty, police pressed on with their investigation, bringing in various people for questioning, including Bob Frentzel (whose blue coupe had reportedly been seen in front of the Withers home on the morning of the murder) and the former husband of the dead woman, Mr. Charles Withers of Seattle, who himself was highly dubious of the suicide theory. "I do not believe she would have done such a thing," declared Mr. Withers, who, like Frentzel, turned out to have an airtight alibi.

Other people acquainted with Beata Withers shared her ex-husband's point of view. One of her neighbors, for example—a woman named Miriam Wright—had spoken to Mrs. Withers just hours before her death. "She was working out in the yard in her dahlias," Mrs. Wright told reporters. "She appeared unusually happy, talking about her plans for her garden this winter and next spring. Why, it seems impossible that a few hours later she would have crawled into the trunk and committed suicide."

Police agreed that Mrs. Withers, "apparent happy attitude" argued against suicide. Still, as Deputy Coroner Ross pointed out, "such a mental attitude on the part of one who is about to take his or her own life is not unknown."

And indeed, as their investigation continued, police began to uncover convincing reasons why Beata might have been driven to suicide. According to some of her friends, the thirty-two-year-old divorcée had been in desperate financial straits, deeply in debt and in danger of losing her house. In an effort to generate income, she had decided to take in boarders. Indeed, just a few days before her death, she had placed a "Room to Let" ad in the *Morning Oregonian*.

The most explosive evidence of all, however, was a personal notebook discovered in the top drawer of Beata Withers' bedroom bureau. This so-called "love diary" (as the tabloids immediately tagged it) was a fervid chronicle of her ill-fated love affair with Bob Frentzel, who was revealed to be a thoroughgoing cad, having lied to Mrs. Withers about his marital status.

The first entry, dated January 11, 1925, describes her initial meeting with her seducer: "It is just two years ago New Year's Eve that I first went out with Bob. I met him through————, when she brought him out to the house, and it was a case of love at first sight, at least for me."

Only a few nights later, she is already permitting Bob to make love to her (though, in the parlance of the time, to "make love" was a more innocent activity than it is today, involving passionate wooing, not consummated sex).

Well, Bob and I had a wonderful time, and he put me in a taxi and took me home after the show. I remember it was bitter cold out and on the way home, he took me on his lap and made love to me. Me, who had never let any man make love to me before except Charles, and then not until I had known him for over three years! Yes, I had fallen so desperately in love that it seemed the perfectly right thing for me to let him love me.

When we got home, I made some hot chocolate and we sat over the cups for a while and talked, wholly absorbed in one another. Bob told me he was divorced and had a little girl. Even told me where he got his divorce, which I believe he said was either in Haley, Idaho or in Caldwell, Idaho.

It isn't long, however, before this blissful account takes a sudden, melodramatic turn when Mrs. Withers discovers that her lover has been deceiving her all along.

I had always been lonely, looking for the person who would understand me as well as I thought he did. Poor little me. How happy we can be when ignorance is bliss. I sit here night after night, day after day, without a friend who wants to know me any more, because they all know that Bob is married and living with his wife. Dear God! How I have repented, only too late, for he has been my ruin!

The diary ends on an ominous note, with the poor woman exclaiming "how terrible it is to be killed by this slow process" and wondering darkly how and when she will ever "come out of it."

* * *

For days the Withers case was the biggest news in town, overshadowing every other local story. So bizarre was the Portland "trunk death mystery" that it was reported in newspapers as far away as San Francisco, though the *Chronicle* relegated it to its daily "Oddities in the News" feature, lumping it together with other believe-it-or-not items: the prediction of a prominent Parisian designer, M. Martin, who foresaw a time when fashionable gentlemen would dress in décolleté garb; the discovery of two little girls living in a wolf's den near a Bengalese village; and the announcement by London attorney Mansfield Robinson that he had established a telepathic link with a Martian woman named "Opestinipitia Secomba" who kept him apprised of the latest news from the red planet. Weird and intriguing as the Withers case was, it seemed remote from the immediate concerns of San Franciscans, who were far more interested in a story that broke on the very day that the Portland woman's body was discovered.

The story emanated from San Jose, where another suspect in the "Dark Strangler" murders had been identified and arrested. And this time the police were absolutely certain that they had the right man. His name was J. E. Ross. On Tuesday, October 19, under the pretense of being a salesman, he had gained entrance to the house of Mrs. A. Di Fiori of 181 Fruitvale Avenue, then raped her at gunpoint. Before fleeing in his automobile, he had warned her not to inform the police. "Remember what happened to the other women who squealed," he had said.

In spite of this threat, Mrs. Di Fiori went directly to the police, who quickly arrested Ross, already a suspect in another assault, the August 23 rape of a woman named Edna Johnson in her Delmas Avenue home. Inside Ross' car, detectives found a bludgeon, fashioned from a lead pipe wrapped in sacking, and several articles of clothing which, according to police, "were there to effect a quick disguise." Even more incriminating were certain remarks Ross made under questioning that seemed to connect him to the still-unsolved murder of Laura Beal the previous March.

The very next day, Sheriff George W. Lyle made a riveting announcement. He would "positively be able to link" Ross not only to the attacks on Mrs. Di Fiori and Mrs.

Johnson but to the killing of Laura Beal. On Wednesday, October 20, the *San Francisco Chronicle* trumpeted the news: a San Jose man had been positively identified as the notorious strangler.

But Sheriff Lyle's announcement turned out to be precipitous. J. E. Ross may have been a serial rapist, but he was *not* the "Dark Strangler"—as new and alarming events up in Portland were about to prove.

17

✝

Slowly, the police put two and two together, obtained the
correct answer, and made the cautious pronouncement that
perhaps the Dark Strangler was at work in Portland.

L. C. Douthwaite, *Mass Murder*

On Thursday, October 21, just one day after the discovery of Beata Withers' body, another Portland woman, a fifty-
nine-year-old landlady named Virginia Grant, had been
found dead in the basement of one of her properties, a vacant house at 604 East Twenty-second Street. The circumstances of her death seemed highly suspicious. Her corpse
was found behind the furnace—as though it had been placed
there in a deliberate act of concealment—and two diamond
rings, valued at several hundred dollars apiece, were missing
from her fingers.

Nevertheless, the immediate judgment of the investigating
officers was that the elderly woman had died of natural
causes, possibly a heart attack.

Mrs. Grant's children were justifiably outraged at this
finding and demanded that the police treat their mother's
death as a homicide. Still, the case generated very little attention compared to the controversy surrounding the sensational "trunk death mystery." More remarkably still, no one
seemed to draw a connection between the cases, even
though the initial report of Mrs. Grant's death appeared on
page one of Friday's *Oregonian,* directly adjacent to its daily
update on the Withers investigation.

When Mabel Fluke turned up dead on Saturday afternoon, however, even the Portland police were finally compelled to admit that something sinister might be going on in their city.

The only daughter of prosperous Portland businessman William MacDonald, Mabel Fluke was raised in privileged circumstances. Her recent life, however, had been marked by hardship. After twelve contented years of marriage, her husband, Robert, had been stricken with cancer. The stress of caring for him and of witnessing his rapid decline had taken a toll on her own health, too. Still, she seemed surprisingly girlish at thirty-seven—a slight, pretty woman with a perfectly oval face, milky complexion, and dark, strikingly large eyes.

In the spring of 1925, the couple had sold their ranch in Independence, Oregon, and returned to Portland, purchasing a two-story house in the Sellwood district at 1521 East Twenty-first Street. Fronting the Eastmoreland golf links, the house was a tidy, wood-frame affair with three rooms on the ground floor and, on the second, two more rooms plus a small, unfinished attic. Less than a year after moving into the place, however, Robert Fluke succumbed to his illness.

At her parents' insistence, Mabel had moved back to the family estate in St. Johns, occupying a small bungalow on the property. Though her husband's death was a devastating loss, the young widow refused to retire from life. Her delicate frame and fragile health belied her strength of character. Enrolling in a local business school, she undertook a course in stenography. And she decided to become a landlady, renting out and overseeing the upkeep of her former home in Sellwood.

Several parties had occupied the house since the summer. The most recent tenant, a travelling salesman, had stayed there for only three weeks before leaving in the second week of October. On Saturday, October 16, several days after his departure, Mabel had placed an ad in the *Morning Oregonian:* "5-ROOM bungalow, completely furnished, electric range, garage on paved street. Reasonable to responsible party. 1521 E. 21st S. There Wednesday, 10 A.M. to 5 P.M."

Very early Wednesday morning, before her parents had awakened, Mabel left St. Johns and headed out to Sellwood, intending to do some housecleaning before any prospective tenants arrived. Along the way, she stopped at the plumbing establishment of Leroy Crouchley, who had been hired to install a sewer connection on the property. Mrs. Fluke complained that Crouchley's workers had left some of the pipes exposed. Crouchley promised to send someone out to attend to the matter before the end of the day.

At approximately 11:00 A.M., a woman named Emma Schultz, who lived next door to the Fluke house, stepped onto her porch and saw the young widow on her hands and knees, scrubbing her own front porch. Mrs. Schultz called a greeting to Mabel, who looked up from her work and exchanged a few words with the older woman, explaining that she "might go out to the country after renting the house." Mrs. Schultz—who assumed that Mabel was referring to Independence, Oregon, where Robert Fluke's family lived—spent a few more minutes chatting before retiring into her house.

Another neighbor, a woman named Newton who lived across the street from the Fluke house, noticed the young widow on several occasions that day, the last time at approximately 1:00 P.M., when Mabel came to the front door to admit a young couple who had just driven up to look at the house. Two hours later, Mrs. Newton glanced out her kitchen window and saw another car pull up. A family of four—father, mother, and two teenage girls—emerged from the car and stepped onto the porch. The husband rang the doorbell. When no one answered, he tried again. After another brief wait, the family held a quick conversation, then climbed back into the car and drove away.

When their daughter failed to return home that evening, Mabel's parents weren't alarmed, believing that she had decided either to sleep over in Sellwood or travel on to Independence to visit her husband's family. By Thursday night, however, William MacDonald was anxious enough to send his son, William Junior, out to Sellwood. The young man returned a few hours later. Mabel wasn't there, he reported. The house had been locked, but he had managed to wiggle inside through an unlocked basement window.

The elder MacDonald assumed that his daughter had, in fact, continued on to Oregon. Early Saturday morning, however, Miss Marion Fluke, the eighteen-year-old niece of Mabel's late husband, arrived by train from Independence for a weeklong visit to Portland. Mabel had known of the girl's trip and had, in fact, written a letter to Marion, promising to greet her at the station. When Mabel failed to appear, however, Marion telephoned the MacDonald home and spoke to William Senior.

"You mean Mabel didn't go out to Independence?" Mr. MacDonald asked.

"Why, no," Marion said, surprised. "She said she'd be here to meet my train."

When Mr. MacDonald hung up the phone, his face was clouded with anxiety. "Something's happened to Mabel," he said to his wife.

Minutes later, he was at the St. Johns police station. An officer named C. D. Maxwell was assigned to accompany him to Sellwood. Using Patrolman Maxwell's skeleton key, the two men entered the house and made a quick search of the downstairs rooms. Lying on the kitchen table were a package of tea, a paper sack containing four eggs, and Mabel's keyring. They found her purse inside a cabinet drawer. The sight of it made her father's throat constrict with fear. Clearly, his daughter had not gone off anywhere. A sudden, terrifying image came to him—Mabel's violated body lying in the ditch that had been dug for the sewer line.

The two men proceeded upstairs. It took only a moment to check the two bedrooms. There was no sign of Mabel in either of them. That left only one place to look. The attic was nothing but a narrow space approximately five feet high and nine feet wide, running the length of the house between the eves and the upstairs hallway. It was accessible through a small, hinged panel in the hall. Officer Maxwell opened the panel. It was pitch black inside the attic, but Maxwell had brought along a flashlight. He thumbed on the switch and aimed the beam inside.

William MacDonald had been wrong about one thing. His daughter's body wasn't lying outside in a ditch. She was stretched on her back, clad in the same dress she had been wearing on Wednesday. Her right shoe was still on her foot;

the other was lying on the floorboards nearby. She had died of strangulation. Her silk scarf had been wound tightly around her neck and double-knotted on one side. The stench that suffused the cramped little space made it clear that she had been dead for several days.

The discovery of Mabel Fluke's body, the third mysterious death of a Portland woman in less than a week, sent shock waves through the city. Even the police, who seemed so reluctant to confront the grim truth, admitted that there were significant connections among the cases. All three had occurred in the same section of town, southeast Portland. Each of the women had been offering rooms to let and had recently placed ads in the newspapers. All three bodies had been found in concealed places—crammed inside a steamer trunk, shoved behind a furnace, laid out in a cramped attic.

Mabel Fluke had clearly been strangled, and though opinion remained divided about the other two women, there was a very real possibility that both of them had died the same way. And certain personal items were unaccounted for in each case. Like Virginia Grant, Mabel Fluke had been wearing diamond rings that were missing from her fingers. And her overcoat, like Beata Withers', was nowhere to be found.

For the first time, the Portland authorities were beginning to make another connection, too. Speaking to reporters on Saturday evening, Police Captain John T. Moore acknowledged that the deaths of Mrs. Withers, Grant, and Fluke bore an unsettling resemblance to the recent spate of killings in California's Bay Area. He urged that "women stay away from untenanted houses unless accompanied by a man."

Chief of Police Jenkins issued an even more emphatic warning. "In all of these cases, the women had advertised their places for rent. Whenever a woman has such a place to rent, at least until we find out more about these cases, it is better that she have somebody stay with her until her business is transacted.

"This may frighten many women," Chief Jenkins concluded. "But it is better that some should be frightened than there should be any more lives lost. It appears to me that this is the work of someone who is watching these advertisements."

Even Detective Tackaberry did an abrupt about-face. After sticking to his trunk-suicide theory for several days, he suddenly declared that "Mrs. Withers and Mrs. Fluke were murdered, without a question. And though I haven't investigated the Mrs. Grant case as yet, I believe she met her death at the hands of the same person." Beyond the fact that this person was clearly "of unsound mind," Tackaberry didn't speculate about the killer's identity, though, like Captain Moore, he alluded to the string of landlady murders down in San Francisco, Oakland, and San Jose.

Up in Oregon, of course, most people were unaware of the California crimes. In its Sunday edition, however, the *Morning Oregonian* filled its readers in on the story. For the first time, the citizens of Portland learned the chilling sobriquet of the fiend who had been terrorizing the Bay cities: the "Dark Strangler."

Remarkably, however, there were still some officials in Portland who clung tenaciously, if not desperately, to the belief that the deaths of Mrs. Withers, Grant, and Fluke were simply three unrelated tragedies. Though the irreducible facts of the Fluke case—a strangled female corpse concealed in an attic—seemed like a pretty strong indication of foul play, a deputy coroner named Guldransen opined that the unfortunate woman may well have taken her own life by arranging herself on the attic floor, then knotting the scarf about her own neck. The bruises on her elbows, Guldransen explained, had evidently been caused by her "efforts to draw the knots tight, one arm having struck the side wall of the attic, the other the floor."

The debate over Beata Withers' "trunk death," meanwhile, remained as heated as ever. After consulting several medical treatises on asphyxiation, County Coroner Earl Smith told reporters that, as far as he could see, the Withers case "looked like murder." During the "second stage" of asphyxiation, he explained, the person lapses into unconsciousness, but the body and limbs begin moving spasmodically, even violently, "due to the action of uncirculated blood on the nerves." If Mrs. Withers had suffocated inside the trunk, Smith said, she would have dislodged the tray and trunk lid in her death throes. Her body certainly wouldn't have been lying in the "peaceful, apparently sleeping attitude in which it was found."

There was only one possible conclusion, Smith said. Mrs. Withers was already dead before she was placed in the trunk.

Counter to Coroner Smith's statement, however, was the opinion of a "high police official," who, speaking anonymously to reporters on Sunday evening, pointed out that there were no apparent marks of violence on Mrs. Withers' body. Moreover, her "love diary" proved that she was "hopelessly despondent, that she owed bills amounting to several hundred dollars, and that her house was about to be turned over to the mortgage holders." For these and other reasons—including the testimony of her good friend, Bob Frentzel, who told investigators that she had threatened suicide the previous year—the unnamed official held firm to his belief that Beata Withers had taken her own life.

Over the next few days, the controversy continued to rage. Early Monday morning, Chief Jenkins, pronouncing the situation "the most baffling and mysterious ever to come within the scope of the Portland police," met with Mayor Baker to request an emergency appropriation of $1,000. The funds, the chief told reporters, would be used "to bring to the city some nationally known criminologist to take charge of the case." Expressing his belief that the three deaths appeared to be the work of a "methodically working pervert," Jenkins declared that "if such a killer is at large, the matter of money should be our smallest worry."

To be sure, there was no indication that any of the women had been sexually molested, a fact which, in the view of certain officials, seemed to undercut the murder theory. Asked about this aspect of the case, Chief Jenkins replied that there were "numerous varieties of perverts," including those who killed "solely for the thrill of it."

Every available detective had been assigned to the case. In addition to James Tackaberry and his partner, Robert Phillips, the team consisted of a dozen investigators including, by a bizarre coincidence, one named Earl Nelson. "As of now," Chief Jenkins declared, "all other police work is secondary."

Other members of the department, however, continued to

take issue with the chief, insisting that Beata Withers had committed suicide and that Virginia Grant, who suffered from heart disease, had died of natural causes. As for Mabel Fluke, these skeptics conceded that she may have been killed, but her death, they argued, was unrelated to the others. Whatever similarities existed among the three cases were "merely coincidental."

Of course, the skeptics had trouble explaining away certain inconvenient facts, such as the missing overcoats and jewelry. On Monday evening, Mrs. Withers' cousin, Carl Duhrkoop, made another discovery that cast serious doubt on the suicide theory. Going through Beata's belongings, Mr. Duhrkoop discovered that every piece of the dead woman's underwear was gone.

Late Tuesday afternoon, Mayor Baker met in his office with a group of officials, including Police Chief Jenkins; Detective Lieutenants Thatcher and Graves; County Coroner Earl Smith; and the three physicians in charge of the autopsies, Drs. Robert Benson, Harvey Myers, and Frank Menne. The purpose of the conference, the first of its kind in Portland history, was (as the newspapers reported) "to coordinate the scientific and medical features of the cases with the police angles."

Nothing, however, came out of the meeting but more ambiguity. While Jenkins and his subordinates saw the deaths as the work of a single killer—"someone using some cunning method"—the physicians were inclined to the opposite view, that the three cases were unconnected. According to their preliminary findings, "Mrs. Fluke met death by strangulation, possibly self-imposed; Mrs. Grant died of natural causes; and Mrs. Withers died of suffocation, possibly self-inflicted."

The coroner's jury investigating the Withers case was riven by the same conflict of opinion. Convening on Wednesday evening, the six jurors heard the testimony of various witnesses, including Mrs. Withers' fifteen-year-old son, Charles; her good friend, Bob Frentzel; her neighbor, G. C. Cook (who, along with Frentzel, had found the body); coroner's physician Benson; and a police inspector named R. H. Craddock (the officer who, at Detective Tackaberry's orders, had squeezed inside the trunk).

After deliberating for more than an hour, however, the jury failed to reach a verdict, with three members reportedly voting for suicide, the others for murder.

The matter remained unresolved the following day, when funeral services for Beata Withers were held at the Miller and Tracy chapel. Immediately afterwards, her body was transported to the Portland crematorium for its final disposition.

On Friday, October 29, 1926, Portlanders were briefly distracted from the case of the three "mystery deaths" by some sad news from Detroit.

One week earlier in Montreal, Harry Houdini had been visited backstage by a young McGill University student named J. Gordon Whitehead, who took a dim view of Houdini's debunking crusade against Spiritualism. Whitehead asked Houdini if it were true that, as the magician often claimed, his stomach was so solid that it could sustain the hardest punches. Raising his arms, Houdini invited the young man to feel the muscles.

Without warning, Whitehead delivered a flurry of savage blows to Houdini's body, directly above the appendix. By that night, the fifty-two-year-old magician was suffering from agonizing abdominal pains. In spite of a temperature of 104 degrees, he performed in Detroit on Sunday, October 24, but collapsed as soon as the show was over. The following day, he was rushed to the hospital, where his ruptured appendix was removed. By Friday morning, peritonitis had developed.

Houdini's dire condition was front-page news everywhere in the nation, including Portland, where the *Oregonian* reported that physicians attending the Great Escapologist had "expressed doubts about his recovery." It wasn't long before those doubts were confirmed. By Sunday, Harry barely had strength to talk. "I'm tired of fighting," he whispered to his brother, Theo. "I guess this thing is going to get me." The next day, Monday, October 31—Halloween—the "master mystifier" passed on to the "other side," though not before promising his beloved wife, Bess, that he would do his best to contact her from the "great beyond."

*   *   *

The day before Houdini's death, a Portland policeman named James Russell received a letter from his cousin, George, who lived in Santa Barbara. By a grim coincidence, this cousin was the same George Russell whose wife, Ollie, had been killed by the "Dark Strangler" the previous June. Included in the letter was a description of the suspect that had appeared in the Santa Barbara papers: "Thirty-five years old, 5 feet 8 or 10 inches tall, heavy build, especially shoulders and chest, and very dark. Said to be of Greek nativity, though speaking excellent English and to be a restaurant worker—either a cook or dishwasher—and also a construction worker."

As Patrolman Russell read this letter, he suddenly recalled that, while making his rounds on the previous Tuesday, he had spotted someone matching this very description in the vicinity of Mabel Fluke's house in Sellwood. At the time, of course, Russell had thought nothing of it, but now he wondered if the man he had seen was really the "Dark Strangler."

Russell's story immediately made it into the *Oregonian*, which published the description of the strangler suspect in its Saturday edition—too late to do any good. By that time, the elusive killer, whose escapist skills had once earned him a comparison to Houdini himself, had already vanished from the city.

18

✝

Five million words were written and sent from Somerville, New Jersey, during the first eleven days of the trial. Twice as many newspaper men were there as at Dayton. . . . Over wires jacked into the largest telegraph switchboard in the world traveled the tidings of lust and crime to every corner of the United States, and the public lapped them up and cried for more.

Frederick Lewis Allen, *Only Yesterday*

If asked to name the most famous trial of the 1920s, most people would immediately think of Leopold and Loeb, or Sacco and Vanzetti, or possibly the so-called Dayton "Monkey Trial," whose defendant, John T. Scopes, was found guilty of teaching evolution. For sheer sensationalism, however, none of these matched the proceedings that got underway in a New Jersey courtroom in early November 1926. The case in question was a double homicide, the most notorious since Mr. and Mrs. Andrew Borden were hacked to death by a mysterious assailant who may or may not have been their daughter, Lizzie. It would be another seventy years before a different double slaying, that of O. J. Simpson's estranged wife and her waiter-friend, Ron Goldman, generated such frenzied fascination.

The murders themselves had taken place four years earlier in New Brunswick, New Jersey. On the morning of September 16, 1922, a young couple strolling on a dusty back road had stumbled upon two bodies in an apple orchard. Sprawled on their backs under a crab apple tree, the corpses were those of a man and a woman. The dead man was dressed in a dark blue suit and a clerical collar. His Panama hat had been placed over his face, as though to shade him from the sun. Beside him lay the woman, her legs demurely crossed, her head resting on her companion's outstretched right arm. She was wearing a polka-dotted blue dress, the hem tugged as far below her knees as the fabric would allow. A brown scarf had been draped over her throat. Beneath the scarf, her throat was slashed from ear to ear and was swarming with maggots. The autopsy would later reveal that her tongue, larynx, and windpipe had been cut out. She had also been shot three times in the face at point-blank range. Though the dead man had not been subjected to the same mutilations, he had been killed with chilling deliberation, executed with a single .32-caliber bullet to the brain.

It was not the savagery of the killings that made the case so sensational, however, but rather the identity of the victims. The dead man turned out to be the Reverend Edward Wheeler Hall, pastor of St. John's Episcopal Church and a pillar of the community. He was married to Mrs. Frances Hall, née Stevens, daughter of one of New Brunswick's most prominent families. The dead woman found at his side, however, was not his matronly, forty-eight-year-old wife. She was Mrs. Eleanor Mills, a pretty thirty-four-year-old who sang in the congregation choir and was married to the church's sexton.

The exact nature of their relationship was made explicit in a batch of torrid love letters that had been scattered around their corpses. "Sweetheart, my true heart," Eleanor Mills had written in one. "I know there are girls with more shapely bodies, but I'm not caring what they have. I have the greatest part of all blessings, a noble man's deep, true, eternal love, and my heart is his, my life is his; poor as my body is, scrawny as my skin may be; but I am his forever. How impatient I am and will be! I want to look up into your dear face for hours as you touch my body close."

The pastor's replies were equally ardent. "Darling Wonder Heart," he had written. "I just want to crush you for two hours. I want to see you Friday night alone by our road;

where we can let out, unrestrained, that universe of joy and happiness we call ours." He signed himself "D.T.L.," short for *Deiner Treuer Liebhaber* ("Thy True Lover" in German). Mrs. Mills, preferring a less formal endearment, referred to the pastor as "Babykins."

This steaming porridge of sex, murder, and scandal proved irresistible to the tabloids, which began dishing up great, daily gobs to their readers. New Brunswick was overrun with reporters. The nationwide coverage turned the old Phillips farm, where the bodies were found, into a major tourist attraction. On weekends the crime scene became a virtual carnival with vendors hawking popcorn, peanuts, soft drinks, and balloons to the hordes of the morbidly curious.

After two months of investigation, the killer's identity remained unknown, though the likeliest candidates were the pastor's wronged wife and her two brothers, one of whom was reputed to be a crack shot. When Mrs. Hall—a wealthy socialite with many powerful friends in the community—let it be known that she wanted the circus to end, a grand jury was quickly convened. After five days of hearings, it failed to issue an indictment. Mrs. Hall promptly set sail for Europe, and the nation was compelled to seek its titillation elsewhere.

Four years later, however, in a bid to boost its circulation, William Randolph Hearst's fledgling tabloid the New York *Daily Mirror* dredged up some new evidence in the case and plastered the front page of its July 16, 1926, edition with a sensational headline: HALL-MILLS MURDER MYSTERY BARED. Over the course of the following week, the tabloid trumpeted one frenzied charge after another: HALL'S BRIBERY REVEALED, MRS. HALL'S SPIES HELD TOWN IN TERROR, HOW HIDDEN HAND BALKED HALL MURDER JUSTICE.

The strategy worked. Not only did the *Mirror*'s circulation jump, but its strident calls for action forced the governor of New Jersey to reopen the case. Finally, on July 28, 1926, Mrs. Frances Stevens Hall—along with her brothers, Willie and Henry—was arrested for the murder of her husband, Edward, and his inamorata, Mrs. Eleanor Mills.

"The Trial of the Century" (as it was immediately dubbed by the press) began on the morning of Wednesday, November 3, 1926, in Somerville, New Jersey. The courthouse was crammed with hundreds of reporters, who would file more than twelve million words during the trial's spectacular twenty-three-day run. The notoriously stodgy *New York Times,* which normally sniffed at such lurid matters, not only kept four full-time stenographers on the scene but actually covered the case more extensively than the tabloids. (When asked about this seeming contradiction, publisher Adolph S. Ochs loftily replied, "The yellows see such stories only as opportunities for sensationalism. When the *Times* gives a great amount of space to such stories, it turns out authentic sociological documents.") Among the celebrity spectators were evangelist Billy Sunday (whose campaign against "Demon Rum" had helped bring about Prohibition); novelist Mary Roberts Rinehart; and legendary newsman Damon Runyan.

The trial offered more than its share of melodramatic moments, including the public reading of the Reverend Hall's steamy love letters; the questioning of Mrs. Hall (nicknamed "The Iron Widow" because of her stolid demeanor); and— most sensationally—the testimony of a purported eyewitness, a farmwife named Jane Gibson, dubbed "The Pig Woman" because she raised Poland China hogs. Dying of cancer, Mrs. Gibson, attended by a doctor and two nurses, was carried into the courtroom on a stretcher and placed on an iron hospital bed facing the jury box. During her testimony—a gripping (if highly dubious) account of the grisly double murder—her own aged mother sat in the front row of the gallery, wringing her gnarled hands and muttering, "She's a liar! She's a liar! She's a liar!"

For three solid weeks, the dramatic doings in Somerville kept the whole country in thrall. Every morning, Americans followed the case in their daily papers as though devouring the latest installment of the world's juiciest potboiler. During the height of the Hall-Mills hysteria, only the most extraordinary news could dislodge the trial from the headlines or distract the public from the sensational proceedings, from the Iron Widow's steely testimony and the Pig Woman's shocking tale.

In the end, the jury would believe the former over the latter. Mrs. Hall and her brothers would be acquitted of the charges (and would promptly sue the *Mirror* for three million dollars). Before that happened, however, something extraordinary *did* take place in San Francisco—something so purely alarming that, when it made the headlines on November 19, even the Pig Woman's riveting story was relegated to second place.

Almost three months had passed since the murder of Mary Nisbet, the last of the strangler's Bay Area victims. During that time, occasional scare stories would appear in the papers—reports of women who had been attacked in their homes, ostensibly by the strangler.

In late October, for example, the *Chronicle* ran a piece about Mrs. Josephine Allen, a thirty-four-year-old war widow who rented rooms in her house at 1463 Post Street. On the morning of October 26, a strange man appeared at her front door and asked to see a room. No sooner had Mrs. Allen led him up to the second floor than he suddenly seized her by the throat and began choking her. Putting up a fierce struggle, Mrs. Allen managed to break free and dash for the staircase. But her assailant overtook her, and the two began to grapple again at the head of the stairs.

The noise attracted one of the tenants, a Filipino man named Cruz Marcuse, who poked his head out of his room. Spotting him, the stranger shoved Mrs. Allen aside, then whipped a straight razor from his pocket and came at Marcuse, who ducked back into his room and slammed the door.

Mrs. Allen, meanwhile, had stumbled down the stairs and made for the telephone. She had just been connected to the station house when the stranger came bolting down the stairs and out the front door. By the time the police arrived, he was long gone.

Just a few days later, at around eight in the evening, a thirty-five-year-old woman named Glady Mullins stepped out of her house to deposit some trash in her backyard garbage bin. Suddenly, she was seized from behind. Powerful hands clapped a gag to her mouth and began binding her arms with a length of rope. At that moment, however, her next-door neighbor, Frank Hicks—who was just arriving home from his job—pulled his car into the alleyway between the two houses. In the glare of his headlights, he saw Mrs. Mullins lying on the ground, a hulking figure looming above her. As Hicks jumped from his car, the stranger turned, leapt over the backyard fence, and vanished into the night.

Both these episodes were reported in the *San Francisco Chronicle* as the work of the "Dark Strangler." In truth, however, it was impossible to know who had really attacked the two women, or even if it had been the same man. In spite of its inflammatory headline—S.F. WOMAN ATTACKED IN HOME BY STRANGLER—the *Chronicle* conceded that Mrs. Allen's description of her assailant did "not tally in many points with that" of the notorious landlady killer. And Mrs. Mullins, who had been jumped from behind, hadn't gotten a look at her attacker at all.

Indeed, some police officials firmly believed that the strangler was long gone from the Bay Area, which had presumably gotten too hot for him. The recent crimes up in Portland certainly suggested that he had decamped for new hunting grounds. It was more than likely, so these authorities opined, that he had left California for good.

Others, however, including Police Chief O'Brien, believed that it was only a matter of time before the strangler struck again in the Bay City. On Thursday, November 18 (the very day that the Pig Woman was delivering her dramatic sickbed testimony on the other side of the continent), Chief O'Brien's prediction came true.

The victim was Mrs. William Anna Edmonds, who occupied a spacious, two-story house at 3524 Fulton Street, directly across from Golden Gate Park. The middle-aged widow had been more-or-less housebound for the previous three weeks, having slipped down the main staircase and broken her shoulder blade. Even before the accident, Mrs. Edmonds had been thinking of selling her house and moving into smaller, more manageable quarters. With her husband gone and her grown son Raoul living on his own, the house had come to seem oppressive—too big and empty for a lone, aging woman. As a result, she had recently placed a classified ad in the *Chronicle* and a "For Sale" sign in one of the big bay windows fronting the park.

At around six on Thursday evening, Raoul arrived at the house to discuss the plans for his mother's fifty-sixth birthday, which was to fall on the following day. He rang the doorbell but received no response. Puzzled, he walked around to the rear of the house and discovered that the back door was open. That seemed very odd. His mother, nervous under the best of circumstances, had felt even more vulnerable since her accident. She always made sure to lock her doors when she was alone.

Inside the house, Raoul called out to his mother, but she did not reply. Quickly, he began searching the rooms. By the time he reached the second floor, he was already in the grip of alarm. He checked the bedrooms, but they were empty. That left only one place to look, the "radio room," where his mother liked to relax in her armchair and listen to music on her handsome RCA console.

Trying the door, Raoul was startled to discover it locked. He had never known his mother to lock it before. Doing his best to control the trembling of his hands, he used his pocket knife to jiggle open the lock.

Inside, his mother's dead body lay sprawled on the floor, her gray hair in a tangle, her ankle-length skirt yanked up to her knees. A closer examination of Mrs. Edmonds' corpse revealed that the jewelry she normally wore, two diamond rings and a pair of diamond earrings, were missing from her body. The police later ascertained that her purse had also been stolen from her bedroom.

At first, the police hesitated to impute the crime to the "Dark Strangler." True, the circumstances of the case seemed chillingly familiar, a lone matron murdered in her home after placing a classified ad. But except for two faint bruises on the victim's neck, there were no apparent signs of a violent struggle. Nor had the killer gone to extraordinary lengths to conceal the body. The missing jewelry led some investigators to believe that Mrs. Edmonds had been killed during a robbery.

Three things happened on Friday, however, that dispelled any doubts about the crime. First, a witness came forward— a neighbor named Margery Patch, who appeared at police headquarters early Friday morning. According to Mrs. Patch's story, at around 1:30 the previous afternoon, she had dropped by Mrs. Edmonds' house and found the widow in her first-floor sitting room talking to a "strange man." When Mrs. Edmonds explained that she was "engaged in a business deal" relating to the sale of her house, Mrs. Patch excused herself and left—but not before getting a good look at the stranger. The description she gave the police—well-dressed working man, about thirty-five to forty years old, smooth-shaven, with dark hair and olive complexion—corresponded closely to that of the "Dark Strangler."

That robbery had not been the motive behind the murder was further confirmed on Friday afternoon when pathologist Z. E. Bolin ascertained that Mrs. Edmonds had not only been throttled to death but sexually assaulted as well.

The most dramatic development of all, however, occurred on Friday evening. At approximately 6:00 P.M., a pregnant, twenty-eight-year-old woman, Mrs. H. C. Murray of 1114 Grove Street, Burlingame, was viciously attacked in her home. This time, there was absolutely no doubt that the culprit was the "Dark Strangler." Everything about the incident conformed precisely to his previous attacks, except for one crucial difference. Mrs. Murray lived to tell her tale.

She told it to reporters from her hospital bed, where she was recovering from the trauma of the episode. Mrs. Murray's house had been on the market for the past several months. Like Mrs. Edmonds, she had taken out an ad in the papers. There was also a hand-painted "For Sale" sign planted on the front lawn.

At around five o'clock on Friday evening, while her husband was still at work, someone came to the door.

"He saw the sign and rang the bell," Mrs. Murray told the newsmen who were gathered at her bedside. "I opened the door. I had not the slightest thought of meeting the strangler, but I always make it a practice to take every precaution when showing strange men the house. I kept a considerable distance from him from the moment I let him in—at least six or eight feet. I also left the front door open."

The dark-haired man, standing about five feet seven or eight inches tall, looked perfectly presentable. He was dressed in a decent blue serge suit with a white shirt, mustard-colored tie, tan shoes, and brown fedora. Doffing the hat, he began to converse in a polite, well-spoken way that, while not entirely disarming her suspicions, served to put the young woman at her ease.

"He first asked the price of the place," Mrs. Murray continued, "and then said he would like to look at it. I let him in, and he examined the rooms in much detail. He is evidently very familiar with building and construction, for he used expressions relating to such things that I did not understand myself."

While touring the rooms, the stranger began chatting about himself, explaining that he was planning to get married in just three days. "This will be my third marriage," he said. "The first time my wife nagged me to death. The second one I took to dances and would find sitting on the laps of other men." He gave a bitter grunt. "I couldn't stand that."

There was something in his tone that made Mrs. Murray pause and take a closer look at the stranger. "I was curious to see the sort of man the woman was going to get." She judged his age to be around thirty-two or thirty-five. He was nicely groomed—clean-shaven, his receding black hair neatly trimmed, as though he had just been to the barber. He had thick black eyebrows and an olive complexion, though he was clearly not a foreigner. His two most striking features were his dark, piercing eyes and strong, white, perfectly even teeth.

Though Mrs. Murray did not feel at all threatened by the dark-complexioned stranger, she continued to keep her distance from him as they toured the house, taking care to remain "six or eight feet away from him during the whole interview." She was struck by the close attention that he paid to certain details—closets, door locks, and especially ceilings. Only in retrospect did she perceive the diabolical cunning behind the stranger's behavior.

"I realize now," she told the reporters, "that he was trying to get me to look up towards the ceiling, so that he could get behind me and grab my throat."

Mrs. Murray had deliberately left all the window shades up. Entering the main bedroom, the stranger stepped over to the window and casually put his hand on the shade-pull. "Whoever designed this house sure put the windows in places to give plenty of light," he said. Then, as if testing to make sure that the roller functioned properly, he pulled down the shade and left it that way.

As Mrs. Murray was quick to admit, she then did something exceptionally foolish, carelessly letting it slip that her husband would not be home from work until around six. Reaching into his pocket, the stranger pulled out his watch and consulted it. "I wonder if I have the right time," he said, frowning. "My watch has been running kind of slow lately. It says five-thirty." Checking the alarm clock on her night table, Mrs. Murray confirmed that his watch was accurate.

Propped up on several pillows in her hospital bed, Mrs. Murray (who had just entered her eighth month of pregnancy) paused in her recitation for a sip of water. Then, as if gathering her strength, she drew a deep breath and related the dramatic climax of her tale.

"The final place we inspected was the screened porch in the rear of the house. He seemed particularly interested in this and several times called my attention to the ceiling. I kept my distance, however, though I never once dreamed he was the strangler. After exhausting every pretext for lingering, he started out.

"When he reached the front door, he suddenly turned and said, 'There's something about that porch I'd like to see again.' I returned there with him. As we stepped onto the porch, he suddenly pointed through the screen to the garage outside. 'What sort of roof is that on the garage?' he asked."

The suddenness of the question caught Mrs. Murray off guard. "For the first time, I turned my back to him—and in that instant I felt his hands closing around my neck from the rear." The realization hit her with sickening force. She was in the grip of the "Dark Strangler."

But unlike his previous victims, Mrs. Murray was a strapping young woman. Screaming wildly, she tore at his hands with her fingernails. "Fear must have given me strength, for I succeeded in breaking that terrible grip." Turning on him, she clawed at his face, then threw herself "through the screen door and nearly fell down the steps leading from the porch. Bleeding from his scratches, the strangler turned and dashed through the house, fleeing through the front door."

Still screaming for help, Mrs. Murray ran to the front of the house, reaching Grove Steet just as the strangler disappeared around a corner. At that moment, an automobile came cruising along the street. "Stop that man!" Mrs. Murray screeched. Instead of giving chase, however, the car slowed down.

Leaping onto the running board, Mrs. Murray began shouting at the driver. "That man! He attacked me! He's the strangler!" Other neighbors, meanwhile, had come bursting out of their houses to see what the commotion was about. Suddenly, the shock of the episode seemed to hit the pregnant woman in one overpowering blow. Sliding from the car, she collapsed onto the pavement, while a neighbor ran to call the police.

Within the hour, the entire police forces of Burlingame and San Mateo, assisted by a large contingent of armed volunteers, was scouring the area. A cordon was thrown around the entire district. Roadblocks were erected, vehicles stopped, passengers checked. A posse of men armed with shotguns patrolled the wood and marshes. Hospitals and doctors were alerted, in the event that the killer sought medical treatment for the injuries Mrs. Murray had inflicted. In spite of these efforts, however, the "Dark Strangler" managed to slip away again.

With the killer on the loose somewhere in the Bay Area, San Francisco Police Chief O'Brien called a press conference the following morning. Calling the strangler "the most dangerous criminal now at large," Chief O'Brien urged "women who have houses for sale or rooms for rent to use the utmost caution in admitting strangers of the general description of the strangler." He placed special emphasis on the deceptive, Jekyll-Hyde nature of the man. "He is not of a repulsive appearance. It is a mistake to believe that he has the features of an ape or gorilla, or that he is uncouth in speech or manner. He is able to gain an amicable footing with women through his suave manner."

With a canniness "typical of criminals of his type," the strangler had evidently modified his usual m.o. "A month ago," said the chief, "I figured that it was about time for one of the strangler's periodical outbreaks in this city, and I asked that an order be issued, instructing members of the department to warn women lodging-house keepers. The strangler seems now to have switched his operations from rented rooms to houses for sale."

The chief concluded his speech with a grim reminder that "no woman in San Francisco is safe with this man at large. The Police Department is doing everything possible to capture him, but it must have the cooperation of the citizenry to the fullest extent."

While Chief O'Brien had to strike a delicate balance in his pronouncements—sounding an alarm without provoking a panic—the press labored under no such constraints. The back-to-back outrages, the rape-murder of a middle-aged invalid and vicious assault on a young mother-to-be, touched off an orgy of tabloid sensationalism.

Though Mrs. Murray had escaped from the strangler's clutches with little more than a badly bruised neck, the papers reported that she was in critical condition, desperately fighting for her life as well as that of her unborn infant. Her assailant—the same "vile killer" who had murdered not only Mrs. Edmonds but five other Bay Area women—was a "human cobra," a "moron with a strange twist in his warped brain," who nevertheless possessed a "fiendish cunning and audacity" that had allowed him to "effect an easy escape through a cordon of police and a shotgun posse of highly aroused volunteer citizens."

The *San Francisco Chronicle* even coined a colorful new nickname for the killer, one that echoed the most infamous pseudonym of modern times. It first appeared on November 21 in the account of Mrs. Murray's ordeal. The article was published without a byline, but whoever wrote it clearly perceived something essential about the killer.

The headline of the article read: WOMAN TELLS OF HER FIGHT WITH "JACK THE STRANGLER."

19

†

In none of these cases was murder necessary. . . . It is simply
that the killer took delight in his work—he killed for the
satisfaction it gave him.

Charles Tennant

The new nickname never caught on, possibly because it
lacked the ominous ring of "the Dark Strangler." But in
certain ways, it was more apt. It suggested that the strangler
belonged to the same deadly breed as the Whitechapel Monster, to that psychopathic species we now call serial killers.
Moreover, it acknowledged the strangler's extreme cunning,
his ability (like Saucy Jack's) to stay a step ahead of the
police and make a mockery of their efforts to catch him.

Nevertheless, there were important differences between
the two killers. While the Ripper's name remains synony-
mous with serial sex-murder, his final tally of victims was
relatively modest by modern-day standards: five women slain
over several months. By November 21, 1926, the "Dark
Strangler" had already exceeded that total, indeed, had
nearly doubled it. Mrs. A. C. Murray, the pregnant young
housewife from Burlingame, had barely escaped becoming
his tenth murder victim. Mrs. Florence Fithian Monks of
Seattle wouldn't be as lucky.

According to acquaintances, it was vanity that got Mrs.
Monks killed, her insistence on flaunting her fanciest jewelry

even when performing the most routine of chores. To make a simple trip to the grocers, she would deck herself out like Queen Marie of Rumania. Her hands were adorned with no less than four diamond rings worth at least $5,000. In addition, she habitually wore a diamond bracelet and earrings, a triple-strand choker of genuine pearls, a cluster of jeweled lodge pins, and—on the bosom of her camisole—a large diamond sunburst valued at over $3,000.

Her friends, people like Mr. and Mrs. Harry G. Allen, repeatedly cautioned her about the dangers of such ostentation. The gems she insisted on displaying so freely were, they warned, "a temptation to almost any thief." The Allens felt especially anxious because Mrs. Monks, a forty-eight-year-old widow who suffered from a heart ailment, was often alone. Several times a week, she made the long drive from her country estate in Echo Lake Park to her home on Capitol Hill, staying by herself in the big, empty house. But Mrs. Monks scoffed at these warnings. "I'm not afraid," she would say with a carefree little wave of one ring-laden hand.

Unbeknownst to the Allens and her other good friends, Mrs. Monks had even more jewels on her person than the ones she kept on constant display. Strapped to her right leg, just below the knee, was a small sack of diamonds. Other valuable items of jewelry, including two diamond-studded brooches, were wrapped in a handkerchief and pinned to her underclothing.

The twice-widowed woman had inherited money from both her husbands. She had relocated to Seattle from New York City five years earlier with her second spouse, John J. Monks. Mr. Monks had died soon after the move, leaving his wife with substantial real estate holdings in Manhattan. Such was the size of her fortune that when, in late 1925, she suffered a $35,000 loss through a failed investment, she did not even blink, dismissing the sum as "a trifle." Among her friends, she was rumored to be worth at least $500,000.

Having decided to make her country place her sole residence, Mrs. Monks had been trying to dispose of the Capitol Hill house, located at 723 12th Avenue North, since early fall. She had placed a "For Sale" sign in the parlor window and taken out weekly ads in the *Seattle Times*. The most recent had appeared on Monday, November 22. The ad indicated that Mrs. Monks would be at the house between 11:00 A.M. and 3:00 P.M. on Wednesday the twenty-fourth to show the property to interested parties.

She showed up a day early, driving down from Echo Lake Park first thing Tuesday morning. Not long after her arrival, she placed a telephone call to her friend, Mrs. Elsie Allen of 4230 11th Avenue, N.E. The two women discussed plans for several upcoming social functions, including a dinner party Mrs. Monks was organizing for members of her lodge, the Order of Amaranth (of which she was royal matron).

Soon afterwards, she called another friend, Mrs. S. P. Brautigan of 4419 Dayton Avenue. During this conversation, Mrs. Monks mentioned that she was expecting a visit later in the day from a fellow lodge member named J. M. Coy.

Mrs. Monks' neighbors were a couple named Edward and Anna McDonald. At around noon on Tuesday, Mrs. McDonald glanced out her kitchen window and saw a "shabby-looking" automobile pull up in front of the house next door. A tall, thin, gray-haired man—dressed in a wrinkled gray suit and threadbare raincoat—emerged from the car, climbed the front-porch steps, and rang Mrs. Monks' bell. Seconds later, Mrs. Monks came to the door and, after exchanging a few words with the stranger, let him in. Mrs. McDonald, assuming the man was there to see the house, returned to her cooking.

Approximately one hour later, a couple named Carpenter arrived to view the property. They were admitted by Mrs. Monks, who proceeded to lead them on a tour of the house, beginning in the basement, then moving up to the first-floor rooms. They were just about to ascend to the second story when the doorbell rang. Excusing herself, Mrs. Monks hurried to the door and admitted a tall, blond man with a ruddy face and the air and appearance of a laborer. When they departed about twenty minutes later, Mr. and Mrs. Carpenter noticed the man seated in a small room off the main hallway waiting to speak with Mrs. Monks.

Whatever business the blond man had with Mrs. Monks must have been concluded by 2:30 P.M. That was when she telephoned her caterer, Otto Kirchbach of the Art Bake Shop, to discuss arrangements for a party she was planning for sixty members of the Order of Amaranth. It was scheduled for December 4 at the Rainier Masonic Temple.

"It was to be very elaborate," Kirchbach later recalled. "I had bought turkeys and other things for it, and she wanted the turkeys carved in front of the guests. She also asked me to change her order for punch to one for cider and to supply small raisins."

After about fifteen minutes, Mrs. Monks suddenly broke off the conversation. "I've got to go now, Otto," she said, interrupting him in the middle of a sentence. "There's someone at the door." Bidding him goodbye, she hung up the phone.

Later, Kirchbach would wonder if that "someone" had been Mrs. Monks' killer.

At approximately 8:00 P.M. that evening, J. M. Coy, Mrs. Monks' fellow lodge member, showed up as promised to discuss the plans for the big dinner party. He rang the bell again and again. But much to his surprise, Mrs. Monks did not respond.

Proceeding to a nearby drugstore, he called her from a pay phone but got no answer. He returned to the house and walked all around it. The windows were dark. Puzzled, Mr. Coy headed back to his house.

At around 6:00 P.M. the following evening, Wednesday, November 23, 1926, Edward McDonald looked out his parlor window and saw a middle-aged couple standing on the front porch of Mrs. Monks' house. The man, who wore an angry scowl, was pounding on the door. Mr. McDonald went out to investigate.

The man, who gave his name as Hansen, explained that he and his wife had called Mrs. Monks the previous week and made an appointment to inspect the house. They had come a long way and were much put out to find that she was not there.

Since Mrs. Monks spent only part of each week in the city, she had arranged for McDonald to show the house when she wasn't there. Fetching his key, McDonald let the couple inside and began to lead them around the premises, but the house was clearly not to their liking. Before they had finished viewing the first floor, Mr. Hansen announced that he and his wife had seen enough. Thanking McDonald for his trouble, the couple departed.

McDonald headed back to his own house, wondering where Mrs. Monks had gone. It was completely unlike her to forget an appointment. He could only surmise that she had been called away on an urgent matter.

About an hour later, however, it occurred to him to check her garage. The instant he saw her car parked inside it, he grew worried. Clearly, Mrs. Monks could not have gone very far. Perhaps something had happened to her. He knew that she suffered from dizzy spells. She might be lying unconscious somewhere in the house.

Hurrying to the home of another neighbor, a man named B. E. Gordon, McDonald explained his concern. The two men proceeded to Mrs. Monks' house and made a quick search of the premises, beginning in the attic and working their way down to the cellar. McDonald, who had never been in the cellar after dusk, couldn't find the light switch. Striking a match, he and Gordon peered around the dank, musty room, empty except for the big, silent furnace that loomed in the shadows. But they saw no sign of the widow.

At approximately 8:00 P.M., however—less than an hour after the two men had given up and gone back to their homes—someone else showed up at Mrs. Monks' front door, Thomas J. Raymond, the caretaker of her country estate. He had been trying to contact his employer by telephone since the previous evening. Raymond, too, knew about Mrs. Monks' heart condition and, fearing that some accident had befallen her, had driven down from Echo Lake to investigate.

After receiving no response to his insistent knocking, he let himself into the house with an emergency key and quickly searched the first floor. Inside the kitchen, he discovered a whole loaf of bread, an untouched marble cake, and a wilting bunch of celery—provisions for a meal Mrs. Monks had obviously never gotten around to eating.

The house was largely devoid of furniture, most of it having been removed in anticipation of the sale. The only exception was Mrs. Monks' second-floor bedroom. Switching on the electric light, Raymond was startled to see something that McDonald and Gordon had mysteriously overlooked.

The bureau drawers had been opened and apparently ransacked, as had the closet. But Mrs. Monks was nowhere to be seen.

Raymond made his way down to the cellar. Unlike McDonald, he had no trouble finding the light switch. As soon as he clicked it on, his heart constricted with alarm. Something heavy had been dragged across the dirt floor. There was a trail leading from the foot of the stairs to the rear of the furnace.

Even before he crossed the floor and peered behind the furnace, Raymond knew what he would find. When his worst fears were confirmed, he spun on his heels, bolted back up the staircase, and made a frantic call to the police.

The murder of Florence Monks was a milestone in the "Dark Strangler" case. Not only did it cause an uproar in Seattle, but it even made the pages of the *New York Times*, which ran a half-column story about the slaying on Friday, November 26. For the first time, the strangler case was national news.

Not that everyone assumed that the wealthy widow *had* been slain by the "Dark Strangler." Indeed, like the recent "trunk-death" case in Portland, the killing of Mrs. Monks set off a highly public controversy among local authorities.

To be sure, the crime bore obvious parallels to previous strangler murders—an aging landlady killed in "lonely surroundings" (as the *Seattle Times* put it), her body stuffed into a cramped, concealed space. Other aspects of the case, however, seemed to depart from the pattern. For one thing, it wasn't at all clear that Mrs. Monks had died of strangulation. True, there were finger marks on her throat. She had obviously been choked. But there was also (as Coroner Willis H. Corson told reporters) "a large contusion on her head, resulting in a hemorrhage between the scalp and skull." Corson, who was openly skeptical of the "strangler" theory, believed that Mrs. Monks may have been bludgeoned to death, possibly with a coal shovel found a few feet away from her body. Given her heart condition, it was also conceivable that she had died of shock.

The postmortem conducted the following day seemed to bolster Corson's position. As the newspapers delicately put it, "the examination failed to disclose the slightest evidence that the woman had been subjected to any indignity." Evidently, as Corson asserted at a press conference Friday evening, robbery—"not lust"—was the motive for the crime.

His theory received additional support when police ascertained that, shortly before her murder, Mrs. Monks had emptied her safety deposit box at the Seattle National Bank of all its contents, including a collection of diamond rings, pins, and bracelets appraised at somewhere between four and five thousand dollars. Besides the jewelry he had stripped from Mrs. Monks' body, the killer had apparently made off with these valuables, too—a fact which suggested not only that he was "actuated by greed" (as Corson insisted) but that he was someone with "an intimate knowledge of the widow's habits."

Over the next few days, detectives focussed their attention on several suspects, primarily the gray-haired man who had driven up to Mrs. Monks' house on the day of the murder and the blond, ruddy-faced laborer who had dropped by while the Carpenters were touring the premises. But both men had airtight alibis. So did J. M. Coy, Mrs. Monks' fellow member of the Order of Amaranth lodge, who fell briefly under suspicion but was quickly cleared.

That left the police with only one tantalizing lead, provided by Louise Baker, Mrs. Monks' niece. Several weeks earlier—according to Mrs. Baker—a "dark, round-faced stranger" had appeared at her aunt's door holding "some kind of a paper which had Mrs. Monks' name on it." Just as the widow was about to close the door on him, the stranger "asked her if she lived there alone, and she told him that it was none of his business and slammed the door in his face."

When Mrs. Monks had recounted this story, Mrs. Baker had remonstrated with her aunt. "It is dangerous for you to spend so much time in that big house all by yourself. Particularly with so much valuable jewelry in your possession." But Mrs. Monks had only laughed at her niece's fears.

For Captain of Detectives Charles Tennant, the Monks case was a grim object lesson in the perils of female preening. At a press conference on Friday afternoon, he vented his scorn at the vanity of women like Mrs. Monks, suggesting that if anyone was to blame for her death, it was the victim herself. Her fate, he declared, should stand as a warning to others.

" 'Come and take them!' That's what these women are saying to every cut-purse and sneak thief that comes along," said Tennant, his voice edged with contempt. "They load themselves up with a lot of bar pins, diamond sunbursts, and expensive rings—an open and never-failing invitation to some crook to help himself. In New York City alone there are scores of such women robbed every day, many of them killed. We have been fortunate here, but the woman who is known to carry large amounts of gems around with her, as Mrs. Monks did, is never safe."

Some of Tennant's colleagues, however, including Chief William H. Searing, had a very diferent view of the matter. Taking issue not only with Tennant but with Coroner Corson as well, Searing declared his conviction that the slayer of Mrs. Monks was the same "fiend" who had already killed a string of landladies in San Francisco and Portland.

"There is no question in my mind," he told reporters, "but that the man we're looking for is the same criminal who has had such uncanny success in covering up his tracks in California and Portland. The methods of working are exactly parallel with the procedure in the murder of Mrs. Monks." Searing went on to describe the suspect, "the most cunning and cold-blooded killer in the annals of Pacific Coast crime," as a killer "whose perverted senses delight in the throttling of helpless women. He speaks good English, is ingratiating in the extreme, is of vigorous constitution, brawny of build although fairly short of stature, and has the smooth olive complexion of a man of Italian or Serbian descent."

When a reporter raised the question of the coroner's findings—Dr. Corson's conclusion that Mrs. Monks, unlike the strangler's previous victims, had not been sexually violated—Searing simply shrugged and said, "I don't take much stock in these scientific reports."

His belief that the "Dark Strangler" had killed Mrs. Monks was bolstered by Detective Archie Leonard of Portland, who arrived in Seattle on Saturday, November 27, to aid with the investigation. After conferring with Searing and other officials, Leonard met with newsmen and announced that he was "greatly impressed by the similarity between the murder of Mrs. Monks and the slaying of three Portland women last month. In every case, the murderer entered a house that was either for sale or for rent. The victim was between forty-five and sixty years of age and was alone in the house when the slayer called. Jewels were also taken in one of the three Portland cases."

For the next few days, the controversy over the Monks case continued to rage. Had the aging widow been murdered by a jewel thief or by the strangler who had been prowling the Pacific Coast for months, preying on unwary landladies?

Even a visiting performer found a way to get in on the act. On Monday, November 29, nineteen-year-old Eugenia Dennis, billed as the "Amazing Girl Psychic," arrived from Kansas for a week-long engagement at Seattle's Coliseum Theatre. Miss Dennis' telepathic powers had brought her international renown. No less a celebrity than Sir Arthur Conan Doyle had proclaimed her "the eighth wonder of the world."

On the afternoon of her arrival, a reporter for the *Seattle Times* came to interview her in her dressing room, where—in the presence of her manager, William "Billy" Morrison—he asked her about the "Monks murder mystery."

Without having read or heard anything about the case—so she maintained—Miss Dennis immediately asked, "Wasn't she a middle-aged woman?"

"That is correct," exclaimed the reporter.

Shutting her eyes, the Amazing Girl Psychic remained silent for a long moment, her brow furrowed in intense concentration. Suddenly she began to speak in a deep, unfaltering voice: "I see a tall, rather heavy-set, dark man. His eyebrows are conspicuous. He had admired her very much, but they had a quarrel. She is holding a box in her hand. It has a lot of money in it.

"I can see him standing outside a cellar door. Was there a cellar in the house? Yes, he carried her in the cellar to where it is dark. He came out the front door later. It must have happened around six o'clock. He has her jewels and a lot more money than anyone now supposes.

"I see him go to a boat where he gives a man a package

containing the jewels. They are taken to Canada. Yes, they are still in Canada. The man has the money in his pocket. He still is carrying it."

Informed of Miss Dennis' assertion that the killer of Mrs. Monks was an acquaintance who stole her jewels and sold them to a Canadian fence, Chief Searing responded with a derisive snort. Mrs. Monks' killer was no thief, he repeated, but a "degenerate"—the same "beast-man strangler" who had recently slain the three Portland women.

"In none of these cases was murder necessary," Searing insisted. "There was no necessity of killing Mrs. Monks. There was none in any of the Portland cases. It is simply that the killer took delight in his work. He did not kill for profit. He killed for the satisfaction it gave him."

20

✝

If you ever find me lying dead, please don't take my body
up to the morgue.

Blanche Myers

The doorbell rang a few minutes past noon, Monday,
November 29, 1926. Excusing herself, Blanche Myers rose
from the table and headed for the front entryway, leaving
the kitchen door slightly ajar.

Her lunch guest, Alexander Muir, remained seated at his
place, finishing off his plateful of liver and eggs. Though the
kitchen was just down the hall from the entryway, the house,
located at 449 Tenth Street in Portland, was of such solid,
thick-walled construction that Muir could barely make out
Mrs. Myers' voice as she spoke to the caller—obviously a
male, judging from the muffled words spoken in reply.

Using a chunk of pumpernickel to swab his plate clean,
Muir washed down the bread with the last of his coffee.
Then, settling back in his chair, he removed a cigar from his
shirt pocket, bit off the end, and lit it with a long wooden
match.

The tidy, two-story house belonged to Muir, who leased
it to Blanche Myers, who in turn rented out the two spare
rooms on the second floor. She had begun taking in lodgers
four years earlier when her husband, Frederick, a veteran of
the Spanish-American War, dropped dead of a heart attack,
leaving her with two adolescent boys to raise. At the mo-

ment, the smaller of the spare bedrooms was vacant, and Mrs. Myers had placed a "Room to Rent" sign in the front-parlor window facing Tenth Street.

Muir, a balding, broad-shouldered man in his thirties, had come by that morning to do some repair work on the roof of his property. Afterwards, Mrs. Myers had invited him to stay for lunch. Muir, himself recently widowered, was only too glad to accept. He enjoyed spending time in Mrs. Myers' company, liked chatting with her, liked *looking* at her. At forty-eight, she was still a strikingly handsome woman with thick, dark hair, almond eyes, a soft, full-lipped mouth, and a dimpled chin he found entrancing.

Muir was almost halfway through his smoke before Mrs. Myers reappeared in the kitchen, around fifteen minutes later. Reaching out her cupped right hand, she dumped a bunch of big silver coins onto the checkered oilcloth covering the table. Muir put out a finger and counted the change, seven silver half dollars in all.

"Just found a renter for that empty room," Mrs. Myers said, reseating herself across from her visitor. Nodding at the $3.50, she added, "Paid a week in advance."

"Who is he?" Muir asked, puffing on his stogie.

"Some fellow that came by last Saturday, asking about the room. Looks like a logger."

Muir's brow wrinkled. "Funny for a logger to take a room so far uptown. He a drinking man?"

"I asked," said Mrs. Myers. Raising her cup to her mouth, she sipped and made a face. Her coffee had gone tepid since she'd left the room. "Said he did, but only a little now and then. Seems respectable enough."

The lodger had decided to lie down for a nap, Mrs. Myers explained. Muir hung around for another five minutes or so, then, after checking his pocket watch, rose from the table, thanked his hostess for the meal, and departed. By then, it was nearly 1:00 P.M.

Sometime within the next hour (according to the coroner's subsequent estimate), Mrs. Muir was evidently summoned to the second-floor room by her new tenant. She must have still been in the kitchen when he called, perhaps cleaning up after lunch, since her pink tea apron was on when she entered his room.

Precisely how he diverted her attention is unknown, though he had, of course, a good deal of practice in such deadly ruses. It seems likely that, as he had with Mrs. H. C. Murray, he tricked her into glancing at the ceiling. There were a dozen ways he could have done it. "Look at that big waterstain right over the bed," he might have said, gesturing upwards. "That plaster's about to go."

Mrs. Myers, caught unawares, would have reflexively obeyed, tilting her head towards the spot he was pointing to, exposing her throat. It would have taken only a few seconds for her to realize that there was no loose plaster about to fall onto the bed—but that was all the time he needed.

In that instant, he was upon her.

Mrs. Myers' older son, Robert, who had just turned twenty-three, was away at school, majoring in political science at Whitman College in Walla Walla, Washington. His younger brother, Lawrence, however, still lived at home. It was Lawrence who notified the police after his mother had been missing for twelve hours.

Two officers named Chase and Miller responded to the call. They found Mrs. Myers in the upstairs room. Lawrence himself had looked into the room while searching the house for his mother. But he had failed to see her body—unsurprisingly, since it was shoved beneath the single bed and concealed by the low-hanging quilt.

The forty-eight-year-old widow had been strangled to death with her tea apron. It had been savagely twisted around her neck, five times in all, and secured with two square knots. Some splotches of blood that had leaked from her ears (a common occurrence in strangulation cases) had been covered by the throw rug in the center of the room. There was also a thin trail of blood on the floor. The killer had obviously garrotted Mrs. Myers in the middle of the room, then hidden her body beneath the bed.

Whether he had raped her as well wasn't immediately clear. Though her skirt was hiked above her knees, police believed that the garment might have become disarranged when the killer dragged her body feetfirst across the room.

Unaccountably, there were still a few people in the Pacific

Northwest who refused to accept that the recent rash of landlady deaths was the work of a single, elusive killer. In Seattle, close friends of Florence Monks continued to maintain that she had been slain for her jewelry by someone who knew her. Coroner Willis Corson, too, remained stubbornly attached to his theory, that the widow's weakened heart had given out when she was assaulted in the course of the robbery.

In Portland, however, the universal consensus, even among those officials who had formerly been most skeptical of the "strangler" theory, was that the same phantom killer had just claimed another victim. The circumstances surrounding the deaths of the four Portland women were too similar to ignore. And indeed, on the day that Mrs. Myers' death was blazoned on the front page of the *Morning Oregonian,* the paper ran a comparative chart showing the glaring similarities among the four murder cases: Mrs. Beata Withers, thirty-five-year-old landlady, her body found jammed inside a trunk; Mrs. Virginia Grant, fifty-nine-year-old landlady, her body found stuffed behind the furnace; Mrs. Mabel Fluke, thirty-seven-year-old landlady, her body found hidden in the attic; and now, Mrs. Florence Myers, forty-eight-year-old landlady, her body found stuffed beneath a bed.

In the latest case, as in each of the others, a few items belonging to the victim had been taken by the killer, who had made off with Mrs. Myers' diamond engagement ring, her wristwatch, and a total of $8.50 from her purse. It was the opinion of Chief Thatcher, however, that robbery was not the motive in the crimes, since some of the items stolen from the victims (Beata Withers' hat, for instance, and Mabel Fluke's coat) were of no intrinsic worth. Evidently, as Thatcher told reporters at a Wednesday morning news conference, the killer had taken the items "more as curios or souvenirs than for their value."

Exactly why a homicidal maniac would be interested in such paltry mementoes was something of a puzzle to the police, though it wouldn't be at all surprising to their counterparts today who know that it is common for a serial killer to remove "trophies" from a murder scene: fetishistic objects associated with the victim (anything from a driver's license to a body part) that help the killer relive his crime in fantasy.

In each of the three previous cases, the Portland police had been strikingly slipshod in their procedures, traipsing around the crime scene, mishandling evidence. Detective Tackaberry's impromptu experiment of having his man climb into and out of Beata Withers' "death trunk," thereby obliterating any hope of recovering fingerprints, was typical.

This time was different. Reflecting their new (if belated) conviction that something dire was afoot in their city, the investigators exercised a thoroughgoing professionalism. The small, second-floor bedroom where Blanche Myers' body had been found was immediately sealed off and protected. No one was permitted to touch anything in the room until the coroner arrived and fingerprint expert Harold A. Anderson had completed his work. Even the cigarette butts found in an ashtray were collected for analysis.

This diligence had an immediate payoff: Anderson was able to discover and photograph three perfect fingerprints on the iron headboard of the bed. By Tuesday evening, the police were busily checking the prints against the thousands in their files.

In the meantime, Portland Chief of Detectives John T. Moore issued a public warning to all Portland landladies. "Do not show your houses or rooms for rent while alone," Moore declared. "If necessary, call a policeman to accompany you. Crimes such as these should be prevented and *could* be prevented if women would be more careful. I do not wish to unduly alarm the people of Portland. But there is no denying that the situation is grave."

By Wednesday morning, Captain Moore was in touch with his counterparts in San Francisco and Seattle. There was no longer any doubt in the minds of these three lawmen that they were hunting for the same homicidal maniac. "I am confident that the man operating in Portland is the same slayer who murdered the women here," declared Captain Duncan Matheson of the San Francisco police bureau. Speaking to newsmen in Seattle, Captain Charles Tenant concurred, "You don't have to be much of a sleuth to know that the murders are the work of the same man."

While Moore, Tenant, and Matheson conferred by phone, coordinating their investigations, the entire Portland detective squad launched into what the newspapers described as "a manhunt unrivaled in Pacific Coast police annals." Alexander Muir, the last person to see the victim alive, came forward at once. Unfortunately, he wasn't a particularly valuable witness, since he had not caught so much as a glimpse of the suspect. He did, however, provide one potentially useful lead, recalling something Mrs. Myers had mentioned—that the stranger had initially come by her house on the previous Saturday to inquire about the room.

Pursuing this lead, detectives discovered that one of Mrs. Myers' oldest friends—a Seattle resident named Nellie Stengl, who taught at a school for the deaf and dumb—had visited the victim on Saturday. They immediately sought out and interviewed Miss Stengl at her home. Much to their disappointment, however, Miss Stengl had not seen the suspect, having apparently departed before he arrived.

With his entire city in a panic, Mayor Baker of Portland announced that he would furnish $100 of his own money for information leading to the arrest and conviction of the "Dark Strangler." His offer was quickly matched by three others, from Portland Post No. 1 of the American Legion, a dairy farmer named Charles Eckleman, and Mrs. Myers' brother, John A. Lawrence. On the following day, the reward fund ballooned to $1,300, when the city council pledged $1,000 to the fund (prompting Mayor Baker to withdraw his own personal offer).

While Mrs. Myers' older child, Robert, made the mournful journey home from college to attend her funeral, her younger son, Lawrence, made an eerie disclosure. His mother, he told reporters on Wednesday afternoon, had apparently experienced a strange premonition of her death. Just one month earlier, she had handed him a sealed envelope, instructing him to open it "in case of an accident."

Inside, as Lawrence had just discovered, were a brief obituary notice, handwritten by his mother, and a request that she be buried in a vault at the Portland cemetery in "an inexpensive coffin."

That Mrs. Myers, for whatever odd reason, had been mulling over the possibility of her own untimely death was confirmed by deputy coroner Ben Guldransen, who, as it happened, was a friend of the victim. About a year before her murder, Guldransen revealed, he and Mrs. Myers had been talking about his work. "Well, Ben," Mrs. Myers had said in all apparent seriousness. "If you ever find me lying dead, please don't take my body up to the morgue. I want it to go to the Holman & Lutz undertaking parlors."

At the time, Guldransen had made light of her concern, wondering why a vigorous, youthful woman would even entertain such morbid thoughts. Now, remembering her wishes, he made sure to comply.

21

✝

I never spoke to a nicer mannered fellow.
                    Russell Gordon

Even as the morticians at Holman & Lutz were readying
Blanche Myers' body for burial, a major break was occurring
in the murder investigation. Indeed, it was the most significant turn in the "Dark Strangler" case since Mrs. H. C.
Murray—the pregnant California woman who had survived
a terrifying encounter with the killer—provided police with
the first detailed account of his insidious m.o.

Two elderly widows—Mrs. Edna Gaylord, proprietress of
a ramshackle rooming house on Third Street in Portland,
and her longtime tenant, Mrs. Sophie Yates—revealed that,
during the four days preceding the most recent slaying, they
had been sharing their living quarters with the strangler.

According to the two women, who told their story to the
police on Wednesday afternoon, December 1, a man calling
himself Adrian Harris had shown up at the boardinghouse
exactly one week earlier, at around 10:00 A.M. on the day
before Thanksgiving. They described him as a short but
stocky fellow in his late twenties, with a swarthy complexion,
dark hair, and "piercing black eyes." In one hand, he
clutched a shiny, new suitcase of a clearly inexpensive make.
Though somewhat shabbily dressed, he comported himself
like a "perfect gentleman," doffing his brown cap as he
stood on the threshold and introduced himself. He was a

carpenter, he explained, who would be working in Portland for an indefinite period of time. Mrs. Gaylord noticed that he spoke with a slight lisp, his thick lips "bulging" slightly when he talked.

When the landlady confirmed that she had a room available on the second floor, he took it sight unseen, paying her a week's rent in advance—$2 in silver coins. Mrs. Gaylord led him up to his room and left him there to get some rest. He had been travelling all night, he explained, and felt "dog-tired."

Later that day, he appeared in the parlor, where Mrs. Gaylord and her tenant were chatting companionably by the fireplace. Settling into a chair, he pulled out a pack of Lucky Strike cigarettes and joined in the conversation. Before long, the talk turned to the women's Thanksgiving Day plans. Somewhat sheepishly, the landlady confessed that she was not in a financial position to make much of a fuss, but that she would do her best to put together a nice meal, which Mr. Harris was welcome to share.

Harris conversed easily with the two women, telling them a bit about his background as he puffed on his "coffin nail" (as the abstemious Mrs. Gaylord thought of cigarettes). He was Danish by birth, he explained, his parents having emigrated from Copenhagen when he was five years old. He had been married for a brief time, but his wife couldn't stop flirting with other men, so Harris had divorced her about a year ago. Mrs. Gaylord and Mrs. Yates made commiserating noises as the young man provided several shocking examples of his ex-wife's shameless behavior.

Since the breakup of his marriage, he had been moving around a good deal, making his living building bunkhouses in logging camps. Having managed to salt away a tidy sum—$1,200, which he had just deposited in a local bank—he now intended to start his own construction business, putting up and selling small houses in Portland.

After fifteen minutes or so, the well-spoken young man—whose only fault, as far as the landlady could see, was his fondness for smoking—excused himself and returned to his room. Not long afterwards, he reappeared in the parlor, dressed in his slightly oversized brown coat and floppy cap.

"I will be back in a short while," he said. "I have some

errands to run." Then he turned and headed for the front door.

When he showed up at the house again an hour or so later, he was clutching several overstuffed grocery bags. Carrying them into the kitchen, he set them onto the counter. The two women came bustling after him, exclaiming with surprise.

"Here," he said, as he beamed with an almost childlike pleasure. "Tomorrow we will have a real holiday feast." Then, so excitedly that he reminded Mrs. Gaylord of a little boy unwrapping his birthday gifts, he began emptying the bags, which were packed with Thanksgiving provisions.

When Mrs. Gaylord protested at his extravagance—"But Mr. Harris, there's so much food!"—the burly young man admitted that he had "gone whole hog," spending no less than fourteen dollars.

The women had a happy time the following day, filling their bellies to the point of discomfort while the young man regaled them with amazing tales of occult, theosophical, and Spiritualistic phenomena, drawn from a seemingly inexhaustible fund of arcane knowledge. He was evidently a deeply religious individual, whose speech was laden with references to Scripture.

When the two women queried him more closely about his beliefs, Harris replied that he had recently been to some Holy Roller meetings and had attended a service at the spectacular Angelus Temple of Sister Aimee Semple McPherson, the golden-haired revivalist whose name had been continuously in the headlines for almost half a year. (The previous June—following a mysterious, month-long disappearance— a bruised and blistered Sister Aimee had suddenly appeared in Arizona, claiming that she had been kidnapped and held captive in Mexico. As investigators delved into her story, however, it became increasingly evident that the self-described "World's Most Pulchritudinous Evangelist" had actually absconded for a prolonged romantic interlude with one of her married employees.)

Altogether, the young man remained at the boarding-house for four and a half days. For the most part, he stayed shut up in his room, emerging only at dusk, when he would briefly leave the house to buy the daily *Oregonian*. At one point, he came down with what seemed to be a touch of the flu and spent much of the following day seated by the fireplace, a blanket draped around his shoulders.

At around 10:00 A.M. on Monday, November 29 (the day of Blanche Myers' murder), he appeared in the front hallway, suitcase in hand. He was leaving for Vancouver, Washington, he declared. Since he had paid a full week's rent in advance, this sudden departure, less than five days after his arrival, struck the women as peculiar. It seemed doubly surprising in light of his earlier statements, that he planned to settle in Portland and go into the construction business.

It wasn't until Wednesday afternoon that Mrs. Gaylord realized with a shock just who the young man was. She was seated in the parlor, reading the newspaper account of Blanche Myers' murder. When she came upon the description of the "Dark Strangler" suspect, she let out such a startled cry that Mrs. Yates came hurrying in from the kitchen to see what was wrong.

Mrs. Gaylord did not own a telephone. Throwing on her overcoat, she hurried to a neighbor's house and called police headquarters.

Under ordinary circumstances, the police wouldn't have attached any undue weight to her story. After all, they had been inundated with similar reports ever since Mrs. Myers' death—breathless accounts from dozens of lone, local women who had found themselves confronted (often in the secrecy of their bedrooms) by dark, menacing strangers. In this case, however, there was a compelling cause to take the testimony of Mrs. Gaylord and Mrs. Yates seriously.

For reasons explicable only to himself, the man who called himself Adrian Harris had decided to bestow an extravagant gift on the two women. He had done it on the day after Thanksgiving. Descending from his bedroom in mid-morning, he had summoned them to the parlor and presented each of the astonished women with several costly pieces of jewelry.

He had given the landlady a triple-strand choker of pearls and a white-gold necklace along with several smaller items, including a gold pin and a silver-mounted fountain pen. Mrs. Yates received a diamond bracelet with matching earrings, plus a gold perfume bottle and a jeweled brooch.

Though the women had demurred, the young man was insistent. According to Mrs. Gaylord's account, Harris had said that he "had no use" for the jewelry and wanted to share it with them because they "had so little."

Less than fifteen minutes after receiving Mrs. Gaylord's call, two detectives, James Mulligan and Bernard LáSalle, arrived at her home to examine the jewelry. The moment they laid eyes on it, they exchanged an excited look. Like every other police agency in the Pacific Northwest, the Portland department had received a detailed bulletin from Seattle, describing the valuables that had been stolen by the slayer of Mrs. Florence Monks.

Even at a glance, Mulligan and LaSalle could see that the jewelry which "Adrian Harris" had lavished on the two elderly widows appeared to be a precise match.

By Wednesday evening, the confiscated loot was on its way to police headquarters in Seattle, where the three most striking pieces—the white-gold necklace, triple-strand string of pearls, and diamond bracelet—were arranged on a black velvet jeweler's tray and photographed. The picture appeared on the front page of the following day's *Seattle Times,* along with an article explaining that the "gems were thought to be the ones stolen from slain Seattle widow, Mrs. Florence Fithian Monks." Any of her acquaintances who recognized the jewelry were urged to contact the police without delay.

Less than forty-five minutes after the paper hit the stands, Detective Sergeant W. B. Kent received a call from Mrs. Harry G. Allen, a close friend of the victim. "Those look like Florence's jewels," Mrs. Allen declared. She was brought down to headquarters by squad car, where—after making a firsthand examination of the gems—she tearfully confirmed that they had belonged to her murdered friend. Later in the day, several more of Mrs. Monks' intimates—including a neighbor, Miss Mattie Nelson, and Charles McMinimee, executor of the slain widow's estate—positively identified the jewels.

Meanwhile, down in Portland, investigators were pursuing another lead involving Mrs. Monks' stolen property. Shortly after the publication of Wednesday's *Morning Oregonian,* which ran a page-one story on the recovered jewels, no fewer than four pawnshop owners had contacted the police with precisely the same story. On the previous afternoon, a dark-complexioned young man had appeared in each of their stores, attempting to sell a white-gold woman's lodge pin—an item which (as the brokers now realized) had been part of the loot taken from the murdered widow. None of the pawnbrokers had purchased the pin, since the young man, though apparently eager to unload it, had sniffed at their offers.

A special police detail, under the supervision of Inspectors Howell and Abbott, was immediately assigned to check out every hockshop and secondhand store in Seattle in the hope of locating the pin and tracking its seller. But this effort proved unavailing. The police *did* manage to haul in over a dozen suspects, including a forty-four-year-old Serbian who bore a striking resemblance to the published descriptions of the strangler. But all these men were promptly released when their fingerprints failed to match the ones retrieved from the iron headboard in the room where Blanche Myers had been killed.

On Thursday afternoon, the coroner's inquest into the death of Mrs. Myers took place in Portland. Three witnesses testified at this pro forma affair—Dr. Robert Benson, the coroner's physician who conducted the autopsy; the victim's younger son, Lawrence, who had reported her disappearance to the police; and Alexander Muir, the owner of the boardinghouse, who had been sharing lunch with the landlady when her killer appeared at the front door. It took the jury only a few minutes to reach its foregone conclusion: "That Mrs. Blanche Myers met death by strangulation at the hands of a party or parties unknown."

At virtually the same time in Seattle, the funeral of Florence Monks was underway in the Corinthian room of the Masonic Temple, located at Harvard Avenue and Pine Street. In accordance with Mrs. Monks' will, the services were conducted under the auspices of Seattle Chapter No. 95, Order of the Eastern Star, the Reverend Maurice J. Bywater officiating. The temple was packed with more than 400 mourners, including the slain woman's sister, Vivian Drummond of Flushing, New York, who had arrived the previous afternoon with her husband, Charles. Following Mrs. Monks' interment at Lakeview Cemetery—where she was laid to rest in a plot adjoining that of her late husband, John—Charles Drummond spoke to reporters, declaring that it was his firm intention to "devote his energies to unraveling the mystery veiling the brutal murder of his wife's sister."

Any doubts that Florence Monks and Blanche Myers had been strangled by the same fiendish killer were resolved on Saturday afternoon, when Detective Sergeant W. J. Sampson of Seattle's Police Identification Bureau confirmed that fingerprints lifted from a black pocketbook in Mrs. Monks' bedroom precisely matched the ones discovered on the iron headboard in Mrs. Myers' rooming house. Over the next few days, police up and down the Pacific Coast made what the papers described as a "frantic effort" to locate the killer. But the manhunt led nowhere. The strangler's whereabouts remained completely unknown, though Portland investigators did manage to turn up another eyewitness who had come into direct contact with the killer.

This was a grocer named Russell Gordon, who owned a little store on Third Street, the very one where "Adrian Harris" had purchased fourteen dollars' worth of dinner provisions on the day before Thanksgiving. According to Gordon, "Harris" was such a pleasant, soft-spoken, and polite individual that it was almost impossible to believe he could be the notorious strangler. "Why, I never spoke to a nicer mannered fellow," Gordon told the officers who interviewed him.

Gordon's testimony only confirmed what the police already knew from Edna Gaylord, Sophie Yates, and others (like Mrs. H. C. Murray) who had spent time in the strangler's company and lived to tell about it. "When not in the midst of his heinous crimes," as the *Seattle Daily Times* reported, "the Dark Strangler has an engaging personality, quiet habits, and pleasing manners."

In attempting to account for such a singular being, a monstrous killer whose daily demeanor gave "no intimation that he possessed any talent for crime," the authorities were clearly at a loss. "The murderer isn't a maniac in the sense that he is mentally deranged," Chief of Detectives Charles Tennant of Seattle told a gathering of reporters on Saturday, December 4. "But there must be a screw loose somewhere."

The best explanation that authorities could come up with was that the strangler "possessed a dual personality," making him a "real-life Dr. Jekyll and Mr. Hyde." In 1926, a criminal who could seem perfectly ordinary one moment and turn into a maddened sex killer the next was clearly so extraordinary that he seemed like a creature out of fantasy. The time had not yet arrived when psychopathic lust murderers, capable of concealing their malevolence behind a mask of bland normality, would be a grimly familiar feature of American society.

In the week following Blanche Myers' murder, the main detective room on the third floor of Portland's central police station was (as the *Oregonian* reported) "a veritable 'mad house,' with clerks and operators taking hundreds of telephone calls from citizens who had reports to make on suspicious characters, and a score or more of detectives working frantically, taking reports from citizens who visited the office." Investigators dutifully followed through on all of these leads, even the most far-fetched. But none of them panned out.

On Monday, December 6, newspapers reported the arrest of a drifter named Morris Yoffee, who had arrived in Eugene, Oregon, a few days earlier. Engaging a room in a local boardinghouse, he had promptly aroused the suspicions of the proprietress, who, like virtually every other landlady in the Pacific Northwest, lived in constant vigilance of the "Dark Strangler."

There was something furtive about Yoffee's behavior. Since his arrival, he had remained sequestered inside his room, emerging only at mealtimes. He had also betrayed a disquieting interest in the murder of Florence Fithian Monks, sending out each afternoon for the *Seattle Daily Times,* so that he could follow the latest developments in the investigation. At the table, he conversed about the case with an enthusiasm that struck the landlady as distinctly unhealthy.

On the morning of December 6, she put in a telephone call to police headquarters. That afternoon, Chief Jenkins himself, disguised in plain clothes and posing as a prospective tenant, showed up at the rooming house to check out the suspect. Convinced that Yoffee bore a passable resemblance to the descriptions of "Adrian Harris," Jenkins revealed his identity and took the startled man into custody. "Am I wanted in Seattle?" Yoffee asked as he was led off to jail.

Within twelve hours, however, following a telephone conversation between Chief Jenkins and Detective Captain William Justus of Seattle, Yoffee was released. According to Justus, the suspect's appearance did not, in fact, jibe with the strangler's. "The man arrested at Eugene has light, watery eyes and is slender," Justus explained to reporters on Tuesday morning. "The man we think killed Mrs. Monks had dark, penetrating eyes and was of a husky build."

Two days later, papers trumpeted the arrest of another suspect, a thirty-one-year-old Nebraskan named James Ford, who strolled into Seattle police headquarters early Thursday morning and announced that he was the "beast man" who had slain Mrs. Monks. As the police began questioning Ford, however, it quickly became clear that he was ignorant of the most basic facts about the case. Ford—who eventually admitted that his imagination had been overly stimulated by a combination of bootleg liquor and the gruesome crime stories he had been reading in *Thrilling Detective* magazine—was deemed "mentally unbalanced" and held for a sanity hearing.

The media attention given to such a flagrant crank as Ford was a sign of how little of real substance there was to report about the case. As the Myers investigation entered its second week, the killer's trail had grown completely cold. Though police were now armed with a detailed description of the "beast man's" appearance, mannerisms, and m.o., he continued to elude them.

Speaking to reporters on Friday morning, December 11, Chief of Detectives Charles Tennant of Portland couldn't conceal his frustration. "It's uncanny the way this killer operates," Tennant declared.

Indeed, Tennant was so discouraged over the state of the investigation that he made what amounted to a complete admission of defeat. In a front-page story headlined POLICE FEAR "DARK KILLER" WILL RETURN, an anonymous reporter for the *Seattle Daily Times* who had attended Tennant's Friday-morning press conference wrote: "So baffling have been the murders, so cunningly has their perpetrator covered up his tracks that Tennant confessed yesterday that his greatest concern was that another woman would be found mysteriously slain here."

Indeed, it was only a matter of time, Tennant was convinced, before the "Dark Strangler" reappeared in Portland or one of the other Pacific Coast cities and claimed "victim number twelve."

22

✠

Which way I fly is hell; myself am hell.
John Milton, *Paradise Lost*

But Detective Chief Tennant was wrong. The killer
would never return to Portland or to any of his previous
hunting grounds. By now the Pacific Coast really *had* gotten
too hot for him.

By the time of Tennant's news conference, the killer had
already embarked on an odyssey that would eventually take
him to the opposite end of the continent and halfway back
again. Keeping on the move, however, was not a problem
for the homicidal maniac now variously known as the "Dark
Strangler," the "Phantom Killer," and the "Beast Man."
Ever since adolescence—when he would disappear from the
home of his long-suffering family for weeks at a time—he
had been possessed of a powerful wanderlust.

Three weeks after Blanche Myers' murder, he would show
up in Council Bluffs, Iowa, at the precise midpoint of the
country. For the next six months, he would trace a roughly
trapezoidal course, heading southward to Kansas City, Missouri, then straight across to Philadelphia, up into Buffalo,
and westward again to Detroit and Chicago. And everywhere he went, women died.

On the day before Christmas, 1926, Mrs. John Brerard of
Council Bluffs became the strangler's twelfth victim. The

forty-one-year-old woman lived with her husband and their nineteen-year-old daughter, Corene, in a simple two-story house at 351 Willow Avenue, within earshot of the city's business district. The house had been built for them four years earlier when the Brerards had moved to Council Bluffs from their previous home in Emerson, Iowa.

To supplement Mr. Brerard's modest earnings as a passenger agent for the Burlington Railroad, the couple rented out the two spare bedrooms on the second floor. The larger of these had originally been occupied by their older daughter, Evelyn, a nurse at the Methodist Hospital in Omaha, who had recently gotten married and moved into a home of her own. For the past few months, Evelyn's former bedroom had been rented out to a thirty-four-year-old fireman for the Burlington Railroad named Robert Moore, an old family friend.

The other, smaller room had been vacant for nearly a year. As in most of the previous murder cases, there was a hand-lettered "Room to Rent" sign prominently displayed in a front window of the Brerard home.

At approximately 3:15 P.M. on December 24, Moore headed downstairs on his way to work. As he passed by the living room, he saw Mrs. Brerard chatting with someone he had never laid eyes on before, a burly, dark-complexioned man dressed in somewhat shabby clothing.

Beckoning to Moore, the landlady introduced him to the stranger, whose name, she said, was "Mr. Williams." Moore, who was late for work, barely took note of the other man. As he later explained to police, he assumed that the fellow "was probably some worker in the Seventh Day Adventist Church, of which Mrs. Brerard was an active member." Giving the stranger's hand a quick shake, Moore said that it had been nice to meet him, then hurried from the house— never to see Mrs. Brerard alive again.

The discovery of her body followed what was by now a dismayingly familiar pattern. At around four in the afternoon, the Brerards' younger daughter, Corene, returned from her job as a salesgirl in a local millinery shop and found the house empty. Though her mother was normally home at that hour, engaged in dinner preparations, Corene was not concerned. There was a big family gathering

planned for the following day in celebration of both Christmas and Mrs. Brerard's birthday, which fell on December
28. Corene assumed that her mother must have gone out to
do some last-minute shopping.

When Mr. Brerard returned from work shortly after five,
father and daughter headed out on an eleventh-hour shopping expedition of their own. It wasn't until they returned
to the house an hour or so later, expecting to find Mrs.
Brerard in the kitchen, that they began to get worried. She
was still nowhere in sight.

While John Brerard descended to the basement, Corene
headed upstairs to check the vacant rooms. Moments later,
she was rushing back down the staircase in response to a
sound she had never heard before in her life—her father's
terrified shrieks, so loud and piercing that they carried
throughout the entire house.

She had just reached the ground floor when her father came
stumbling up the stairs from the basement, half-delirious with
fear. "It's Mother!" he cried. "Go for help!"

There was no telephone in the Brerard house. Dashing to
the home of a neighbor, Mrs. Henry Frandsen of 207 Fourth
Street, Corene called the police. Within minutes, Sheriff P.
A. Lainson and two of his deputies were at the crime scene,
where they found John Brerard almost cataleptic with shock.

He was staring fixedly at the furnace. Peering behind it,
Lainson saw Mrs. Brerard's lifeless body wedged between
the back of the furnace and the basement wall. She had
been strangled with a man's cotton shirt, which had apparently been plucked from a clothesline strung across the ceiling beams.

Though Mrs. Brerard was a frail, small-boned woman, she
had clearly put up a terrific struggle. Her face and arms
were badly bruised, the floor was stained with blood, there
were clumps of her hair stuck to the furnace door. Her husband's neatly organized workbench had been overturned,
and his tools lay scattered across the basement floor.

In spite of this evidence, one local official, County Attorney Frank Northrop, made an astonishing pronouncement.
Shortly after the discovery of Mrs. Brerard's body, Northrop
met with reporters and revealed that the victim had recently
been discharged from St. Bernard's mental hospital, where

she had been treated for a "nervous disorder." Given her fragile emotional state, Northrop declared, it was possible "that the shirt may have been knotted about her throat in a suicide attempt."

But Northrop (whose deductive skills clearly rivalled those of James M. Tackaberry, the Portland detective who hypothesized that Mrs. Beata Withers had taken her own life by stuffing herself inside an attic trunk) was alone in this opinion. Everyone else, from Sheriff P. A. Lainson to the victim's overwrought husband, believed that she had been slain by the mysterious "Mr. Williams," possibly in the course of a thwarted rape.

"It seems very plain to me," Lainson told newsmen shortly after examining the murder scene, "that her attacker intended to commit a criminal assault and, failing in his effort, killed her for fear she would report the attack to us."

The question, of course, was the true identity of "Williams." Some investigators believed that he was himself a former inmate of St. Bernard's who had developed a deadly obsession with Mrs. Brerard. But a search of the hospital's records turned up no one matching the suspect's description.

Sheriff Lainson—who had been following the recent rash of killings on the West Coast—offered another, much more chilling theory, which was reported by the local paper, the *Council Bluffs Nonpareil,* on Christmas morning, the day after Mrs. Brerard's murder. Prominently featured on page one was a black-bordered box headlined WARNING! The text read as follows:

Saying it was possible that Mrs. John Brerard was killed by a "strangler" such as has killed women in California, Oregon, and Washington during the past few months, Sheriff P. A. Lainson this afternoon asked *The Nonpareil* to warn housewives of this city against admitting to their homes a man of the description of the "Mr. Williams" known to have called at the Brerard home shortly before Mrs. Brerard was found dead. The description is:

Height—Five feet, eight inches.
Weight—180 pounds.
Complexion—Dark.

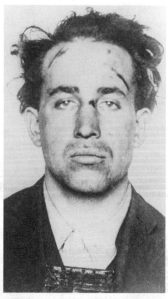

Mug shots of Earle Leonard Nelson, aged twenty-four, at the time of his arrest for assaulting twelve-year-old Mary Summers in May 1921. *UPI/Corbis-Bettmann.*

A GALLERY OF
EARLE LEONARD NELSON'S VICTIMS

Clara Newman, murdered
February 20, 1926,
in San Francisco.
UPI/Corbis-Bettmann.

Mrs. Beata Withers,
murdered October 19,
1926, in Portland. With
her is her son, Charles.
UPI/Corbis-Bettmann.

Mabel Fluke, murdered
October 23, 1926, in
Portland.
UPI/Corbis-Bettmann.

Mrs. Florence Monks,
murdered November 24,
1926, in Seattle.
UPI/Corbis-Bettmann.

Mrs. Blanche Myers, murdered November 29, 1926, in Portland. *UPI/Corbis-Bettmann*

The body of Mrs. Emily Patterson, murdered June 10, 1927, in Winnipeg. *Provincial Archives of Manitoba.*

MURDER

$1500.00 REWARD

PROVINCE OF MANITOBA

The Attorney-General of the Province of Manitoba has authorized the payment of $1,000.00 (One Thousand Dollars), and the City of Winnipeg $500.00 (Five Hundred Dollars), for information leading to the arrest and conviction of the criminal degenerate who is wanted for the murder of

Mrs. Emily Patterson
Miss Lola Cowan

The following is a dependable description of a man who murdered Mrs. Emily Patterson, at 100 Riverton Avenue, Elmwood, City of Winnipeg, on Friday afternoon, the 10th day of June, 1927, by strangulation, and also Miss Lola Cowan, at 133 Smith Street, City of Winnipeg, on or about the 9th of June, 1927, who was also strangled. In each case a sign was displayed on the house either "House for Sale" or "Rooms to Rent."

DESCRIPTION

28 to 30 years, 5 ft. 7 or 8 ins., 150 lbs., dark sallow complexion, has Jewish or Italian appearance, peculiar eyes, fairly well built, hair thin on top and brushed back in long pompadour, newly barbered and inclined to be curly, believed to have very bad corns or bunions on feet.

1 top shirt, either blue or mauve check, size 15), "Wearanfit" trade mark, collar to match.

1 pair of socks, seconds, size not known, greyish brown, light weight.

1 pair fleece lined combinations, bluish colored top, "Didsknit", size 28.

1 pair light brown tan boots, bulldog style, rubber heels, size 9½, "Leader" brand.

1 fawn wool coat sweater, "V" neck style, four pockets, two at top and two at bottom, with one button each, five buttons down front of sweater, match the colour of the material, conspicuous.

1 leather belt, size 34, nickle tongue buckle, green and white stripe in centre.

1 silk scarf, grey and white.

1 silk neck tie, with grey stripe.

Gent's second-hand two-piece suit, very light grey, plain with no visible stripe.

Gent's overcoat, very light grey colour, rough material, lined shoulders and inside front.

All goods are brand new with the exception of the two-piece suit.

This man has a very pleasing manner in presenting himself when entering houses. Upon entering he does not have the appearance of being vicious. He reads and speaks of religious missions. Is an inveterate cigarette smoker, usually smoking Lucky Strike or other American cigarettes.

In the first case he took a room on Wednesday, the 8th of June, 1927, at 133 Smith Street, and paid $1.00. He said he was religious and wanted a quiet bright room where he could study. He gave his name as "WOODCOATS". Next day, the 10th June, Lola Cowan, 14 years, living a few blocks away, went for a walk and never returned. Woodcoats left his room tidy on Thursday night, promising to pay Two Dollars more on Friday morning. Friday noon he murdered Mrs. Patterson, strangling her, robbing the house and pushing her dead body under the bed. Clothes disarranged, apparently assaulted, changed his clothes, taking her husband's suit. Her body was discovered 12 hours after. On Sunday night, the 12th June, the body of Lola Cowan was found stripped naked under the bed in Woodcoats' room at 133 Smith Street, City of Winnipeg. She had been brutally strangled and raped. Not a stitch of her clothing was found.

The murderers, following the Patterson crime, changed again into the clothing described above.

This man is the most dangerous criminal at large today. I ask every Police Officer to help bring this man to Justice. There is ample evidence to convict.

In the first case he has been beating his way by freight, walking and getting lifts from autoists, stopping at rooming houses. He goes over lists of advertisements for rooms in local papers and then commences visiting them. Other houses with "For Sale" or "For Rent" signs he enters on some pretext.

The above reward is not payable to any Peace or Police Officer of the Province of Manitoba.

If located, communicate immediately:

CHRIS. H. NEWTON,
Chief Constable, Winnipeg, Manitoba

13th June, 1927

WANTED poster for the Winnipeg strangler. *Private collection.*

Main Street of Killarney. *UPI/Corbis-Bettmann.*

Earle Leonard Nelson in custody.
Western Canada Pictorial Index.

Earle Leonard Nelson, the "Gorilla Murderer."
Winnipeg Free Press.

Eyes—Dark, piercing.

Clothing—Pearl-colored hat, mouse-colored coat, over-
shoes.

Sheriff Lainson's theory was bolstered that very day when
another witness came forward. After seeing Lainson's warning in Saturday's *Nonpareil*, a Council Bluffs matron, Mrs.
O. H. Brown, telephoned his office with a chilling tale.

Just thirty minutes before the Brerard slaying, according
to Mrs. Brown, a squat, swarthy man had appeared on the
doorstep of her house at 232 Tenth Avenue, which had a
wooden "For Sale" sign planted on the front lawn. Introducing himself as "Mr. Williams," the man—who was perfectly
polite and well-spoken, if somewhat shabbily dressed—explained that he was a railroad switchman, originally from
Milwaukee and currently living in Omaha. He was about to
be transferred to Iowa and was thinking of buying a house
in Council Bluffs to be "nearer to his work."

Mrs. Brown, whose husband was at work in his bakery a
few blocks away, invited him inside. After examining every
room in the house, "Williams" asked to see the basement
furnace. By then, however, Mrs. Brown had grown wary of
the dark-complexioned stranger. "I was afraid of him," she
would later explain to a reporter for the *Nonpareil*. "His
eyes were so black and piercing, with an odd glint in them,
that I became afraid and hurried him to the door, asking
him to call the store and talk to my husband."

If it had not been for her suspicions, the shaken woman
now realized, it would have been she, not poor Mrs. Brerard,
lying dead behind a furnace. As it turned out, Mrs. Brown
was not the only local woman to have had a close brush
with the killer. Late Saturday afternoon, Council Bluffs Fire
Chief James Cotter received a phone call from a Mrs. J. B.
Walters, who said that a man matching the published description of the suspect had visited her home the previous
Thursday afternoon, claiming to be an "inspector of furnaces" for the fire department. Mrs. Walters, who was alone
at the time, refused to admit him to her house. As it happened, this wasn't the first time that Chief Cotter had received such a report. Indeed, for the past few days, he had
been contacted by at least a half-dozen housewives who had

been approached in precisely the same way by the fraudulent "furnace inspector."

By Saturday evening, even County Attorney Northrop had discarded his suicide theory and conceded that the mysterious "Mr. Williams" was undoubtedly the notorious "Dark Strangler," responsible for eleven brutal murders up and down the Pacific Coast. Police Chief E. N. Catterlin had conferred with his counterparts in San Francisco and Seattle and obtained a detailed description of the strangler suspect. Point for point, the description fit the man Robert Moore saw speaking to Mrs. Brerard just before her death.

Even as the slain woman's corpse was making its way by the Rock Island Railroad to its final resting place in Hennessey, Oklahoma, the Brerards' hometown, a small army of law enforcement agents was scouring every city from Omaha to Des Moines for the suspect. An apparent breakthrough occurred on Sunday, December 26, when a drifter named John O'Brien, who bore a vague resemblance to the strangler, was arrested in Creston, Iowa, after trying to force his way into the home of a local housewife. Within hours, Robert Moore, accompanied by Council Bluffs Police Chief E. N. Catterlin and several newspaper reporters, was on his way to Creston. But after viewing the suspect in the Creston city jail, Moore announced that O'Brien was "positively not the man I saw with Mrs. Brerard."

With that, the Iowa authorities found themselves in the same baffled situation as their counterparts in the West—"as far away as ever from a solution to the case," as the *Nonpareil* reported.

23

✝

Bring in the slayer, dead or alive.
L. R. Toyne, Chief of Detectives,
Kansas City, Missouri

Even before Moore and his escorts arrived in Creston, the strangler had already migrated southward to Kansas City, Missouri, where, within twenty-four hours, he added three more victims to his tally.

At approximately 2:00 P.M. on Monday, December 27, a twenty-eight-year-old workman named Raymond Pace returned to his home at 3920 Hammond Street after cashing a $7.50 paycheck for a construction job he had completed that morning. The instant he stepped through the front door, he was greeted by a feeble cry from the bedroom of his son, Victor, an alarmingly frail six-year-old who suffered from a tubercular spine.

"Mamma fell down the stairs," the bedridden boy whimpered when his father hurried to his side. Pace rushed to the stairwell, but his wife, Bonnie—a slender, twenty-three-year-old brunette—was nowhere in sight.

He found her in an upstairs bedroom, her body sprawled across the mattress, her house dress yanked above her hips, ugly bruises on her throat. Later, Deputy Coroner C. S. Nelson confirmed that she had died of manual strangulation. Her body temperature indicated that she had been slain sometime between 10:00 A.M. and noon.

When Detectives W. S. Shumway and Roy Bondure arrived to question little Victor, the boy explained that he had heard someone arrive at the house earlier in the day. The caller—a grown man, judging by the sound of his voice—had been admitted by Mrs. Pace, who presently led him upstairs. Soon afterwards, Victor had heard a muffled commotion from above, then a heavy thud on the staircase. Seconds later, the front door slammed as the man fled the house.

Victor called out to his mother again and again but received no reply. Clearly something bad had happened to her. Judging from the noises he had heard, the six-year-old thought that she might have fallen down the stairs.

When the detectives asked Victor if he had any idea who the man was, the boy nodded and identified him as a truck driver named Robert McKinley, an old family friend. Victor hadn't actually seen the caller but assumed it was McKinley, since (as he told the police) the truck driver "was always coming around to visit Mamma when Poppa was away at work."

McKinley immediately became the prime suspect but was able to provide an airtight alibi. Though Raymond Pace was so broken up that he had to be sedated, he, too, fell under suspicion after investigators learned that he had known about and been fiercely jealous of his wife's friendship with McKinley. As soon as Pace was coherent enough for questioning, however, he was able to supply a solid account of his whereabouts at the time of the murder.

Precisely twenty-four hours after the discovery of Bonnie Pace's corpse—at 2:00 P.M., Tuesday, December 28—a Kansas City man named Marius Harpin returned to his house at 2330 Mercier Street and found both his twenty-eight-year-old wife, Germania, and their eight-month-old son, Robert, dead. The killer had strangled both victims with his bare hands.

Later, police learned that a family friend, J. F. Grofils, had dropped by the house at around noon and been unable to arouse anyone inside, though he had rung the doorbell repeatedly. Grofils had noticed two full milk bottles standing on the front stoop. Since the milkman made his daily delivery to the Harpin home at around 10:00 A.M., the killings had evidently occurred between that hour and twelve.

Over the next few days, the police received the usual torrent of worthless tips, many of them from disgruntled callers, pointing accusatory fingers at their own neighbors, co-workers, and relatives. A string of suspects was brought in for questioning, then promptly released after supplying plausible alibis.

At one point Chief of Detectives L. R. Toyne, who had already issued a "dead or alive" directive to his underlings, took a call from a husky-voiced man who declared, "I killed those people, and I may kill myself." Cupping his hand over the mouthpiece, the chief whispered urgently to the nearest officer, "Trace this call!" Then Toyne got back on the line, hoping to keep the man talking. Suddenly, however, the voice let out a low chortle. "Boy, I'm nutty!" the caller declared before slamming down the receiver in the chief's ear.

New Year's Day saw the Kansas City police no closer to a solution. By then, several of Toyne's men, aware of the recent homicide up in Council Bluffs, were certain that they, too, were dealing with the infamous "Dark Strangler." It wasn't simply that all three Kansas City victims had been choked to death. There were other circumstances linking the murders to the strangler.

While searching the latest crime scene, for example, investigators had found a cigarette butt on the bathroom floor, although neither Marius Harpin nor his wife was a smoker. On the other hand (as authorities knew from the accounts of Edna Gaylord and Susan Yates, the elderly Portland women who had played host to "Adrian Harris" for several days) the strangler suspect *was* a smoker.

More significantly, both the Harpins and the Paces supplemented their incomes by taking in boarders and had hand-lettered "Rooms for Rent" cards displayed in their front-parlor windows.

Of course, the Harpin case *did* differ in one essential respect from the earlier crimes. Up to that point, all the victims had been landladies. Little Robert Harpin was the first child to die at the strangler's hands. He wouldn't be the last.

24
†

A bad man can do a million times more harm than a beast.

Aristotle, *Nicomachean Ethics*

The day after Bonnie Pace was slain, one of her neighbors, an elderly man named C. C. Buck, telephoned the central station of the Kansas City police. Buck reported that, at around ten o'clock on the morning of December 27, the approximate time of the murder, he had glanced out his bedroom window and seen a Ford coupe pull up in front of the Pace residence. A squat man had emerged from the car, mounted the front steps, and, after ringing the doorbell and exchanging a few words with Mrs. Pace, been admitted to the house.

The stranger had been facing away from Buck, so the old man didn't get a good look at him. Nor did Buck remember much about the car, beyond its dilapidated condition. Still, his information confirmed the police's growing conviction that Mrs. Pace's killer was the Pacific Coast strangler, who, on at least one prior occasion, had been spotted fleeing from a crime scene in a beaten-up Ford.

By 1927, Henry Ford's creation was transforming the very character of American life and, in the view of many people, not always for the better. The wayward morality of the country's "flaming youth" was blamed, at least in part, on their easy access to enclosed automobiles, which one outraged critic described as "bordellos on wheels."

Cars were also accused of contributing to the frightening rise in violent crime. In his 1927 magazine article, "What Makes Criminals," George W. Kirchwey, former warden of Sing Sing and Dean of Columbia Law School, observed that the "high-powered motor car, which has given us 'necking' in place of the old-fashioned 'sparking,' has also given us the bandit, with his automatic gun and easy getaway, in place of the old-time footpad."

But cars were conducive to more than motorized banditry and adolescent sex. In America, the advent of the modern serial killer coincided absolutely with the coming of the automobile. Before the 1920s, the closest thing our country had to a serial murderer was the nineteenth-century "arch-fiend," Dr. H. H. Holmes. But though Holmes led a peripatetic life, his atrocities were largely committed in a single locale, his brooding "Murder Castle" in a suburb of Chicago.

By contrast, the "Dark Strangler" preyed on victims from coast to coast, presaging the enormities of such nomadic monsters as Henry Lee Lucas and Ted Bundy, who were able to get away with dozens of murders by keeping constantly on the move. In this, as in other respects, the strangler was a true evil prototype, the first American serial killer of the modern era.

Sometime in the early spring, he reached the East Coast, where, on Wednesday, April 27, he killed his sixteenth victim.

Mrs. Anna Keichline, an elderly invalid who lived alone at 1935 South Sixtieth Street in West Philadelphia, had spent the afternoon seated by an open front window, savoring the sweetness of the day. At approximately 2:45 P.M., she saw a strange man approach the house of her next-door neighbor, a fifty-three-year-old widow named Mary McConnell. Mrs. Keichline assumed that the man was there to inquire about the house, which had been on the market for nearly a year. The wooden "For Sale" sign standing on the front lawn was so weatherbeaten by now that the painted words were barely legible.

About a half-hour later, Mrs. Keichline saw the man stroll out of her neighbor's front door. This time, the elderly woman took a closer look at him. As she would later tell the police, he was a "dark-skinned white man, maybe Greek or Italian, about thirty-five or forty years old, with a chunky build. He was wearing a gray soft hat and a shabby gray coat, a little too big for him." One particular detail caught her eye, a sticky white substance that looked like paperhanger's paste smeared on the front of his droopy gray overcoat.

It was only a few minutes later that Mary McConnell's corpse was discovered. Her son-in-law, John Donovan, who was helping her re-paper an upstairs bedroom, dropped by around 3:30 P.M. to finish the task.

As soon as the young man stepped into the room, he saw the signs of disturbance—an overturned table, a shattered lamp. The paste bucket had been knocked over, and its contents lay puddled on the floor.

He found his mother-in-law's body stuffed under the bed. She had been strangled with a woolen dust rag, knotted so tightly around her throat that Donovan couldn't undo it with his fingers and had to cut it off with scissors. Stuffed deep inside the victim's mouth was an old cotton sock.

It took only a few minutes for Detectives Rogers and O'Kane of the Woodland Avenue station to respond to Donovan's frantic call for help. After examining the murder scene and interviewing Anna Keichline, the investigators concluded that the crime was the work of the Pacific Coast strangler, whose description, by that point, was known to every major police department in the country.

Over the next few days, virtually every officer on the Philadelphia force hunted for the killer. One suspect, a thoroughly bewildered Mexican laborer named Pedro Garcia, who lived on Twelfth and Sixtieth streets, was picked up and questioned for no other reason than his rough physical resemblance to the strangler. Meanwhile, the switchboard of the central police station was flooded with the usual rash of strangler sightings. At least two dozen housewives called in to report that their homes had been invaded by dark, sinister men while their husbands were away at work.

One of the few apparently authentic reports came from a woman named Foy. On Thursday, April 28, Mrs. Foy was hanging out her wash when she saw a "swarthy-looking stranger" ringing the bell of the next-door house, at 5583 Locust Street. The house, owned by a widow named Sophie Freeman, had a "For Sale" sign displayed in its front window. Mrs. Freeman, however, was away for the week, vacationing in Atlantic City with her son, Franklin.

"There's no one home," Mrs. Foy called out to the man.

The man, who wore a gray hat and oversized gray coat, looked over at Mrs. Foy, then turned his attention to her house, which was identical in design to Mrs. Freeman's.

"Your place laid out inside the same as this one?" he called out to her.

Mrs. Foy confirmed that it was.

"Can I come over and have a look?" asked the man, smiling pleasantly. Mrs. Foy was struck by how white his front teeth looked in contrast to his olive skin.

Suddenly, she felt her insides go cold. She had read that morning's *Inquirer,* which had run a front-page story about the "throttling fiend" along with a warning to all Philadelphia housewives from Police Captain McMichael of the Woodland station.

"No," said Mrs. Foy. "You may not." But the man was already headed in her direction. Suddenly, when he was just a few yards away, he came at her with a lunge.

Letting out a scream, Mrs. Foy turned and bolted into her house, slamming the door behind her. Her screams roused her husband, John, a police officer attached to the Fifty-fifth and Pine Streets station, who had just gotten home from his shift and was upstairs in their bedroom. By the time Foy got hold of his gun and rushed downstairs, however, the stranger had fled.

Meanwhile, the murder victim's husband, William McConnell, had learned of his wife's death in a particularly painful way. A travelling salesman, he had just arrived in Wilkes-Barre, Pennsylvania, on the day of the murder. The following morning, he came down to the hotel dining room, stopping off first at the front desk for a copy of the local newspaper. Seating himself at the table, he unfolded the paper. The first thing that caught his eye was a front-page headline: PHILADELPHIA WOMAN FOUND STRANGLED IN HOME. Then he read the story.

Stunned and disbelieving, McConnell ran to a telephone and called his son-in-law, who confirmed the terrible news. Within the hour, McConnell was on a train back to Philadelphia. He was so overcome with grief by the time he arrived that he could not bring himself to view his wife's body at the morgue.

By then, Captain McMichael had received reports that the strangler had been spotted travelling along the Baltimore pike. A squad of homicide detectives was immediately dispatched to Delaware County. But on Monday, May 2, the weary captain conceded defeat. Meeting with reporters, he praised the efforts of his men, who had been devoting "every waking hour to the pursuit." But in spite of their exertions, they had lost the strangler's scent. As the *Inquirer* reported on Tuesday, May 3, "the suspect's identity and whereabouts" were "still as much of a mystery to police as when they started to search for him."

25

She would not move from this home. She always said she
would live here forever.

Gideon Gillett

By the time the strangler struck again, Charles A. Lindbergh had made his epochal transatlantic flight from New
York to Paris. Indeed, the momentous exploit of the heroic
"Lone Eagle" was still dominating the headlines when the
killer claimed his seventeenth victim, Mrs. Jennie Randolph
of Buffalo, New York.

To her family and friends, the fifty-three-year-old widow
was a loving, almost saintly, woman. She and her only child,
Orville, had moved into a two-story house at 175 Plymouth
Avenue eighteen years earlier, after the death of her husband, Earl. Six years later, in 1915, Orville—a bright, handsome teenager who had just graduated from the Normal
public school—died during an operation to remove a ruptured appendix.

The loss of her son was such a devastating blow to Jennie Randolph that her loved ones feared she might suffer
a complete emotional collapse. After weeks of anguished
mourning, however, she managed to wrest herself from the
grip of despair and discover a new purpose in life, plunging
into church work and dedicating herself to the welfare of
others.

The primary outlet for her philanthropy was the Cradle

Roll program of the Plymouth Methodist Episcopal Church. Each week, along with other members of the church, Mrs. Randolph would equip herself with a bagful of baby clothes and, venturing into the city's poorest slums, distribute the garments to needy young mothers. Once a year, the program also sponsored a "cradle party" at the church, to which all the new mothers of the neighborhood were invited.

To make ends meet, Mrs. Randolph worked as a part-time waitress in the YMCA restaurant. At the same time, she had begun taking in tenants, who provided her not only with a supplementary income but also with another outlet for the maternal care she could no longer lavish on her child. One of these was her own older brother, Gideon Gillett, himself a widower, who had occupied a room in his sister's house for nearly ten years. Another was twenty-two-year-old Fred Merritt, a night watchman in a Delaware Avenue apartment building. Merritt, an orphan, had been living in the house for so long—over three years—that Mrs. Randolph had come to regard him as a surrogate son.

In May 1927 there were two other roomers staying in the house, a short-order cook named Michael Malloy and James Bottinger, a carpenter. That left two available rooms, both recently vacated by travelling salesmen. To advertise them, Mrs. Randolph had placed a "Rooms to Let" sign in a living-room window facing Plymouth Avenue. She had spent the better part of Thursday morning, May 26, putting the rooms in trim—dusting, mopping, making up the beds with freshly laundered sheets and clean white counterpanes. She had even hung new chintz curtains on the windows.

At around 11:00 A.M. on Friday, May 27 (just six days after "Lucky Lindy's" monoplane touched down at Le Bourget Airport, transforming the lanky midwesterner into the idol of his age), a man calling himself Charles Harrison appeared at the front door, which was opened by Mrs. Randolph's brother, Gideon Gillett. The man—about thirty-three years old by Gillett's estimate, with a stocky build, dark complexion, and black hair combed straight back—explained that he was a housepainter from New York City who was thinking of moving to Buffalo. He was looking for temporary lodgings and had spotted the rental sign in the window as he was passing along Plymouth Avenue.

In spite of his baggy gray overcoat and some yellow paint stains on his fingernails, Harrison cut a perfectly presentable figure. Indeed, to Gillett's eyes, the stranger—who was wearing a dark tan suit, a blue silk shirt with blue-striped tie, and tan oxfords—looked like a "flashy dresser." True, there was something slightly disconcerting about his dark eyes, which seemed to glint in a peculiar way. But on the whole, he appeared thoroughly respectable.

When Gillett told him the cost of the room, five dollars a week, Harrison made a disappointed noise and replied that the rent was too high for him. Thanking Gillett for his time, he was on the verge of leaving when Jennie Randolph came to the door to see who the caller was.

After introducing Harrison to his sister, Gillett explained that the painter had decided to look elsewhere. Harrison, however, suddenly seemed to reconsider. "If it's all right with you, I think I'll have a look at your rooms after all," he said, showing his square, white teeth as Mrs. Randolph invited him inside.

Harrison allowed the landlady to show him both bedrooms. The one on the ground floor, adjacent to the kitchen, did not suit him at all. He liked the upstairs room better, though it was more cramped than the first and located at the far end of a dimly lit corridor. When Harrison casually asked about the other tenants, Mrs. Randolph told him a bit about Fred Merritt, Michael Malloy, and James Bottinger.

Shortly afterwards, Harrison asked Mrs. Randolph if she would consider reducing the rent by one dollar. When she remained firm, he thanked her and departed.

At around six that evening, however, he reappeared with a small travelling bag in hand and announced that he had changed his mind. He gave Mrs. Randolph a five-dollar bill and settled into the second-floor room.

Later police theorized that "Harrison" had spent that afternoon searching for an easier setup, a rooming house with no male boarders and a completely unprotected landlady. Failing to find such a place, he had returned to Jennie Randolph's home, apparently assuming that, at some point, he would meet with an opportunity to get the fifty-three-year-old widow alone.

That opportunity came in the early morning hours of Monday, May 30.

He had slept late on Sunday, emerging from his room just before noon. He spent the rest of the day hanging about the house, making small talk with Merritt and Gillett and, at one point, helping the latter repair a leaky bathroom faucet.

When suppertime rolled around, Harrison accompanied Fred Merritt to a restaurant on Connecticut Avenue, where the two men chatted amiably over a dinner of corned beef hash and beans. Merritt was slightly taken aback by Harrison's eating habits, particularly the ferocious way he shovelled food into his mouth. Still, the housepainter seemed like a decent enough fellow, who could converse fluently on a wide range of topics, from astrology to Spiritualism.

Returning to the house around 6:00 P.M., the two men found Jennie Randolph seated in the living room with Gillett, discussing church-related matters. While Merritt repaired to his room to get ready for work, Harrison sat down with the landlady and her brother. Soon, he was holding forth on religious topics, so impressing Mrs. Randolph with his knowledge of Scripture that she invited him to accompany her to services that night. Harrison, however, demurred.

At around eight, the landlady departed for church, while her brother and the new lodger continued their conversation in the living room. They were still talking when she returned an hour later. After fixing herself a cup of tea, she rejoined the two men in the living room. By then, Fred Merritt had already left for work.

At approximately ten o'clock, Gillett, stifling a yawn, excused himself and headed upstairs to bed. According to his later testimony, he awoke around midnight and got up to use the bathroom. As he shuffled along the hallway, he could hear the muffled voices of his sister and Harrison, who were still seated downstairs, engaged in an animated conversation.

Returning to his bed, the sixty-year-old Gillett slept until approximately 3:00 A.M. Slipping on his bathrobe, he tiptoed downstairs, fetched the empty milk bottles from the kitchen, and set them out on the front porch. Instead of returning to his room, he stretched out on the living-room couch and was soon asleep again.

He was still sleeping when Fred Merritt returned from his

night watchman's job at around 7:30 A.M. Normally, Mrs. Randolph was in the kitchen at that hour, preparing her breakfast before going off to her job at the YMCA. The young man was a bit surprised to find the kitchen empty but assumed that the landlady had stayed up late talking to Harrison and was allowing herself a few extra minutes of sleep.

Leaving the house again, Merritt strolled to a nearby grocery store, where he purchased three hard rolls for his own breakfast, along with the morning paper.

When he returned about fifteen minutes later, Mrs. Randolph was still nowhere to be seen. He immediately roused Gillett. With Merritt at his side, Gillett made for the kitchen, where he instantly spotted something that had escaped the younger man's attention: ugly reddish-brown stains on the kitchen floor.

Rushing to Mrs. Randolph's ground-floor room, the two men were alarmed to discover that her bed was still neatly made. Instantly, they hurried to the staircase where Gillett saw something that made his heart turn to ice: a trail of the same bloody marks leading upstairs.

The bloodstains ended at the locked door of the new lodger's bedroom. Merritt, a muscular youth, battered the door open with his shoulder. Bursting into the room, the two men were greeted by a horrifying sight—a pair of woman's feet protruding from under the bed. With a yell that brought the other tenants running, Merritt and Gillett leapt to the bed and heaved it off of Jennie Randolph's savaged body.

She had been the victim of a bestial assault. Her bulging eyes were blackened, her nose was battered flat, her face was scarred with scratch marks. She had been pounded on the side of the head with a blunt object and garrotted with a kitchen towel, tied so tightly around her neck that it seemed embedded in the flesh. She was naked below the waist, her skirt and undergarments having been violently ripped from her lower body. Later the coroner would determine that (as the *Buffalo Evening News* put it) the fifty-three-year-old had been "maltreated after death." As for her killer, the disarming fiend who called himself Charles Harrison, there was no trace of him to be found.

* * *

From the moment he learned the details of the case, Buffalo Police Chief James W. Higgins knew who the killer was. "Harrison" was none other than the notorious West Coast strangler, who had gone by the name of "Adrian Harris" in Portland. Higgins had only recently seen a flier about the strangler, circulated by the Philadelphia police.

At a news conference on Monday afternoon, the chief shared his belief with the press, announcing that Jennie Randolph had almost certainly been slain by the "long-sought Pacific Coast Bluebeard—perhaps the most brutal killer, and certainly one of the most cunning, in the history of this country."

So apprehensive was Higgins that the strangler would shortly strike again that he wired an alert to police departments in every city within a 500-mile radius of Buffalo. Meanwhile, the entire detective squad was assigned to the manhunt.

Their only significant lead came from a man named Wilkinson, who owned a pawnshop on Seneca Street. According to Wilkinson, who contacted the police on Tuesday, a stranger had come by his pawnshop the previous morning, looking to sell a travelling bag full of clothes. After a bit of haggling, the man had accepted the proffered amount: four dollars. Wilkinson, who was struck by the fellow's "peculiar eyes," took particular note of his appearance, which (he was now convinced) corresponded in every respect to the published descriptions of Mrs. Randolph's killer.

When Detectives Frank Brinkworth and John Steibeck showed up at the pawnshop to examine the items, they saw at once that Wilkinson was right. The clothing, which included a pair of painter's overalls, precisely matched the ones that "Charles Harrison" had with him during his stay at Mrs. Randolph's rooming house.

To Detective Chief Austin J. Roche, the fact that the killer had settled for such a meager sum suggested that he was desperately low on funds and needed whatever cash he could get hold of to flee the city. It was also apparent that he was no longer travelling in his Ford coupe. Through the window of his pawnshop, Wilkinson had seen him out on Seneca Street attempting to hitch a ride with a passing motorist.

On the following day, Jennie Randolph was buried alongside her husband and son in Elmlawn Cemetery. Afterwards, dozens of visitors came by the house to offer condolences to her brother.

Among the callers was a reporter from the *Buffalo Evening News,* who managed to wangle an interview with the grieving man. Gillett, a vigorous sixty-year-old, seemed to have aged twenty years overnight. His gray head bent low, his faded blue eyes welling with tears, his voice breaking with sobs, he recounted the story of his sister's sad life, explaining how she had "moved into the house eighteen years earlier, after the death of her husband. Six years later, Orville, for whom she had dreamed great ambitions, died. Then she was alone. She threw herself into church work and tried to make a home for the roomers and boarders she took in."

He explained how, after arming herself "with broom, mop, and duster," she had spent the previous Friday morning preparing the upstairs bedroom. The reporter asked if he could see the room. Gillett seemed reluctant at first but finally agreed. Climbing the stairs as stiffly as an arthritic, he made his way down the dimly lit corridor. Then, after taking a moment to brace himself, he threw open the door.

Peering into the "cheery, homey-looking room," the reporter took note of its simple furnishings—an oak dresser topped with a lacy, white doily, a green-seated rocker, a single bed with a simple wooden headboard.

Suddenly, Gillett let out a sob and pointed a quivering finger to the floor at the foot of the bed. "There!" he cried. "There I found the body of my sister. And there on the woodwork is her blood!"

The reporter glanced down at the dull, brownish stains in the center of the room. For all their drabness, they seemed "startlingly bright against the floorboards that Jennie Randolph had scrubbed clean on Friday, wholly unaware, of course, that she was making the room ready to receive her own corpse."

26

✝

The crimes we read of every day
Cause many hearts to shiver
But few surpass in magnitude
The murder at Fall River.

Alexander B. Beard,
"The Murder at Fall River"

On the very day of Jennie Randolph's funeral—Wednesday, June 1, 1927—Miss Lizzie Borden (or "Lizbeth" as she preferred to be called later in life) died at "Maplecroft," her stately home in a fashionable district of Fall River, Massachusetts. For the previous thirty-odd years, she had led a semireclusive life, shunned by most of the townspeople, who believed that she had gotten away with murder.

During the decades that followed her acquittal, the wealthy spinster remained an object of morbid curiosity, drawing stares whenever she rode through the streets in her handsome horse-drawn carriage (and later in a chauffeured limousine). A fan of the theater, she made occasional jaunts to Boston, Providence, and Washington, D.C. When she died at the age of sixty-seven, she left a sizable estate. Among her bequests was a $30,000 gift to her favorite charity, the Animal Rescue League of Fall River.

The news of her death came as a surprise to most of her countrymen. Lizzie Borden—who "took an axe and gave her father forty whacks"—had passed into legend so many years earlier that it was hard to think of her as a flesh-and-blood person who had survived into the era of flappers and speakeasies, movies and motor cars.

Of course, even the death of the celebrated parricide was eclipsed by the nation's frenzy over Charles A. Lindbergh, who was being urged to return with all possible speed to his native land, where he would be greeted with something like mass hysteria. One New York newspaper described his flight as "the greatest feat of a solitary man in the records of the human race," while the *Tucson Dispatch* declared that, "One must go back to the fictive times of the gods who dwelt on Mount Olympus for a feat that will parallel that of Captain Lindbergh."

George M. Cohan, the Yankee Doodle Dandy himself, composed a pop paean to the lanky, young idol—"When Lindy Comes Home"—that became an immediate hit. Streets, trains, and even whole towns were rechristened with his name. A new dance, the "Lindy Hop," was invented in his honor. The ticker-tape parade he received in Manhattan on June 13 would generate nearly 2,000 tons of confetti, more than ten times the amount that showered onto the streets when the Armistice was announced in 1918.

With the whole country caught up in the Lindbergh craze, the double slaying of two middle-aged women on June 1 received relatively little attention, even in Detroit, where the killings took place. To a certain extent, the indifference stemmed from the perceived character of one of the victims, a woman of supposedly questionable morals who—as the newspapers initially implied—had brought the tragedy on herself.

Her name was Mrs. Noresh Chandra Atorthy, though she'd been using her maiden name, Maureen Oswald, ever since her divorce. Her ex-husband, described in the papers as "a Hindu physician," had since moved to London to do postgraduate work in medicine.

According to her divorce papers, Dr. Atorthy had severely mistreated his wife—beating her routinely, refusing her money for food, and subjecting her to various forms of public humiliation. "After our marriage," she had deposed, "I found that Dr. Atorthy had married me for spite. He had been going with another girl for four years and when she jilted him, he married me. I now realize that he never loved me.

"Dr. Atorthy forced me to carry fifty-pound blocks of ice up two flights of stairs and made me split big chunks of coal for the furnace. He seemed to despise me and made his patients think I was the scrub woman."

For his part, Dr. Atorthy had charged that his wife was both an alcoholic and a drug addict who had stolen narcotics from his office. Later investigation into the life of Mrs. Atorthy, née Oswald, revealed that, while serving with the Women's Auxiliary Army during the Great War, she had been wounded at Vimy Ridge and had indeed become addicted to morphine.

Following the breakup of her marriage in February 1927, she had taken a room at 640 Philadelphia Avenue West, a boardinghouse owned by an absentee landlord named Leonard Sink and managed by a fifty-three-year-old widow, Mrs. Fannie C. May. On the first day of June, Sink came by to collect the rent, but no one appeared to be home. He tried again on the following afternoon. This time, he rang the bell and knocked on the door for nearly five minutes before giving up. When he failed to get a response for the third consecutive day, he became alarmed, particularly since there was a growing pile of mail and newspapers on the front porch.

Proceeding to the Bethune police station, Sink identified himself as the owner of the house and told the desk sergeant that he "believed the occupants were in some sort of difficulty." Two officers, Patrolmen Roy Tatton and Ralph Morton, accompanied him back to the house. After trying the doorbell with no success, the three men entered with Sink's passkey.

They found Mrs. May first. She was lying facedown on the tiled floor of the upstairs bedroom, her white cotton housedress bunched above her hips, an electric cord knotted around her neck.

Mrs. Atorthy's corpse was stretched out on the floor of the adjacent bedroom. She had been garrotted with a length of black ribbon. The front of her blouse had been ripped open, and her brown cotton skirt pulled up to her waist. Her topcoat and hat were lying on the floor. From the way the two victims were dressed—the landlady in houseclothes, her tenant in street attire—the officers surmised that the killer had found Mrs. May alone, attacked her, then awaited the return of Mrs. Atorthy. As the *Detroit News* reported, "A 'Rooms for Rent' sign had been placed in the front door of the house, and it would have been easy for a stranger to have gained entrance without exciting Mrs. May's suspicion."

The bedrooms had been ransacked, the contents of the bureau drawers spilled onto the floors. After learning about Mrs. Atorthy's background, the police surmised that she had been killed by one of her unsavory acquaintances, a "dope fiend" who had come to the house to steal her supply of drugs and had slain both women to prevent them from identifying him.

On Thursday, June 2, two narcotics addicts well-known to police, Charles Washington of 1943 Wilkins Street and Jacques Helberg of 567 Napoleon Street, were brought in for questioning. Both men, however, were able to account for their whereabouts at the time of the murders. Nor did either of them conform to the description of a mysterious visitor glimpsed by one of Mrs. May's neighbors, Gloria Hopkins, on the day of the slayings.

Mrs. Hopkins had been hanging out her laundry on Wednesday afternoon when she noticed "a man of medium build and dark complexion" ringing her neighbor's bell. A few moments later, Mrs. May came to the door and, after exchanging a few words with the stranger, admitted him to the house. "That was the last I ever saw of her," Mrs. Hopkins told the police.

Several more days went by before Detroit homicide detectives began to entertain a different theory—that the "dark-complexioned" caller seen by Mrs. Hopkins was the "Pacific Coast Bluebeard" who had recently shifted his operations to the East. By the time they came to this realization, however, the strangler was already heading westward again.

On Friday, June 4, he killed a twenty-seven-year-old landlady named Mary Cecilia Sietsema in the living room of her home at 7501 South Sangamon Street, Chicago. At first, two suspects were arrested—Michael Hirsch, a butcher known to have made a delivery to the victim on the day of the murder, and a car mechanic named Jack Grimm, who worked in a garage a short distance from the Sietsema home.

As the *Chicago Tribune* reported, "Suspicion was cast upon Grimm when it was learned that he disappeared from work Friday afternoon and failed to return home that night."

Both Hirsch and Grimm would quickly be cleared. Hirsch, who had fallen under suspicion partly because of some blood on his shoes, was able to prove that it had come from a wound he had sustained while opening a tub of butter in his father's shop. And Grimm's claim that "he had been out getting drunk" at the time of the murder was substantiated by a number of witnesses. The men were released from the Cook County jail on Monday, June 6, while the real perpetrator was moving up into northern Minnesota.

Since the previous February, he had slain twenty victims: nineteen women and one infant boy. Detectives in a dozen different cities, from San Francisco to Philadelphia, were hunting him. Though he had so far managed to elude capture—through a combination of cunning, luck, and the still-primitive state of American police work—the country was becoming a risky place for him.

And so—sometime on the morning of June 8, 1927—Earle Leonard Nelson crossed the border into Canada.

PART 4

†

THE
GORILLA

27

✝

For brief as water falling will be death . . .
brief as the taking, and giving, breath.

Conrad Aiken, "And in the Human Heart"

By the time he reached Winnipeg, he was tired, hungry, and desperate for cash. He had gotten a lift early that morning from a man named Chandler, who had picked him up near Warren, Minnesota, and driven him as far as Noyes, in the northwest corner of the state. From there he had made his way into Manitoba. Just outside Emerson, he had hitched a ride from another motorist, John T. Hanna, who had dropped him off in Winnipeg at around 1:15 P.M.

He spent one of his few remaining nickels on a trolley ride to Main Street, then trudged along the sidewalk until he spotted what he was looking for, a dingy little shop that peddled secondhand clothes.

The store smelled of mildew and was lit by a single bare bulb. It was so gloomy inside that it took him a moment to locate the proprietor, a balding old man named Jake Garber, who was perched on a stool behind the rear counter.

With barely a nod of hello, he launched into his story. He had just arrived from the country and was flat broke. He planned to look for a construction job in the morning but in the meantime needed some cash to pay for a room.

"Tell you what," he said to the old man. "These clothes are too fancy anyways." Here he gestured toward his outfit—red-striped sweater, blue woolen pants, gray felt cap, and tan loafers. "I'll trade them for anything you got, plus a dollar."

Garber appraised the clothes for a moment. Then, with a grudging sigh, as though he were granting an enormous favor, he eased himself off the stool and shuffled around the counter. After rooting around on his shelves for a few minutes, he returned with an armful of musty old clothes, which he laid on the counter. The dark-complexioned stranger changed hurriedly while Garber made his way to the cash register and removed a dollar.

Pocketing the money, the stranger hurried out of the store without another word. Dressed in the secondhand clothing— shabby blue coat with missing buttons, baggy brown trousers, floppy gray hat, and oversized black boots—he looked about as ragged as he felt. He needed to find a house to hole up in, and it had to be his kind of place: cheap, out-of-the-way, and—ideally—run by a nice, defenseless landlady.

From the outside at least, the big wooden house at 133 Smith Street, with its weatherbeaten air and "Rooms for Rent" sign in the window, appeared to be just what he was looking for. He mounted the veranda and pressed the door buzzer. The time was just before 5:00 P.M., Wednesday, June 8, 1927.

The door was opened by a stout, white-haired woman who introduced herself as Mrs. Hill. He gave his name as "Woodcoats" and said that he was looking for a "quiet room in a quiet house."

"My house *is* quiet," Mrs. Hill replied, a note of indignation in her voice. "I don't allow any drinking on the premises. And if you're looking to bring any girls into your room, you'd better go elsewhere."

"Good," said the young, dark-complexioned man. "All I want is quiet surroundings. I don't like to be bothered while I'm studying my Bible."

Mrs. Hill was impressed. "So you're a religious person, are you?"

"Always have been," the stranger said. "A man with Christ in his heart has nothing in this life to worry about."

Though she'd been a little put off by his uncouth appearance, Mrs. Hill liked what she heard. Inviting him inside, she led him upstairs to the second floor and ushered him into the vacant room.

It was clean and simply furnished and suited his needs just fine. But the price, twelve dollars per month, was a little steeper than he'd hoped.

When he asked if she had anything cheaper, she explained that, yes, there was another, smaller room that rented for ten dollars a month. It was currently occupied by a young dry-goods salesman, but he would be gone in a week, at which point Mr. Woodcoats could have it.

"All right," said the man who called himself Woodcoats. In the meantime, he would remain in the costlier room and pay her one week's rent in advance, three dollars.

"Trouble is," he said, looking somewhat abashed, "I'm down to my last dollar." He was working on a construction job just across the river in St. Boniface and expected to get paid the next day. Could he give her a dollar now and the balance tomorrow—maybe Friday at the latest?

"That will be fine," said the landlady, taking the proferred bill and slipping it into her apron pocket.

The young man was in a talkative mood, so Mrs. Hill, who always liked to learn something about her guests, settled herself on the edge of his bed and had a chat. She remained there for another twenty minutes or so, ample time to make a close inspection of the young man. His black hair, dark eyes, and swarthy skin led her to believe he was of foreign extraction, possibly Greek or Italian. He was dressed like a laborer—mud-encrusted boots, frayed serge coat, cheap cottonade trousers. He was clearly destitute, bereft of everything but the clothes on his back. He carried no luggage at all, not even a small travelling bag.

Still, though he cut an unprepossessing figure, he struck her as a young man of character—"high ideals," as she later put it. They talked mainly about religion. He was a Roman Catholic, he said, and liked to spend part of each day studying Scripture. At another point, by way of explaining his straitened circumstances, he told her that, until recently, he had done a thriving business in construction but had been driven into bankruptcy by an unscrupulous partner.

Mrs. Hill clucked her tongue. "Ah, well. A young man like you is better off on your own anyways."

It was almost six by the time she got up to leave. Pausing at the door, she repeated the house rules. "Now mind. No liquor in the room. And no girls."

"No need to worry," he said, smiling. "I'm a straightforward and good-living man who never wants to do wrong by anyone."

He stayed shut up in his room until after dark, when he wandered onto the veranda. He found another lodger, James Phillips, seated outside, enjoying the night air. Like Mrs. Hill, Phillips took the new arrival for an Italian laborer, a "Dago bricklayer," as he would later tell the police. The two men made inconsequential talk for a while, mostly about the weather. Then, explaining that he was "dog-tired" from a long day of travelling, "Woodcoats" wished Phillips good night and repaired to his room.

No one saw him again until teatime the next day, Thursday, June 9. Mrs. Hill was seated at the kitchen table with her husband, John, when the new lodger appeared at the doorway. Seeing the couple together, the burly young man did a little double take, as though he had expected to find the old lady alone.

"Sorry to interrupt," he said, stammering slightly. After an embarrassed pause, he explained that he still did not have the two dollars he owed her but expected to have it by Friday. Mrs. Hill assured him that Friday would be "just fine." Muttering a thanks, he turned on his heels, made for the front door, and headed outside for a prowl.

Lola Cowan was still a few days shy of her fourteenth birthday, which would fall on Sunday, June 12. But with her bobbed hair, shapely legs, and woman's body, she could have passed for twenty.

She still acted like a child, though. On the afternoon of Thursday, June 9, at roughly the time that Earle Leonard Nelson was leaving the Hill house, she lingered in the playground of the Mulvey school to play baseball with some of her fifth-grade schoolmates, a group that included her friends Chrissie Budge, Peggy Robertson, Florence Reid, Douglas Palk, George Little, James and Billy Clement, Arthur Hermans, and Edgar Betson. It was nearly 5:00 P.M. when she scooped up her schoolbooks and headed home. None of her friends would see her alive again.

The Cowan family—mother, father, and four children ranging in age from five to seventeen—shared a little bungalow at 3 University Place. (Another child, the oldest—twenty-five-year-old Archie Cowan—lived in the Manitoba mining area.) Several weeks earlier, Mr. Cowan, a salesman, had been stricken with pneumonia. After a slow recuperation, he was finally getting back on his feet, though he was still too debilitated for work.

With her husband unemployed and the family savings dwindling at an alarming rate, Mrs. Cowan had taken a menial job at the St. Regis Hotel. Lola had also resolved to do what she could. For the past few weeks, she had been going out in the evening to sell the artificial sweet peas that her older sister, Margaret, fashioned out of colored paper.

Arriving home at around 5:20 P.M. from her after-school ball game, Lola settled down to her homework. At around 6:15 she changed into a blue, pleated skirt and peach-colored sweater-coat. Then, placing several bunches of the paper flowers in a tin lunch box, she headed out onto the streets.

Two people would later recall seeing her that evening. At around 6:30, she appeared at the front door of a woman named Regina Bannerman, who, after explaining that she had no money to spend on paper flowers, returned to her supper.

Approximately one hour later, a man named William Arthur Fillingham was seated in his drawing room, composing a letter, when someone knocked at his door. The caller turned out to be a pretty young woman, who held out a tin box full of paper flowers and offered them at twenty-five cents a bunch. Fillingham spoke to her for a while, asking her name, her age, her family circumstances. Then, after declining to make a purchase, he advised her to return home.

Precisely when and where Lola Cowan encountered Earle Leonard Nelson will never be known. Possibly, she was waiting at the corner of Graham Avenue and Smith Street—where she sometimes met her mother after work—when her killer passed by. Nor is there any way to determine exactly how he managed to get her alone, though the likeliest theory is that he offered to buy some of her flowers if she would accompany him back to his lodgings, where he had ostensibly left his money.

The only incontestable fact is that—sometime in the early evening of Thursday, June 9—the dark, malignant man lured the young girl to Mrs. Catherine Hill's boardinghouse at 133 Smith Street. Then, unseen by any of the other occupants, he led her inside and hurried her upstairs to his room.

At approximately eleven that night, as he was climbing the stairs to his flat, James Phillips passed by the new lodger's bedroom and noticed that the door was wide open. From the bulb that burned on the landing, he could see that the darkened room was empty.

When Mrs. Hill came upstairs to do her daily housekeeping the next morning, Friday, June 10, the door was still wide open. And nice Mr. Woodcoats was nowhere to be seen.

The landlady thought nothing of his absence. She assumed that he had headed out early for work. As she glanced around the room, she was impressed with his tidiness. There was really very little for her to do. He had been particularly careful in making up the bed, smoothing out the coverlet and making sure that its bottom edge reached down to the floor. She spent a few minutes dusting, left a clean towel on the dresser, and shuffled from the bedroom, closing the door on the undetected horror inside.

28

✝

The imagination of Zola himself could have conceived of no more overwhelming horror. Patterson was subjected to a trial of faith with which even that of the patriarch Abraham at Jehoval-Jireh is not analogous, for with Patterson there was no last-minute reprieve.

L. C. Douthwaite, *Mass Murder*

A few miles away, across the Red River in Elmwood, William Haberman, an elderly widower who resided at 104 Riverton Street, was just coming home from the corner drugstore, where he'd gone to use the pay phone. As he approached his little cottage, he noticed a thickset man in a gray cap and navy-blue coat standing on the front porch of the house next door, which had recently been rented by a family named Patterson.

The Pattersons, a young husband and wife named William and Emily and their two little boys, were Irish immigrants who had moved into the neighborhood just two weeks earlier. Since their arrival, Haberman had caught only a few fleeting glimpses of the husband, who left early for his job at the T. Eaton Company and often returned after dark. And so, when the old man saw the thickset fellow fiddling with the front door of the neighboring house, he took him for Mr. Patterson.

Unlocking his own front door, Haberman entered his kitchen, filled a kettle with tap water, set it on his stovetop, then repaired to the parlor and put one of his favorite recordings, "My Blue Heaven," on the gramophone. As Gene Austin's warbling voice filled the room, Haberman peered out a window at the Pattersons' front porch. The thickset young man was no longer there. Seconds later, the teakettle shrilled, and the old man headed back to the kitchen.

He spent the next forty minutes or so seated at the table, sipping tea, munching on ginger snaps, and reading that day's edition of the *Manitoba Free Press*. So he didn't see the Pattersons' front door swing open at around 12:30 P.M., nor observe the thickset young man—who was now dressed in completely different clothing—slip outside the house and hurry away down Riverton Street.

Sam Waldman was a licensed secondhand clothes dealer with a little store at 629 Main Street. At approximately 1:15 P.M., the bell over his shop door jangled and a short, barrel-chested man entered. Dressed in a threadbare brown suit and badly in need of a shave, the man looked so disreputable that Waldman took him for a hobo who had come to cadge a dime. So the storeowner was surprised when the stranger strode up to the counter and announced that he was there to purchase clothes.

"What do you need?" asked Waldman.

"Everything," replied the stranger. "Top to bottom."

Waldman gestured towards his crowded shelves. "Have a look."

Perched on his stool, Waldman watched while the grubby young man, whose old whipcord suit looked as though it had been retrieved from a trash barrel, wandered around the store, poking through merchandise. About fifteen minutes later, the stranger approached with an armful of stuff, which he dumped on the counter.

"Tell you what," he said. "I'm a little strapped at present. Give me a good price, and I'll take the whole load off your hands."

Waldman began going through the pile: light gray topcoat, two-piece gray suit, blue shirt, fawn-colored cardigan, gray-and-white silk scarf, beige cap, leather belt, gray gloves, grayish-brown socks, tan boots with bulging (or "bull dog") toes, and a pair of BVDs.

"Thirty's about as much as I can afford," said the stranger.

Waldman gave a little shrug. "So make it thirty."

Reaching into the pocket of his ragged brown pants, the young man pulled out a roll of bills and peeled off half of them, three crisp tens.

"Mind if I change in here?" he asked.

Waldman pointed to a spot in the rear of the store. While the young man was unbuttoning his clothing, Waldman cast a glance in his direction and noticed that his hands were shaking badly.

"You sick or something?" he asked.

"Cold. I just got in from the country."

Waldman could believe it—the bull-necked young man might have easily been a farmhand.

After changing into his new purchases, the stranger rolled his old clothing—suit, shirt, socks, briefs, everything—into a bundle and handed it to Waldman.

"Want me to dump it out back?" asked the storeowner.

"Leave it," said the other. "I'll come by for it in a day or two." Reaching up a hand, he rubbed the bristles on his jaw. "Know where I can get a shave?"

"Come," said Waldman.

Ushering the stranger outside, the obliging clothier walked him across Main Street to a place called Central Billiards. Occupying one end of the cavernous pool hall was a row of barber chairs. Waldman introduced the stranger to one of the barbers, a man named Nick Tabor.

"Fix this fellow up good, Nick," said Waldman. Then, while the stranger settled into the chair and Tabor whetted his blade on the leather strop, Waldman returned to his store, taking note of the time when he got back—precisely 2:05 P.M.

Though Tabor was not a particularly voluble man, he was curious about his customer, never having set eyes on him before. For his part, the stranger seemed happy to talk. In fact, he kept up a steady stream of chatter, almost as if he were "hopped up" on something (as Tabor later reported).

He told Tabor that he was from the States, "born and bred in Frisco," though he'd spent time "all over" the country. He had recently made a trip to several cities in the East—Philadelphia, Buffalo, Washington, D.C. He worked as a commercial traveller, selling "small articles."

When Tabor asked what kind of car he drove, the man said a Studebaker. "I need to travel fast," he explained with a grin.

Daubing lather onto the man's swarthy face, Tabor asked how he came to be in Winnipeg.

He was passing through North Dakota, the stranger replied, and, never having been in Canada before, decided to take a look. "Not much to see, though," he added.

Tabor, a lifelong Winnipegger, bridled at the aspersion.

"There's as much to see here as in the States," he answered.

The dark-skinned man smirked. "Maybe."

He remained in the barber chair for nearly an hour, getting the full treatment—shave, haircut, hot towel, facial massage. At one point, while combing back the stranger's black, receding hair, Tabor noticed that there was blood on his forehead, right by the hairline. There seemed to be some open sores on the man's scalp, or possibly scratches. Tabor wasn't sure. But one thing was obvious. The blood was still fresh.

Rising from the chair at around 3:00 P.M., the stranger settled with Tabor, tipping the barber four bits. Then he went into the café next door for a bite.

Later that day, as he was passing the display window of a haberdashery store called Chevrier's, his eye was caught by a champagne-colored fedora with a gaudy, detachable band. Ducking into the store, he asked the price.

"Four-fifty," said the salesman, Thomas Carten.

He decided to splurge. Removing the cap he had just purchased at Waldman's, he had Carten bag it up in a brown paper sack and wore his flashy new hat out of the store.

Like most of what he had told Nick Tabor, the bit about the Studebaker was a lie. At around six that evening, he boarded a trolley headed west. On the ride, he struck up a conversation with a man named John Hofer, introducing himself as "Walter Woods." Their talk took a strange turn when he asked if Hofer was a minister.

Hofer was taken aback. "No. Why?"

"You've got a clean face."

Hofer didn't know what to say.

"Are you apostolic?" asked the stranger.

Again, Hofer was at a loss, since he didn't know the meaning of the word. Before he could think of a reply, the man said, "You look like a religious person."

"How can you tell?"

"I am the champion of the world at telling faces," said the man, letting out a self-satisfied chortle.

Sometime later, he confessed that he occasionally over-indulged in drink.

"You shouldn't do that," said Hofer.

"I know," he sighed. Then, shaking his head sadly, he added, "Satan has too much power over educated men like me."

Before they parted at Headingly, "Woods" handed Hofer the brown paper bag he was carrying. "You can have this if you want it."

"What is it?" asked Hofer.

"Look and see."

Hofer opened the bag, peered inside, then reached in and extracted the cream-colored cap.

"It's yours if you want it," the other man said again.

"Well, sure, if you don't have any use for it," said Hofer.

They parted at Headingly, where "Woods" stopped off at a soda fountain and drank a Coca-Cola. Outside again, he flagged down a car driven by a man named Hugh Elder, who offered him a lift to Portage La Prairie. Along the way, they spoke about religion.

At approximately 6:25 P.M., around the time that "Walter Woods" was boarding the Portage Avenue trolley, William Patterson returned to his house at 100 Riverton Street in Elmwood.

The house was empty. He found his sons, James and Thomas, ages three and five, at the home of a neighbor, Mrs. Evelyn Stanger, whose own little boys were Jim and Tommy's playmates. Mrs. Stanger had no idea where Patterson's wife was. She hadn't seen Emily since early that morning, when the two women chatted briefly while walking their five-year-olds to school.

Patterson was mildly surprised but not concerned. He assumed his wife had paid a visit to a friend and gotten held up for some reason. Thanking Mrs. Stanger, he took his sons back home, fed them supper, and put them to bed.

By 10:30 that night, however, Patterson was growing frantic. His wife had never shown up. Returning to the Stangers' house, he used their telephone to check with Emily's friends. But no one had seen or spoken to her all day.

When he got back to his own house shortly after eleven, he felt almost sick with anxiety. Pacing the darkened hallways, he glanced into the bedroom of his sleeping boys and, by the glow of the nightlight, noticed something that had escaped his attention earlier, when he'd put his sons to bed.

In one corner of the room stood a little locked suitcase, where Patterson stashed his nest egg—sixty dollars in new ten-dollar bills. Now, he could see that the lock had been tampered with—the latch was twisted and sprung, as though it had been pried open. Hurrying across the room, he crouched by the case and lifted the lid.

His money was gone. In its place was a claw hammer.

Patterson felt dizzy with confusion. A deeply religious man, he made his way to the bed of his younger son, James, and knelt on the carpeted floor. Palms pressed together, elbows propped on the mattress, he implored God for guidance, praying (as he later testified) that the Lord "would direct him to where his wife was."

As he started to rise, one of his knees caught the low-hanging coverlet and thrust it aside, exposing the bottom of the bed. There was something poking out from under the bed. It looked like the sleeve of his wife's woolen sweater, the one she liked to wear around the house.

Patterson reached beneath the bed. What he felt made his throat clench with fear. Fleeing to the Stangers' house, he managed to put in a panicked call to the police before collapsing in a faint.

29

✝

I drew up the blinds when I felt the smell in the room.
                                                    Mrs. Catherine Hill

Like countless Winnipeggers, Catherine Hill reacted with
both wonder and dread to the lead story in Saturday's *Free
Press*. Spread across four front-page columns, it told how
twenty-seven-year-old William Patterson, seconds after en-
treating the Lord "to direct him to his missing wife," had
discovered her strangled and violated corpse beneath the
bed of their slumbering child. The scene, evoked in all its
horror and pathos, sent a shudder through Mrs. Hill. Clearly,
when it came to grotesque tragedy, there was nothing in
gothic fiction that could match the monstrosities of real life.

The article went on to describe the progress of the police
investigation. Officers had arrived at 100 Riverton Street
within minutes of receiving Patterson's frantic call. Inside,
they found several of his stunned neighbors gathered around
the rumpled bed, which someone had shoved about two feet
away from the wall. Patterson himself, almost stupefied with
grief, was being comforted in an adjoining room by his
neighbor, Mrs. Stanger, while another Samaritan attended
to his two sobbing children.

Clearing everyone from the crime scene, the three constables—Mann, Wood, and Gibson—carefully dismantled the
single bed, completely exposing Emily Patterson's corpse.
The twenty-three-year-old woman lay sprawled on her back,

the lower half of her body twisted sideways. She was still fully clad, though her skirt had been yanked above her hips and her stockings rolled below her knees. Her face was smeared with blood from her battered nose and mouth, and there was an ugly bruise on her forehead.

Coroner Herman Cameron, who arrived shortly after the three constables, determined that Mrs. Patterson had been struck on the head with a blunt instrument—possibly the hammer that her husband had found inside his suitcase—then asphyxiated by smothering and strangulation. She also had been raped, apparently after death. Cameron found a glaze of dried seminal fluid on the front of her right thigh.

While the coroner oversaw the removal of Mrs. Patterson's corpse to Kerr's undertaking parlor (where a complete post-mortem would be performed by Dr. W. P. McCowan), two detectives, Charles McIver and Harold Fox, conducted a thorough search of the house. It wasn't long before they made several important discoveries. A threadbare suit belonging to the overwrought husband turned out to be missing from his bedroom. It had evidently been stolen by the killer, whose own discarded clothes—a shabby blue jacket and brown cottonade trousers—were found heaped in a corner of the room. Inside the pocket of the trousers the detectives discovered some crumpled newspaper classifieds torn from the "Rooms to Let" section of the *Winnipeg Tribune*.

From this telltale clue, and the conspicuous thumb marks on the victim's throat, Detective Sergeant McIver quickly deduced that the killer was none other than the infamous "strangler fiend" who had already slain twenty victims in the States. The Winnipeg P.D. had recently received a circular describing the homicides from the Buffalo police.

Mrs. Patterson hadn't been a landlady, but in every other respect her murder bore all the earmarks of the killer's m.o. Surmising that, if the strangler struck again, he would probably seek out his favorite type of victim, Chief Detective George Smith immediately directed all available personnel to visit every rooming house in Winnipeg.

Apprised of these developments by her morning paper, Catherine Hill was not at all surprised when, shortly before noon on Saturday, June 11, two detectives showed up at her home. She invited them into her parlor, where they proceeded to question her about her lodgers. Had any suspicious-looking men rented rooms from her recently? Had any of her boarders checked out in a hurry during the last few days? To both these questions Mrs. Hill answered, "No."

She wasn't lying, at least as far as she knew. Her only new lodger was Mr. Woodcoats. But in spite of his coarse appearance, he had turned out to be such a devout and idealistic young man that it never occurred to Mrs. Hill that he might be a murder suspect. Besides, though she hadn't laid eyes on him since Thursday evening when he'd unexpectedly appeared at her kitchen doorway, she believed that he was still residing at her house. He had certainly never checked out. Indeed, she was still expecting the two-dollar balance he owed on his rent.

By the following morning, however, Sunday, June 12, Mrs. Hill had begun to feel troubled by doubts, which grew stronger by the hour as the day passed with no sign of Mr. Woodcoats. Finally, at around 4:30 P.M., she mounted the stairs and, after knocking on his door and receiving no response, let herself into the room.

Two things struck her immediately. One was the state of the room, which had clearly not been occupied since Friday morning when she had come upstairs to clean. The bed had obviously not been slept in, and the fresh towel she had placed on the bureau was untouched. The other thing that struck her was the stink—a thick, fetid odor like the stench of decay.

Mrs. Hill assumed that she was smelling the lingering reek of the unbathed Mr. Woodcoats, which had intensified in the closeness of the shut-up room. Wrinkling her nose, she crossed to the window, raised the blinds, and threw open the sash. Sunlight and clean air poured into the room. Turning, she headed for the landing, leaving the door wide-open behind her.

Downstairs, she summoned her husband and shared her concern. She was afraid that she might have inadvertently lied to the police. She now believed that Mr. Woodcoats had, in fact, absconcded without paying his rent.

Mr. Hill promised that he would stop off at the police station on his way to church that evening. He left the house at around 5:30 P.M. Arrriving at the Central Station about twenty minutes later, he was interviewed by Chief of Detectives George Smith, who was intensely interested in what the old man had to say. Hoping that the landlady might be able to identify the discarded men's clothing found at the Patterson house, Smith immediately ordered one of his men to convey it to Smith Street.

Even as the detective was on his way to the Hills' boardinghouse, however, a discovery was taking place there that, for sheer sensational horror, almost matched the melodrama of William Patterson's experience.

One of Mrs. Hill's lodgers was a man named Bernhardt Mortenson. Mortenson and his wife occupied a spacious room just off the parlor, one of the nicest in the house. Its only disadvantage was its distance from the bathroom, which was located on the second-floor landing.

After returning from a midday outing with his wife at around 6:00 P.M. on Sunday, Mortenson went upstairs to use the facilities. As he walked back towards the stairwell a few minutes later, he passed the little room at the head of the landing, the one that had been recently rented to the new arrival, Mr. Woodcoats. For the past few days, Woodcoats' door had been continuously shut. Now it stood open.

As Mortenson began descending the stairs, he happened to glance over into Woodcoats' room. In the late afternoon sunlight that slanted through the window, he thought he could make out something peculiar beneath the bed. Pausing, he squinted at the thing, then let out a gasp. The sight was so startling that he had to grab hold of the bannister to keep his balance.

Fleeing downstairs, he shouted for the landlady, who came bustling out of the kitchen in alarm.

"What's wrong?" she cried.

Mortenson was a Dane and, even under the best of circumstances, his English was shaky. Now he was barely coherent.

"Mrs. Hill! Upstairs! Somebody there!"

When the landlady stood frozen in perplexity, he grabbed her by an elbow and urged her upstairs.

Inside Woodcoats' room, Mortenson gestured wildly towards the bed. "Under there!" he shouted. Mrs. Hill had never seen him look so pale. Dread welled up inside her as she lowered herself to one knee and peered beneath the bed.

Wedged beneath the bedsprings was the body of a naked young girl. The slender corpse was curled on its side, turned towards the wall.

"Oh, God!" shrieked Mrs. Hill. "It's dead! Quick! The police!"

Mortenson was so agitated that he forgot there was a telephone in the parlor. Tearing downstairs, he ran to the house of a neighbor, Harvey Pape, who listened in astonishment to Mortenson's frantic story, then put in a call to the Central Station.

By late Sunday afternoon, the Winnipeg police were more convinced than ever that Emily Patterson had been killed by the same itinerant madman who had already slain twenty women throughout the United States. Chief Christopher H. Newton, who was in Windsor, Ontario, attending the annual International Police Chiefs' Convention, had been keeping abreast of the situation in his city by wire and telephone. As it happened, another participant in the conference was Captain of Detectives Duncan Matheson of San Francisco, who had been involved in the strangler case from the beginning.

Matheson not only concurred with the belief that the strangler was now at large in Canada but offered to stop off in Winnipeg on his way back to San Francisco and assist in any way he could. In the meantime, Newton and his second-in-command, Acting Chief Constable Philip Stark, had decided to issue a citywide alert.

By 6:00 P.M. on Sunday, a bulletin had been drafted. Before it could be broadcast over the radio, however, word arrived at Central Station that another victim had been found in a Smith Street boardinghouse.

The discovery of the second slaying confirmed the worst fears of the police. The bulletin was quickly revised. At approximately 6:30 P.M., an announcer broke into the weekly broadcast of the Sunday evening church service with the news that two local women had been strangled to death by a killer, believed to be the same "notorious murderer wanted for twenty similar murders in the United States."

"All women with 'rooms to let' or 'for sale' signs on houses are cautioned," the announcer intoned. "This man may have taken a room from you in the last few days, or he may come to your house for a room or to see the house. Do not admit him if you are alone. Keep your door hooked and put him off. Watch where he goes and notify the police as soon as you can. Don't get excited. If you have a 'for sale' or 'for rent' sign on your house, this man will seek a pretext to enter your home. Do not admit any stranger; you will then be safe. Do the same as we are asking the rooming keepers to do. Put him off and notify the police."

Listeners were warned to be on the lookout for a man "twenty-six to thirty years of age, about five foot six or seven inches tall, weighing about 150 pounds with large dark eyes, full face, sallow complexion, clean shaven, dark brown hair, and broad shouldered. Evidently a transient of Jewish or Italian appearance but might be any nationality. He speaks good English."

The police announcer concluded with a final plea to "all railway men, both passenger and freight crews, to help us catch this fiend, who is a degenerate of the worst type, and protect other defenseless women."

Even before the Sunday evening radio broadcast was interrupted by the special police bulletin, word of the latest murder had swept through the Hills' neighborhood. By 7:00 P.M., Smith Street was so jammed that motorists had to detour around the block. Before the evening ended, more than 500 people—men, women, children, and a growing mob of reporters—would gather at the scene.

While a pair of constables guarded the entranceway—keeping both gawkers and newsmen at bay—the crowd milled around the boardinghouse, exchanging hearsay and straining to see through the glowing, second-story window where grim, blue-coated figures moved about the room. The atmosphere on the block was charged with that peculiar mix of shocked disbelief and morbid excitement characteristic of crime scenes.

One local resident, an early arrival on the scene, held forth with an air of smug authority, passing along the few reliable facts that had filtered from the house. A girl, apparently dead for several days, had been found stuffed beneath a bed, just like that unfortunate Patterson woman in Elmwood. Clearly, the same maniac was responsible for both atrocities.

One of the listeners declared that another Winnipeg woman would undoubtedly die before the madman was caught. After all, murders, like every other kind of bad accident, always came in threes.

Meanwhile, a little boy engaged in a make-believe reenactment of the crime, playfully throttling his little sister until she broke away and ran screaming for her mommy. Nearby, a cluster of teenage girls spoke in spellbound whispers about the titillating rumors of rape. And a sullen-looking stranger, slouching on the outskirts of the crowd, drew more than one suspicious stare from bystanders who wondered if he might possibly be the killer himself, inexorably drawn back to the scene of his heinous crime.

John Hill, in the meantime, was completely unaware of the crisis at his home. After stopping off at the Central Station to convey his wife's suspicions, he had proceeded to church. He had spent the next hour engrossed in the service, while thousands of his fellow Winnipeggers, who preferred the convenience of radio prayer, were being alerted to the latest homicide.

As a result, when Hill stepped off the trolley at around 7:30 P.M. and saw the crowd around his house, he felt a sharp pang of fear, which grew into something like panic when he heard an onlooker refer to "the murdered woman."

Pushing his way through the crowd and into his house, he mounted the stairs, exclaiming with relief when he caught sight of his wife. Pale but clearly unharmed, she was talking to a policeman in the little front room on the second floor. Hill's pleasure, however, was quickly undercut by the sight that assaulted him as he entered the room.

The bed, which normally stood in the southwest corner, had been moved aside. Curled on the floor was a naked female body, stiff and livid. The slender corpse lay on its left side, turned towards the wall, knees slightly flexed, right arm bent, left stretched flat beneath the body. From where he stood, Hill could see a patch of dried blood caked on the left thigh, just below the girl's buttocks.

A man in a brown business suit, who turned out to be Coroner Cameron, was crouched beside the body, while several policemen hovered nearby, conferring in hushed voices. Even with the window wide open, the stench of death was thick in the room.

Hill averted his eyes from the ghastly thing on the floor and, hit with a sudden wave of dizziness, sank onto the straight-backed wooden chair beside the bureau.

At that moment, no one knew who the murder victim was. Constable B. L. Payne, the first officer to arrive on the scene, had made a thorough search of the room. But he had found none of the girl's clothes or anything else that might help with an identification.

Now, after asking Mrs. Hill where her telephone was located, he headed downstairs to put in a call to the Central Station and find out if there had been any recent reports of missing teenage girls.

When Lola Cowan failed to return home on Thursday night, her parents were at a loss. Their first thought was that she had stopped off at a friend's house while making the rounds with her paper flowers. They phoned around to all her acquaintances, but none of them had seen Lola since she'd left for home after participating in the after-school ball game.

Doing their best to stay calm, they wondered if Lola might have gone to visit a schoolchum they weren't familiar with. Mr. Cowan decided to call their daughter's teacher, Miss Morrow, and get the names of all of Lola's classmates. But Miss Morrow, who happened to be away for the evening, didn't answer the phone.

Early the next morning, after a completely sleepless night, John Cowan went off to the Mulvey school, walking into Miss Morrow's classroom just as she finished calling attendance. There was a geography exam scheduled for that day, and Miss Morrow herself was surprised that Lola, one of her best students, was absent. The moment she saw John Cowan's haggard face, she knew that something was wrong.

Addressing the class, he asked if anyone knew where his daughter might be. No one had the slightest idea.

Before returning home, Cowan stopped at the Central Station to report that his daughter had gone off the previous afternoon to sell artificial flowers and had never come home.

When Saturday arrived with no sign of Lola, Mrs. Cowan, more out of desperation than any particular faith in the occult, paid a visit to a neighborhood fortuneteller who, after performing some mumbo-jumbo over her tea leaves, announced "that a dark man in a blue suit would bring news of Lola before Monday."

At around 7:30 P.M. Sunday evening, John Cowan went off to church to say a prayer for his missing daughter. He was riding home on a streetcar an hour or so later when he overheard two other passengers talking about a murdered girl whose body had just been discovered earlier that evening. Cowan's heart quailed.

Disembarking near Smith Street, he found an enormous crowd milling around a three-story house at Number 133. From one of the bystanders he learned that the body of the murder victim, an unidentified teenage girl, had just been removed from the building and was on its way to Thompson's undertaking parlor.

Within minutes, Cowan himself was at Thompson's. As he hurried through the front entrance, he saw something that made his insides turn to ice. His wife, Randy, was being led into an antechamber by two close family friends.

Mrs. Cowan could not bring herself to view the body. She remained in the antechamber in an agony of suspense, still hoping against hope that the victim was not her child, while her husband followed a coroner's assistant into the morgue. Five minutes later, he staggered out again. He was immediately surrounded by a crowd of clamoring newsmen.

"Yes," Cowan rasped in answer to the question they all seemed to be shouting at once. "It is all too true. It's Lola. There is no mistake."

Then, while the newsmen scrambled to file their stories, he made his way into the antechamber to break the news to his stricken wife.

It was only later that Cowan found out how his wife came to be at Thompson's before him.

After telephoning the Central Station and learning that a man named John Cowan had filed a missing-persons report on Saturday morning, Constable B. L. Payne had gone directly from the Hills' to 3 University Place. Mrs. Cowan had opened the door and, at the first glimpse of Constable Payne, had gone deathly pale.

The fortuneteller had been right after all. Randy Cowan *had* received news about Lola from a man in a blue suit—a uniformed police officer, come to tell her that a teenage girl, quite possibly her missing daughter, had been found murdered that evening at a Smith Street boardinghouse.

30

It was then that the legend of a human gorilla being abroad
in the land gained currency.

Winnipeg Tribune

As darkness came on, the crowd around the Hills' boardinghouse began to disperse. Adolescent girls, hugging themselves against the chill, hurried away down the street,
mothers dragged their reluctant children home to bed, elderly couples shuffled off to their rooms. Still, a hundred or
so diehards continued to mill around, as though determined
to extract every last drop of horror from the scene.

As the throng thinned out, the atmosphere around the
boardinghouse underwent a palpable change. At the height
of the stir, Smith Street had been enveloped by an almost
carnival air. Now, as a reporter for the *Winnipeg Tribune*
moved among the remnants of the crowd, he noted a shift
in their mood, from "buzzing excitement" to "sullen dread."

Walking by one small cluster of women, who were gossip-
ing in tense whispers, the reporter was struck by a phrase
he heard passing among them. Already, with the discovery
of the second Winnipeg victim just a few hours old, the
women were wondering if the killer could possibly be the
same homicidal maniac who had left a trail of strangled
corpses across the United States.

One of the women in the little group referred to the unknown killer by a nickname the reporter had never heard

before. He jotted down the phrase in his notepad. In his story that appeared in the next day's *Tribune,* he quoted the phrase. Within a week, it would become permanently attached to the killer, replacing the "Dark Strangler" as the nickname by which Earle Leonard Nelson would forever be known: the "Gorilla Man."

The strangler was not the first "Gorilla Man" to send shivers through Jazz Age America. Indeed, the grotesque figure of the savage, lust-crazed ape-man was a fixture of 1920s culture. The fantasy sprang from several sources. Foremost among these, of course, was Darwin, whose theories on the kinship between humans and primates entered pop lore so rapidly that, by the early 1870s, rakish New Yorkers were already sporting "Missing Link" tie tacks and chuckling at W. S. Gilbert's comic lyrics about a lovesick gorilla who, in order to impress a "Lady fair," decked himself out in white tie and boots and "christened himself Darwinian Man."

> But it would not do,
> The scheme fell through—
> For the Maiden Fair, whom the monkey craved,
> Was a radiant Being,
> With a brain far-seeing—
> While a Darwinian Man, though well-behaved,
> At best is only a monkey shaved!

Of course, Darwin's deflating view of human origins was no laughing matter to millions of people, many of them congregated in the American Bible Belt, where the controversy over evolutionary theory reached its hysterical pitch with the 1925 trial of Tennessee schoolteacher John T. Scopes. Just one year before the "Gorilla Man" made his appearance in Winnipeg, Scopes—an affable twenty-four-year-old who taught high school biology—allowed himself to be arrested in Dayton, Tennessee, for the crime of exposing his young charges to Darwin's sacrilegious ideas. The Dayton "Monkey Trial"—which pitted famed attorney Clarence Darrow (fresh from his triumph in the Leopold and Loeb case) against Fundamentalist champion William Jennings

Bryan—captivated the country, generating millions of words of newsprint and scores of satirical cartoons. In one typical drawing, published in the *Detroit News,* Darrow reaches out to embrace a treed chimpanzee while exclaiming with delighted recognition: "Papa!"

Freudian theory, which (as cultural historian Ann Douglas has written) "seemed to blur the distinction between man and beast," also helped fuel the fantasy of the rapacious ape-man. By the mid-1920s, psychoanalysis had become all the rage among urban sophisticates. After diverting themselves with humorist Robert Benchley's "All Aboard for Dementia Praecox!" in the *New Yorker,* Manhattanites could take in John Barrymore's heavily Oedipal *Hamlet* on Broadway, then cap off the evening by interpreting one another's dreams at a "Freuding party."

Freud's view of the primitive instincts roiling in the undermind of civilized men and women also began to pervade American literature, from Sherwood Anderson's *Winesburg, Ohio* (which portrayed the thwarted urges seething beneath the surface of small-town life) to Eugene O'Neill's *Hairy Ape,* whose brutish protagonist, Yank, identifies so closely with a caged gorilla that he releases the beast (which promptly crushes him to death). "Yuh think I made her sick, do yuh?" Yank rants at one point, after encountering a slumming heiress. "Just lookin' at me, huh? Hairy ape, huh? I'll fix her! I'll tell her where to get off! . . . I'll show her who's a ape!"

The belief that primitive ape-men still stalked the modern world was also reinforced by the theories of Cesare Lombroso, now considered a crackpot but widely esteemed in his own day. In his influential study *L'Uomo Deliquente (Criminal Man),* Lombroso, an Italian physician, argued that criminals were "atavisms"—savage, Stone Age beings born, by some evolutionary quirk, in the modern world. Because they were throwbacks to a prehistoric past, these "born criminals" could be identified by certain physical traits. They actually possessed the anatomical features of apes—thick skulls, big jaws, high cheekbones, jutting brows, long arms, thick necks, etc. As Lombroso wrote, describing the "flash of inspiration" that led to his theory,

> I seemed to see all of a sudden, lighted up as a vast plain under a flaming sky, the problem of the nature of

the criminal—an atavistic being who reproduces in his person the ferocious instincts of primitive humanity and the inferior animals. Thus were explained anatomically the enormous jaws, high cheek bones, prominent superciliary arches, solitary lines in the palms, extreme size of the orbits, handle-shaped ears found in criminals, savages, and apes, insensibility to pain, extremely acute sight, tattooing, excessive idleness, love of orgies, and the irresponsible craving of evil for its own sake, the desire not only to extinguish life in the victim, but to mutilate the corpse, tear its flesh and drink its blood.

Between Darwin, Freud, and Lombroso, it's no wonder that "ape-men" kept popping up in the culture of the twenties, from *The Hairy Ape* to Edgar Rice Burroughs' hugely popular Tarzan series to horror movies like *A Blind Bargain*, in which Lon Chaney is transformed into a simian beastman by a botched "monkey gland operation" (a surgical fad of the 1920s, in which chimpanzee glands were transplanted into male patients in an effort to boost their virility).

One of the most popular entertainments of the twenties was Ralph Spence's Broadway smash *The Gorilla*, which received a tumultuous, five-minute ovation when it premiered in May 1925. A high-spirited mystery farce (which was eventually made into three movie versions), the play cheerfully exploited every cliché in the book, from a stereotypical "feets-don't-fail-me-now" servant named Jefferson, to a wisecracking woman reporter, to a pair of bumbling gumshoes.

Providing the thrills were both a criminal mastermind nicknamed "The Gorilla" ("the most ruthless criminal this country has ever known," according to the script) and an actual gorilla (played by an actor in a monkey suit) who, in the boisterous climax of the play, leaps off the stage and lumbers up and down the aisles. The gorilla is ultimately revealed to be a runaway pet named "Poe," an homage to the classic detective story "The Murders in the Rue Morgue."

The "Gorilla Man" nickname had actually been used as far back as November 1925, when it first appeared in a headline in William Randolph Hearst's *San Francisco Examiner*.

The phrase seemed chillingly apt for a dark, brawny killer who (like Poe's murderous monkey) often shoved his victims' bodies into tight, concealed spaces.

Bay Area authorities, however, did their best to squelch it, believing that it created a serious, and potentially fatal, misimpression of the killer's appearance. Immediately after the murder of Mrs. William Anna Edmonds, Chief O'Brien of the San Francisco police had called a press conference to warn local landladies that it was "a mistake to believe that [the killer] has the appearance of an ape or gorilla, or that he is uncouth in speech or manners." Partly as a result of these efforts, U.S. newspapers had stuck with the "Dark Strangler," an equally sinister and less dangerously misleading epithet.

Up in Canada, however, the situation was different. The "Gorilla" nickname—which had filtered up from the States and circulated among the crowd outside Catherine Hill's boardinghouse on the night of Sunday, June 12—immediately caught on. On Monday the thirteenth, the biggest story in America was the massive ticker-tape parade thrown in Manhattan for Charles Lindbergh. In the *Manitoba Free Press,* however, news of the aviator's frenzied reception would occupy a single column buried on page nine, while the eight-column screamer plastered across the front page read:

KILLER IS STILL AT LARGE

Identify Strangler As Much Wanted Gorilla Man

AMERICAN POLICE

JOIN IN HUNT FOR

ELUSIVE SLAYER

31

Fear stalked in every unprotected home in Winnipeg during
the week of the manhunt, and from not a few vicinities
there was a general emigration of womanhood.

J. H. Stitt

Not since 1913, when a vicious killer named Krafchenko
was on the loose, had such an all-pervading panic gripped
Winnipeg. By Monday morning, the entire city was "seething with fear and excitement" (as the *Free Press* reported),
whipped to a frenzy by the blaring headlines, hourly radio
bulletins, and rampant hearsay, like the alarming—and
wholly unfounded—rumor that a third woman had been
found murdered on Lipton Street.

No sooner did the hardware stores open for business on
Monday than every padlock, deadbolt, and door chain in
the city sold out. Wholesalers quickly ran through their supply, and lock manufacturers as far away as Detroit found
themselves besieged with emergency orders.

Overnight, locksmithing became the busiest occupation in
Winnipeg. Every handyman capable of installing a deadbolt
suddenly found himself with all the work he could handle,
often repairing or replacing locks that had been broken and
unused for years. The *Winnipeg Tribune* described one local
mechanic who—after receiving "a hurry-up call from a terrified spinster"—spent the better part of the morning equip-
ping her house with a half-dozen new doorlocks. Married

men—who suddenly seemed "to think that their wives are more valuable than ever before," in the words of one sardonic hardware salesman—took a few hours off on Monday to install chains on their doors.

Throughout the city, housewives barricaded themselves inside their homes while their husbands were away at work, refusing to open their doors to anyone, even deliverymen they had known for years. Milkmen who would normally take a few minutes to chat with an old customer simply left their bottles on the front stoop and hurried away. Some women even stopped answering their phones, fearing that the strangler might be on the other end. Others kept their children home from school. After spending all of Monday knocking futilely on bolted doors, frustrated callers—house-to-house salesmen, bill collectors, vegetable peddlers—simply gave up the effort, declaring a holiday until the "Gorilla Man" was caught.

Boardinghouse owners exerted particular caution, turning away every stranger who came to their doors. Visitors to the city were forced to look elsewhere for accommodations. Within forty-eight hours, every hotel in Winnipeg, even the most expensive, was booked solid.

Of course, many rooming houses in the city were already full of lodgers. Some proprietresses worked out secret codes with their guests: whenever a roomer returned from an outing, he had to knock in the prearranged way in order to be readmitted. Others had a house key made up for each boarder, so that they themselves would never have to answer the front door. More than one landlady who had recently rented a room to a burly young stranger became convinced that she was harboring the "Gorilla Man" and lost no time in notifying the police.

In general, it was a bad time to be a stocky, dark-complexioned male in Winnipeg. On the streets, men who bore even a passing resemblance to the published descriptions of the "Gorilla Man" were subjected to suspicious looks, hostile stares, and worse. On at least one occasion, a threatening mob surrounded an olive-skinned hobo in a shabby gray suit, who had to be rescued by police. By Tuesday—when the *Manitoba Free Press* ran a story headlined

REIGN OF TERROR HAS CITIZENS OF WINNIPEG IN GRIP—some swarthy, thickset men were afraid to leave their homes.

Assisted by American detectives—who had detoured to Winnipeg on their way home from the International Police Chiefs' Convention in Windsor—the local authorities threw themselves into the search for the "Gorilla Man." Since the discovery of Lola Cowan's body, every member of the Winnipeg force had been on continuous duty, focussing all their energies on what the *Tribune* described as "a man-hunt that for intensity has never been equalled in the history of the city."

Squads of uniformed and plainclothes officers, armed with revolvers and sawed-off shotguns, patrolled the city and suburbs. Others, mounted on motorcycles or packed into cars, roared through the streets in pursuit of the hundreds of leads pouring into the stationhouse switchboards. In the rural districts, provincial police scoured the countryside, setting bloodhounds on the trail of the elusive "Gorilla."

"Everything that can be done is being done to track down the maniac responsible for these revolting crimes against women," announced Police Commissioner John O'Hare. "Every rendezvous for crooks in the city has been combed, and the police are working day and night. Every man on the force has been placed on the job. We will spare neither time nor effort to run this maniac to earth."

By Monday morning, police had visited hundreds of rooming houses and brought in scores of suspects for questioning. All the men were eventually cleared, though a dozen or so, picked up on street corners or rounded up along railway tracks, were fined or imprisoned for vagrancy. On Sunday night, Attorney General W. J. Major authorized a $1,000 reward "for information leading to the arrest and conviction of the criminal degenerate" responsible for the murders of Emily Patterson and Lola Cowan. The following day, the City Council added another $500, bringing the reward to $1,500.

At first, police made encouraging progress. On Saturday afternoon, officers canvassing Main Street had located William Patterson's stolen whipcord suit in Sam Waldman's clothing store. Waldman had supplied the investigators with a complete description of both the dark-skinned stranger who had visited his store on Friday and the apparel he had sold the man. Waldman then led the officers to the barbershop down the block where the owner, Nick Tabor, provided them with additional physical details.

Armed with this new information, Police Chief Christopher Newton had a reward bulletin printed up and distributed to police departments from western Ontario to Alberta.

The bulletin described the suspect as "28 to 30 years, 5 ft. 7 or 8 ins., 150 lbs., dark sallow complexion, has Jewish or Italian appearance, peculiar eyes, fairly well built, hair thin on top and brushed back in long pompadour, newly barbered and inclined to be curly, believed to have very bad corns or bunions on feet."

A detailed itemization of the clothes purchased from Waldman's followed: blue shirt, grayish brown socks, tan boots with "bull-dog toes," fawn-colored cardigan, leather belt with a "green-and-white stripe in centre," gray-and-white silk scarf, gray overcoat, and a "gent's second hand two-piece suit, very light gray, plain with no visible stripe."

"This man has a very pleasing manner in presenting himself when entering houses," the bulletin continued. "Upon entering he does not have the appearance of being vicious. He reads and speaks of religious missions. Is an inveterate cigarette smoker, usually smoking Lucky Strike or other American cigarettes. . . . In the past he has been beating his way by freight, walking, and getting lifts from autoists, stopping at rooming houses. He goes over lists of advertisements for rooms in local papers and then commences visiting them. Other houses with 'For Sale' or 'For Rent' signs he enters on some pretext."

The bulletin concluded with a warning and an appeal: "This man is the most dangerous criminal at large today. I ask every Police Officer to help bring this man to justice. There is ample evidence to convict."

This widely circulated description of the suspect's wardrobe, however, was of limited use, since—as Chief of Detectives George Smith pointed out—"the strangler's chief method of eluding police is by frequently changing his clothes." Meeting with reporters on Monday morning, Smith stressed that the strangler was "a clever man. He is different from any criminal with whom we have ever been called on to deal. He is a man with absolutely no moral sense. He can commit the most atrocious crime and a minute afterwards go on his way without showing the slightest mental trace of the frightful act he has just done." Even with the entire police force pursuing him, a killer of such monstrous cunning wasn't going to be easy to catch.

Smith's sense of caution was justified. As Monday wore on, police found themselves utterly frustrated in their efforts to pick up the murderer's trail. By that evening, Smith was forced to concede that "there is no telling where he is. He may still be in the city, but we have combed it thoroughly and are still searching."

The cheerless news was featured on the front page of Tuesday's *Tribune:* "A thousand clues and a thousand chases have left police no nearer to the strangler's hiding place. . . . He is still at large, and the fear that he might strike again, near or far, still holds a threat."

The "phantomlike" killer who had eluded U.S. police for over a year appeared to have done it again, "vanished," as the paper reported, "like a gorilla in the jungle."

32

✝

He did not seem to hold your glance for any length of time.
He would look at you and look away. But his eyes seemed
to have a sort of magnetism.

Grace Nelson

He had arrived in Regina, the provincial capital of Saskatchewan, about 350 miles due west of Winnipeg, on Saturday afternoon. As always, his first order of business was to purchase a copy of the local paper and check out the "Rooms to Let" section of the classifieds. One ad in particular caught his attention.

Asking directions of the newsvendor, he had found his way to 1852 Lorne Street, reaching his destination at approximately 3:00 P.M.

When Mrs. Mary Rowe answered her front door, she found herself facing an olive-skinned stranger, nattily attired in a pale-gray topcoat, two-piece suit, blue shirt, striped tie, silk scarf, and a snappy fedora with a fancy headband. Flashing a smile that revealed a striking set of even, white teeth, he explained that he had read her ad in the *Regina Leader* and had come to see about the room.

Inviting him inside, the young widow led him up a flight of stairs and ushered him into a clean, spacious room, furnished with a single bed, oak bureau, wooden chair, and night table.

After taking a quick look around, the stranger asked if

Mrs. Rowe had something smaller and more secluded, perhaps in the rear of the house.

Mrs. Rowe shook her head. This was her only vacancy. The rent was four dollars a week.

The olive-skinned man spent a few more minutes looking around, then—after saying he'd "think it over"—left the house. Twenty minutes later, he was back. He had decided to take the room after all.

At the foot of the stairway, he handed Mrs. Rowe a five-dollar bill, got a single in return, then repaired to his room. A few minutes later, he descended again and headed outside. Mrs. Rowe watched him through the parlor window as he made his way down Lorne Street. He hadn't gone more than a hundred yards when he stopped abruptly, did an about-face, and came back.

"Can't buy anything without money, can I?" he said with a grin as he reentered the house and hurried up to his room.

She did not see him again until shortly before 6:00 P.M. She was in the kitchen, preparing dinner, when he suddenly appeared at the doorway, wearing his topcoat and fancy hat.

"Excuse me," he said. "Let me tell you my name in case any mail comes for me. I'm Harry Harcourt." With a tip of his hat, he turned and disappeared. Mrs. Rowe heard him go out the front door.

She stayed up late that night, reading *Lost Ecstasy*, the new bestseller by Mary Roberts Rinehart that all her friends had been raving about. She was seated in the parlor at around 10:45 P.M. when she heard the front door open and close. Glancing up from the book, she saw the dark-skinned lodger pass through the front hallway on his way to the stairs and silently climb to his room.

Mrs. Rowe had another lodger, a twenty-three-year-old woman whose name (coincidentally) was Nelson—Grace Nelson. At around 10:30 A.M. on Sunday, June 12, Miss Nelson, still dressed in her nightclothes, was reclining in bed, reading the latest issue of *American Mercury* magazine. She was so engrossed in an essay by Sinclair Lewis that she did not hear the door open.

Suddenly, she became aware that there was someone in her room. She looked up from her magazine, and her eyes widened. A strange, foreign-looking man was looming in the doorway.

Grabbing her blanket and yanking it up to her chin, she began to utter something indignant. But before the words were out of her mouth, the strange man stammered an apology—"Beg pardon"—then turned on his heels and hurried away.

Shaken by the intrusion, the young woman stayed frozen in place, clutching the bedclothes and feeling her heart knock against her breastbone. After a few moments, however, she began to calm down. No harm had been done. The dark-skinned man was undoubtedly a new lodger who had opened the wrong door in his search for the bathroom.

Still, there had been something peculiar, even disconcerting, about the way he had stared at her. After a few more moments, Grace Nelson pulled back the blankets, swung her feet onto the floor, then quickly crossed the room and closed the door, making sure to throw the lock before returning to her bed.

The next day was a balmy one. At around 11:00 A.M., the landlady, Mary Rowe, stepped outside to savor the soft morning air. Seating herself on the running board of her beat-up old Ford, she watched as her nine-year-old daughter, Jessie, stalked an orange-winged butterfly in the little backyard garden.

Suddenly, the back door swung open and the new lodger, Mr. Harcourt, emerged from the house. Spotting Mrs. Rowe, he strolled over for a chat. The two spent a few minutes discussing automobiles, and Mrs. Rowe told him that her Ford was for sale. He replied that he had no need for a car, since he owned a fine, six-cylinder Studebaker that he kept on his ranch at Indian Head.

And all the time they spoke, he kept his eyes fixed on Mrs. Rowe's little girl.

At around 2:00 P.M., while Mrs. Rowe was in the kitchen preparing a cup of tea for herself, she suddenly realized that she had not seen her daughter for several hours. Frowning, she walked out onto the porch, but Jessie was nowhere in sight.

Hastening to her room, she changed from her housedress into street clothes and rushed from the house.

There was a little park not far from the house, where Jessie often went to play. Mrs. Rowe made it to the park within minutes. She looked all around but saw no sign of her child. Suddenly, something caught her eye. Through the trees, she thought she spotted the little powder-blue parasol that her daughter liked to carry on sunny days.

Hurrying across the park in the direction of the powder-blue object, Mrs. Rowe emerged onto Twelfth Street. Sure enough, there was her daughter, strolling along the sidewalk, her open parasol resting on one shoulder.

Beside her walked Mr. Harcourt.

When Mrs. Rowe strode up to the pair, the man greeted her with a big, innocent smile. "I was just bringing her home," he said.

Mrs. Rowe said nothing in reply. Taking her daughter by the hand, she led her home in silence. It wasn't until they were seated alone in the kitchen that Mrs. Rowe began lecturing her child, telling her that she must never, *never* go off like that with a strange man.

"But he's not a stranger," the child protested. "He's one of our guests."

"Where did he take you?" Mrs. Rowe demanded.

Jessie named a local sweet shop. "He bought me an ice cream soda," she said.

After repeating her warning, Mrs. Rowe sent her daughter out to play.

Later that afternoon, sometime around 4:00, Mrs. Rowe decided to take a break from her housework. Stepping onto the veranda, she found Mr. Harcourt seated out there on an Adirondack chair. They fell into a conversation, and she learned that he was originally from the United States, a native of San Francisco.

They remained outside for over an hour. By the time Mr. Harcourt rose to go inside, it was nearing suppertime. Though he and the landlady had engaged in a perfectly pleasant conversation, there was something about him that made her uneasy. With the other tenants away for the day, she felt reluctant to be alone in the house with him. Fetching her purse from her bedroom, she called to Jessie and took her out to eat at a nearby restaurant.

Harcourt was on the veranda again when they returned. "Glad you're back," he said. Stroking his stubble, he asked if there was a barbershop in the neighborhood. "Yes," said Mrs. Rowe, but she doubted that it would be open on Sunday evening.

"Hope you're wrong," he said, rising from his chair. "I've got a hot date. Met her just last night." He gave Mrs. Rowe an insinuating wink. "I'm a quick worker, you know." Then he hopped down the steps and headed off along Lorne Street.

Sure enough, he was freshly shaven when he returned about forty-five minutes later. When Mrs. Rowe expressed surprise that the barbershop had been open, Harcourt explained that, after grabbing a bite at "Chink's restaurant" on Twelfth Street, he had struck a deal with the owner. For the price of two cigars, he had borrowed the Chinaman's razor and shaved himself in the kitchen.

Proceeding upstairs, he donned his overcoat, gray silk gloves, and gray-and-white silk scarf, then went off to meet his date. Less than twenty minutes later, he was back. Mrs. Rowe could see from the look on his face that something had gone wrong with his plans.

"Stood me up," he said with a scowl when she asked what had happened. Without another word, he disappeared up to his room.

She didn't see him again until early the next morning, Monday, June 13. She was eating breakfast at the kitchen table at approximately 7:50 A.M., when she noticed him pass down the hallway on his way to the front door.

Twenty-five minutes later, he burst back into the house and hurried to his room, taking the stairs two at a time. Though Mrs. Rowe couldn't see it, he was clutching a copy of that morning's *Regina Leader*. Shortly afterwards, he descended the stairs again, dressed in his blue shirt, fawn-colored sweater, gray trousers, and flashy fedora. Mrs. Rowe had just buttered a slice of sourdough bread and was raising it to her lips when she saw him headed for the front door.

Since he had left his other belongings behind, it never occurred to Mrs. Rowe that he wouldn't return. By the end of the day, she would learn the startling truth about the foreign-looking stranger who called himself Harry Harcourt. But at that moment—approximately 8:30 A.M. Monday, as she sat in the kitchen enjoying her breakfast—the young widow had no way of knowing just how lucky she was to be alive.

33

†

He is the fastest ghoul that ever wore shoe leather.
Chief of Detectives George Smith

When Earle Leonard Nelson had arrived in Regina on Saturday afternoon, his two most recent atrocities had not yet been brought to light. William Patterson hadn't made his appalling discovery while praying at his child's bedside, and Lola Cowan's naked corpse still lay undetected in Mrs. Hill's boardinghouse. From Nelson's unhurried behavior on Sunday—the leisurely way he passed the hours, lounging on the veranda of Mrs. Rowe's rooming house and taking long strolls around the neighborhood—it seems clear that he felt no particular sense of urgency. Apparently, he was biding his time, waiting for an opportunity to ambush another victim—the landlady or Grace Nelson or possibly nine-year-old Jessie Rowe.

Everything changed on Sunday night, however, after the discovery of Lola Cowan's body. By Monday morning, the entire population of western Canada was on the lookout for the "Gorilla Man," alerted by periodic radio bulletins and blaring newspaper headlines. When Nelson went out to purchase the *Regina Leader* early Monday morning and saw the front page, he made a sudden change of plan. Regrettable though it may have been to forgo the pleasures available at Mrs. Rowe's rooming house, he had little choice. It was time to clear out of Regina.

*   *   *

His first stop after leaving the rooming house was a jewelry shop called England's. Approaching the counter, he shoved a hand inside his pocket and extracted a plain, eighteen-karat gold wedding band. He had taken it from Emily Patterson's finger just before stuffing her outraged corpse underneath her younger son's bed.

Nelson asked the proprietor, Fred England, to weigh the ring and tell him what it was worth. Bringing out his scales, England placed the ring on one tray and laid several small metal weights, one at a time, on the other. "Five pennyweights," he announced when the trays were evenly balanced.

"What does that mean?" asked Nelson.

"It means that it's a five pennyweight ring."

"Well, what is it worth?"

England fished a scrap of paper and a stubby pencil from his shirt pocket and did a quick calculation, muttering under his breath: "Four cents a karat . . . seventy-two cents a pennyweight . . . five pennyweights." He looked up at Nelson. "About three dollars and fifty cents."

It was less than Nelson had hoped for, but he wasn't in a position to haggle. "I'll take it," he said, extending a hand.

England stepped to his cash register, removed the money, and placed it in the upturned palm. Without another word, the stranger turned and left the store.

Fred England stood there for a moment, staring out through the display window at the man's receding form. In his long career as a jeweler, he had taken countless finger-measurements and seen hands of all shapes and sizes.

Never, however, had he encountered hands as grotesquely oversized as the burly, dark-skinned stranger's.

Shortly after leaving the jeweler's, Nelson found a little thrift shop, where he swapped his dressy clothes for a khaki shirt and a pair of bib overalls. As he left the store and hurried along the streets, he drew some funny stares from passersby. Pausing at a shop window and peering at his reflection, he saw why.

Instead of looking more nondescript, as he had planned, he cut a distinctly conspicuous figure. In the workshirt and overalls, he might have been a mechanic or a farmhand. On his head, however, he was still sporting his dandy's fedora. He hated to part with the hat—it was the snazziest one he'd ever owned, a real attention-getter. But, of course, attention was the last thing in the world he needed right now.

Making his way to Broad Street and Eleventh Avenue, he spotted another used-clothing place called The Royal Second-hand Store, where he exchanged the fedora for a black cloth cap, plus fifty cents. He was going to trade his bull-dog shoes for something plainer, too, but the storeowner—who had taken a closer look at the fedora and noticed the "Chevrier's" label inside—began asking all kinds of goddamn nosy questions: Did he come from Winnipeg? How long had he been in Regina? Was he planning to stay long?

So when another customer entered the store just then and the owner went to wait on him, Nelson slipped out the door and strode away down Broad Street, still wearing his bull-dog shoes.

With his simple workman's garments and four dollars in his pocket, he hit the road. By 10:00 A.M. he had hiked a mile and a half southeast of Regina. He was plodding along the asphalt when he heard a car approaching from behind. He stopped, turned around, and held up his hand. When the car rolled to a halt, he stepped to the driver's window and asked the man for a lift.

"Where you headed?" asked the driver, a salesman named William Davidson.

"Weyburn," said Nelson, naming a town about seventy-five miles south of Regina and less than fifty miles from the U.S. border.

Davidson wasn't going that far, but he offered to take the hitcher partway there. They rode together for over an hour, not speaking much. Nelson told the driver that he'd been unemployed for a while and was travelling south in the hope of finding farmwork.

"You from Regina?" asked Davidson, who had spent a fair amount of time in the city.

Nelson affirmed that he was.

"Whereabouts?"

Nelson, who knew next to nothing about Regina, named

the only place he was familiar with—1852 Lorne Street, Mrs. Rowe's address.

It was almost 11:30 A.M. when the salesman reached his destination, a little town called Davin about twenty-five miles south of Regina. With a grunt of thanks, Nelson climbed from the car and proceeded southward on foot.

It was a hot, cloudless day. Within minutes, sweat was stinging his eyes and darkening the armpits of his long-sleeve khaki shirt. About a mile or so south of Davin, he came to a halt. He was resting by the roadside when a car appeared and pulled up beside him. The driver—another travelling salesman, Lyle Wilcox by name—leaned his head out the window and asked directions to the home of a local farmer.

Nelson explained that he himself was a stranger to those parts. He was making his way to Arcola, about ninety miles away, and wondered if he could hitch a ride with the salesman.

Wilcox was happy to oblige, though he wasn't driving all the way to Arcola.

That was fine, Nelson said, walking around to the passenger side. In that heat, he'd be glad just to get off his feet for a while.

They travelled only a few miles together, until they came to an intersection about three-and-a-half miles southeast of Davin. Wilcox was heading south, down an unpaved country road. "Stick to the main road," he told the hitcher. "It's more travelled. You'll get a lift for sure."

Wilcox was right. Nelson had barely begun trudging along the roadside when he flagged down an east-bound car driven by a junk dealer named Isadore Silverman, who was canvassing the local farms for scrap metal.

Silverman and Nelson, who gave his first name as "Virgil," hit it off at once. When Silverman explained what his business was, Nelson offered to help him out in exchange for nothing more than transportation and meals. Silverman leapt at the offer. Collecting old lead and scrap iron was heavy work, particularly during a heat wave, and the sturdy young man at his side had an impressive set of shoulders.

The two spent the remainder of Monday together, travelling around the backroads of southeastern Saskatchewan, purchasing, packing, and loading the car full of scrap metal. At around 10:30 that night, they arrived in Arcola where they checked into the local hotel, Nelson signing the register with the name "Virgil Wilson." They shared a spacious room with two single beds, paid for in advance by Silverman. Early the next morning, Tuesday, June 14, they hit the road again and spent another day buying scrap metal. That night, they shared a hotel room in Deloraine, Manitoba.

After breakfast the following morning, the two set out once more, travelling east towards Winnipeg, where Silverman made his home. Nelson, of course, had compelling reasons to steer clear of Winnipeg, though he couldn't exactly share them with Silverman. Instead, he told the junk dealer that he was broke and wanted to look for farmwork in the countryside.

They parted ways a few hours later. Silverman dropped his travelling companion off in the town of Boissevain, Manitoba. The time was approximately 10:30 A.M., Wednesday, June 15, and Earle Leonard Nelson was less than twenty miles away from the U.S. border.

34

If the wanted man had deliberately set out to put the police
on his trail, he could hardly have left more clues.

James H. Gray, *The Roar of the Twenties*

According to criminologists, the typical mass murderer—
the seemingly normal man who suddenly snaps and goes on a
wildly destructive rampage—is motivated not just by homicidal
impulses but by suicidal ones as well. The disgruntled worker
who shows up at the office one morning and guns down everyone in sight is a kind of human time bomb, erupting in insane,
random violence. When the explosion is over, there are
corpses scattered everywhere—his own included, since most
killers of this kind either take their own lives to avoid capture or die in a barrage of police gunfire. Essentially, these
are men who—having reached some psychological breaking
point—decide to go out in an apocalyptic blaze, taking as
many people with them as they possibly can.

The case tends to be different with serial killers. To be
sure, some of them are actively self-destructive. In the view
of many crime historians, Jack the Ripper's reign of terror
ended abruptly when the notorious harlot butcher—over-
whelmed with revulsion after his final enormity—took his
own life. And other homicidal maniacs have clearly wished
to be stopped—most famously, the 1940s "Lipstick Killer,"
William Heirens, who left a desperate message scrawled at
one crime scene: "For heaven's sake catch me before I kill
more, I cannot control myself."

For the most part, however, serial murderers aren't interested in stopping. They try to keep killing as long as they can, for a very simple reason: they enjoy it. Lust murder is their ultimate thrill. Even when their behavior borders on the reckless (on one occasion, for example, Ted Bundy abducted two young women from a crowded public beach in broad daylight), pleasure is their primary motivation. The risk-taking only adds to the excitement.

Earle Leonard Nelson typified this pattern. Since embarking on his deadly spree in early 1926, he had done everything possible to avoid arrest—keeping constantly on the move, assuming a string of false identities, changing his wardrobe every time he hit a new town. Endowed with the usual traits of his breed—cunning, intelligence, and an abnormal sang-froid—he had managed to elude pursuers throughout the United States.

From the moment he crossed into Canada, however, his behavior almost guaranteed his capture. Though it is possible that he was possessed by self-destructive impulses—a secret desire to be punished for his crimes—there are other, equally plausible explanations for his actions. Arrogance is one—the disdainful belief that, after failing to nab him for a year and a half, the police were simply no match for him. It is also the case that, as far back as 1921, Nelson (then known as Ferral) had been diagnosed as a "constitutional psychopath with outbreaks of psychosis," a man with a profoundly disordered mind.

Whatever the reason—suicidal feelings, hubris, or delusional thinking—Earle Leonard Nelson had left clues in his wake from the moment he arrived in Winnipeg on Wednesday, June 8. And by the following Tuesday, the police had finally picked up his trail.

They had located John Hofer, the man who had struck up an acquaintance with Nelson on the streetcar from Winnipeg. Hofer turned over the beige cap he had gotten from the garrulous stranger—the one Nelson had purchased at Waldman's and wore until he traded it for the champagne-colored fedora from Chevrier's. The cap was still redolent of the pomade that Nick Tabor had massaged into Nelson's hair.

Not long after locating Hofer, detectives tracked down Hugh Elder, the motorist who had picked up Nelson in Headingly and driven him as far as Portage La Prairie. The testimony of the two men, Hofer and Elder, made it clear that the suspect had been headed due west. Knowing the "Gorilla's" m.o.—his preference for cities, where he could blend with the populace (and find an ample supply of landladies), police deduced that he must have been making for Regina.

The Regina police were alerted at once. Chief Constable Martin Bruton immediately assigned his entire force to the manhunt. At the same time, three carloads of Winnipeg detectives were dispatched to the Saskatchewan capital. One of the cars carried the barber, Nick Tabor, who had volunteered to travel to Regina to identify the suspect, should the "Gorilla" be apprehended in that city.

By Monday evening, the Regina police, canvassing every boardinghouse in the city, had located Mary Rowe. The landlady provided a detailed description of the lodger, "Harry Harcourt," who had vanished that morning. Inside his room investigators found the clothing he had left behind. Even at a glance, they could see that the garments—pale gray topcoat, gray suit jacket, gray-and-white silk scarf, striped necktie—precisely matched the ones described in the reward bulletin. They also discovered why "Harcourt" had left in such a hurry. Lying on his bed was a copy of that morning's *Regina Leader*, its front page plastered with accounts of the "Gorilla Man."

It didn't take long for the Regina police to turn up a string of other witnesses: Fred England, the jeweler who had paid $3.50 for Emily Patterson's wedding band; Harry Fages, proprietor of The Royal Secondhand Store, who had traded Nelson a black cap and four bits for the champagne-colored fedora; the owner of the thrift shop where Nelson had acquired the khaki shirt and bib overalls.

It quickly became clear that the suspect had hightailed it from Regina. Surmising that he had continued his flight westward, Chief Bruton ordered a carload of his men to the nearest city which lay in that direction, Moose Jaw, about forty miles away.

Meanwhile, new circulars—containing updated information about the "Gorilla Man's" change of clothing—were printed up and dispatched to police throughout western Canada, as well as to departments in North and South Dakota, Montana, Idaho, and Oregon. Customs officials on both sides of the border were asked to assist in the hunt, as were members of the Royal Canadian Mounted Police. The U.S. Border Patrol was put on alert, and agents of the Great Northern and Northern Pacific Railways were urged to keep on the lookout for the suspect.

An army of constables, carrying revolvers and sawed-off shotguns, scoured western Canada from Winnipeg to Calgary. Southern Manitoba in particular was, as one newspaper put it, "practically under police occupation, with every acre being raked for the killer." Squad cars patrolled the roadways, while ordinary citizens equipped themselves with every weapon at hand—ax-handles, hunting rifles, hatchets, and sheath knives—and banded together in roaming vigilance committees.

Throughout Tuesday, police announcers regularly interrupted the normal radio programming to broadcast the latest description of the suspect, "last seen wearing blue bib overalls sewn with white stitching, a khaki shirt, brown boots with bull-dog toes, and an old black cloth cap." Drivers were warned "to refuse rides to anyone who may resemble the strangler and notify police at once if asked for a lift."

These bulletins brought dramatic results. On Tuesday evening, a call came in to the Winnipeg Central Police Station from William Davidson, the salesman who had given Nelson a lift from Regina to Davin on Monday morning. From Davidson's account, it seemed clear that the "Gorilla" wasn't making his way to Moose Jaw after all but was headed the opposite way, in a southeasterly direction.

Chief Constable Christopher Newton quickly convened a late-night meeting at Winnipeg headquarters. After conferring with his subordinates—Chief of Detectives George Smith and Assistant Chief Constable Philip Stark—Newton decided to dispatch several carloads of reinforcements to Saskatchewan. Shortly after midnight, a convoy carrying Inspector William Smith of the Manitoba Provincial Police, two city detectives, three provincial officers, and six men from the Morality Department headed out of the city and sped towards Arcola.

On Wednesday morning, the *Winnipeg Tribune*—which only twenty-four hours earlier had published such discouraging news about the investigation—ran a headline whose tone was positively triumphant: POLICE CLOSING IN ON SLAYER, the paper trumpeted. PURSUERS DRAWING NARROWING CIRCLE AROUND MAD KILLER. POLICE OFFICIALS SAY HE CANNOT ESCAPE.

The story quoted Chief Detective George Smith, who expressed his belief that the "Gorilla" might attempt to "break back toward Winnipeg, where a thickly settled territory would offer him more hiding place than the prairie country to the west.

"If he tries this tactic, he will run dead into our hands," Smith assured the reporters. "We have taken every possible precaution to head him off."

Here, Smith—who had sounded so grim at his previous press conference on Monday—allowed himself a little smile. "The Gorilla's career of strangling is about to end suddenly," he declared. "He has blundered along a road that will take him to the gallows."

35

My opinion is that Armstrong was anxious to secure the reward for himself.

>   Hon. W. J. Major, attorney general of Manitoba

A few hours after Smith's press conference—at around 11:30 A.M., Wednesday, June 15—a man named Roy Armstrong was driving to his farm a few miles southeast of Boissevain when he spotted a thickset stranger hiking along the roadside. Pulling up beside him, Armstrong offered him a lift.

"Where you headed?" asked Armstrong as the man settled into the passenger seat.

There was a momentary pause before the stranger answered, "Sparting."

Armstrong's brow furrowed. "Sparting? Never heard of it."

The stranger said nothing.

"Who're you working for?" From the man's dress—khaki workshirt, bib overalls, and wide-brimmed straw hat—Armstrong assumed he was a farmhand.

"Nobody," the stranger replied. "Me and a pal own a ranch down there."

"Ranch? What kind of ranch?"

The stranger shrugged. "Just a ranch."

Armstrong was struck by his choice of words. It was more characteristic of the western United States than of Manitoba, where people spoke of farms, not ranches.

The drive didn't last long. When Armstrong reached his front gate just a few miles away, the stranger thanked him, climbed out of the car, and headed eastward along the unpaved country road.

By then, Armstrong's suspicions were fully aroused. Like virtually everyone else in southern Manitoba, he was on the lookout for the "Gorilla," having been alerted by the police bulletins coming over the radio every few hours. Putting his foot to the accelerator, he sped to his farmhouse, brought his car to a stop, and dashed inside to the telephone.

A few calls to his neighbors would have alerted the entire community and brought dozens of armed men converging on the suspect. But Armstrong knew about the $1,500 reward. The way he figured it, the fewer people involved in the "Gorilla Man's" arrest, the better.

Still, he wasn't about to try capturing America's most dangerous killer all by himself. So Armstrong placed a single call—to Constable Joe Young at the Boissevain police house. Young, whose automobile was out of commission, told Armstrong to pick him up immediately. Leaping back into his Ford, Armstrong made it to town in record time. Then, with Young seated beside him, he turned his car around and roared back in the direction of his farm.

Since the suspect was travelling on foot, the two men felt confident that they could overtake him without any difficulty. Allowing for the time it had taken Armstrong to drive to Boissevain and back, they calculated on finding their man about a mile or so east of Armstrong's front gate. When they arrived at the spot, however, the thickset stranger was nowhere in sight.

A big grain elevator stood just off the road. Armstrong stopped his car, and he and Young got out to make a thorough search of the area. After satisfying themselves that the stranger was not hiding in the vicinity of the elevator, they got back into the Ford and proceeded to a nearby schoolhouse, where they asked the teachers and pupils if anyone had seen a man answering to the stranger's description. No one had.

Their next stop was the farmhouse of a man named Reg Noble. Neither Noble nor his housekeeper had seen the stranger that morning. Just north of Noble's house stood a thick grove of trees, a perfect hiding place for the fugitive. Armstrong and Young spent almost an hour prowling through the grove. But they turned up no trace of the stranger.

Still unwilling to summon reinforcements, the two men continued their search of the district. They questioned everyone they encountered—farmers, housewives, travellers, a group of Bible students out for a midday jaunt.

But none of them had set eyes on the thickset stranger.

Even as Armstrong and Young were scouring the countryside to the south, the "Gorilla's" two most recent victims, Emily Patterson and Lola Cowan, were being laid to rest in Winnipeg.

An enormous crowd—more than a thousand people, according to one estimate—packed Old St. Andrew's Church on Elgin Avenue for Mrs. Patterson's funeral service. Her simple gray casket—topped by a single spray of red and white flowers, a farewell token from her stricken husband—rested at the front of the church. It was surrounded by scores of floral tributes from the many citizens who had been stirred to their depths by the tragedy, her "sacrificial death at the hands of the most horrible murderer of modern times" (in the words of the *Manitoba Free Press*).

The service was conducted by Rev. J. S. Miller, pastor of the church. He was assisted by Rev. W. L. Reese of the Church of Christ's Disciples, who offered the opening prayer. Following the reading of Scripture, the choir sang an anthem, "The Souls of the Righteous in the Land of God." Then the Reverend Miller spoke.

Taking as his text the second verse from the fifteenth chapter of Jeremiah—"Her sun is gone down while it is yet day"—he referred to the "suddenness with which the dead has been snatched from the midst of her loved ones," and how the "horror of the deed has exposed the awful depths to which a human being may sink when his life is lived in disregard of God and his fellow man.

"Her passing has stirred the city as it has never before been stirred," the Reverend continued. "You have been drawn here because you feel in your hearts that had chance brought you or yours face to face with the miscreant, you or they would be in her place."

Following the sermon, Miss Agnes McCullough sang "Shadows," an old hymn that had been a favorite of Mrs. Patterson's. Other hymns, sung by the entire congregation, included "God Moves in Mysterious Ways," "Lead Kindly Light," and "Forever with the Lord."

When the service was over, the coffin was borne to Elmwood Cemetery, while thousands of spectators lined the route, watching in silence as the motorized cortege made its solemn way along the streets.

At the same time, a simple service was taking place for fourteen-year-old Lola Cowan in the little chapel of Thompson's funeral home on Broadway. Only relatives and immediate friends had been invited, including a dozen or so of Lola's schoolmates who huddled on the benches, weeping unrestrainedly. Outside the funeral home, at least 400 people milled about on the curbstones, waiting to pay their respects.

The Rev. G. A. Woodside, minister to St. Stephen's congregation, officiated, taking for his text the Twenty-third Psalm. Following the service, the people that had gathered on Broadway were permitted inside. Forming a somber line that snaked around the block, they filed into the chapel and, heads bowed, moved silently past the flower-heaped bier. It took more than an hour for the entire crowd to view the teenage victim in her open coffin.

Afterwards, the casket was driven to the Elmwood Cemetery, where a brief service was held at the gravesite. Once again the Reverend Woodside spoke. Like Chief Detective Smith, he expressed absolute confidence that the "Gorilla" would be brought to justice. The reverend's remarks made it clear, however, that his faith was entirely in the Lord, not in the local constabulary.

"I know what is in the minds of those present," he proclaimed. "They have a thousand questions. I am not going to say what is going to be the outcome of the one who brings tragedy to a home. I am satisfied that God will deal with that person. No one shall escape His eye. They may flee successfully from the law. But they cannot evade the reckoning day."

* * *

Lola Cowan's body had just been interred when Roy Armstrong and Joe Young finally picked up the suspect's trail.

After refueling the Ford in Boissevain, they came upon a farmer named Pettypiece, who had seen the stranger walking eastward at around 1:30 P.M. Another farmer named Hawkings was driving his team home at around 2:30 P.M. when he was approached by a dark-skinned man in bib overalls and a straw hat who asked to borrow some matches. According to Hawkings—who couldn't oblige, since he wasn't a smoker—the man had immediately headed off eastward. Hawkings had watched until the stranger disappeared around a hill.

Armstrong and Young lost the suspect's trail for a while but picked it up again at around 4:30 P.M., when they came upon a farmhand who had been plowing a field when he noticed the stranger hiking along the roadside about an hour before. According to the farmhand, the man had been "walking very rapidly, going east."

Continuing their pursuit, Armstrong and Young arrived at the farmhouse of a man named Doug Chapman, who invited them in for supper. It was already after 5:00, and both men felt in serious need of refreshment. After bolting down some food, they thanked Chapman warmly, hopped back into the Ford, and took off again.

It wasn't long before they came to Matthew Chester's farm. As they drove up to the house, Mrs. Chester appeared on the front porch. "He just came by here," she called to them, gesturing excitedly toward the south. "Keep on going and you'll catch him for sure!"

Two miles further on, as they approached the next farm down the road, the owner, Fred Kendrick, came out to meet them. "Go straight south, Roy," he shouted. "He's just ahead of you." Apparently, Doug Chapman had phoned ahead to both Mrs. Chester and Kendrick and told them to keep their eyes peeled for the stranger.

By then, the two men could barely contain their excitement. They were so close to their quarry that they could almost feel their pockets bulging with the reward money.

They hadn't travelled more than a mile or so beyond Kendrick's farm, however, when the Ford got stuck in a mud-hole. Cursing, they climbed from the car and tried to wrestle it out of the mire.

The time was approximately 5:45 P.M., and they were only a few minutes away from Wakopa, a tiny hamlet at the extreme southern edge of Manitoba province, just five miles north of the U.S. border.

36

✝

Thank God he is captured—the fiend, the animal!

Mrs. Catherine Hill

At the same time that Roy Armstrong and Joe Young were struggling to free their car from the mud, a stocky, olive-skinned man entered Leslie Morgan's general store just a dozen yards from the train station in Wakopa.

In a town consisting of fewer than ten houses, any stranger would have piqued the storeowner's interest. But Morgan, who had been listening to his radio all afternoon, had particular reason to pay keen attention to the thickset fellow in bib overalls, brown khaki shirt, and wide-brimmed, white straw hat.

Approaching the counter, the stranger asked for some cheese. Morgan sliced a healthy chunk from a brick of cheddar.

"That's about twice what I need," said the stranger.

Without a word, Morgan split the chunk, then wrapped one-half in brown paper. The stranger then asked for two bottles of Coca-Cola, a package of Millbanks cigarettes, and a box of matches. The total came to seventy cents. Fishing a handful of coins from his pocket, the stranger counted out the exact change and handed it to Morgan.

"You walking or driving?" the storekeeper asked casually as he dropped the coins in to his money drawer.

The stranger said nothing. Popping open one of the bottles, he took a long swig, then stuffed the rest of his purchases into his pockets, turned, and headed for the doorway.

There was another customer in the store—a commercial traveller named Mr. Martin. As soon as the stranger disappeared out the doorway, Morgan strode up to the table where Martin was just finishing up a ham sandwich and coffee.

"You think that man could be the one that's wanted up in Winnipeg?" Morgan asked.

Martin, however, could only answer with a shrug. He had been immersed in his newspaper and had barely caught a glimpse of the stranger.

Not far from the general store, a man named Albert Dingwall was working on the grain elevator beside the Wakopa station when he spotted the stranger. Like Leslie Morgan, Dingwall had been listening to the radio on and off during the afternoon and had heard several special bulletins relating to the "Gorilla." If that is not the fellow, Dingwall thought, it looks much like him.

The man was sipping from a Coke bottle—evidently purchased at Morgan's—as he strode along the railroad tracks that led south toward Bannerman, a small town less than two miles from the International Boundary Line. Dingwall watched until the man was a few hundred yards down the tracks, then made for the general store.

Morgan was standing by a window, peering out at the stranger's receding form.

"What do you think about that fellow?" Dingwall asked.

"I think he's the one," Morgan replied.

"So do I."

Telling Dingwall to stay by the window and keep an eye on the man, Morgan put in a call to the Provincial Police station in Killarney. The phone was answered by a constable named Wilton Gray. After identifying himself, Morgan asked if the constable could provide him with information on the suspect wanted for double murder up in Winnipeg.

Gray described the suspect, reading from the only circular he had received, the one issued on Monday, June 13, when Nelson was still garbed in the clothes he had purchased in

Winnipeg—pale-gray suit, fawn-colored sweater, fancy fedora.

"The clothes are different," Morgan said after hearing the description. "He was dressed more like a hobo or a farmhand. But that sounds like him, all right."

"Sounds like who?" asked Gray.

"The fellow who was in my store just a few minutes ago. He's hiking south along the tracks towards Bannerman."

"I'm on my way," said Constable Gray.

After hanging up the phone, Morgan and Dingwall held a hurried conference. They decided that Dingwall would trail the suspect, while Morgan rounded up some reinforcements.

Borrowing Morgan's revolver, Dingwall trotted back to the grain elevator, got hold of a co-worker named George Dickson, and quickly filled him in on the situation. Then, mounting Dickson's buckboard, the two men headed south at a gallop, following the tracks.

About a half-mile south of town, the railroad passed by the farm of a man named Duncan Merlin. By the time Dingwall and Dickson reached Merlin's property, the stranger was nowhere in sight.

"He knows we're after him," muttered Dingwall. Evidently, the stranger had left the open railway embankment and ducked into the bushes that ran along the opposite side of the tracks.

Riding up to the farmhouse, Dingwall and his companion alerted Merlin, who immediately offered the use of his Ford. Piling into the car—Merlin at the wheel, Dickson beside him, Dingwall in back—the three men roared off in the direction of Bannerman, certain that the stranger was making a break for the International Boundary Line. They hadn't driven more than a quarter-mile or so when they spotted him loping along the railroad tracks, about a hundred yards up ahead.

Hearing the car coming up behind him, the stranger cast a quick look over his shoulder, then bolted for the undergrowth again.

Dingwall shouted for Merlin to stop. As the Ford came to a halt, he and Dickson leapt out of the car.

"You go on ahead," said Dingwall, drawing the revolver

he had borrowed from Leslie Morgan. "We'll keep him in sight."

Merlin put his foot to the pedal and sped southward towards Bannerman, while his comrades headed for the bushes.

Within minutes of receiving Leslie Morgan's telephone call, Constable Gray had set out for Bannerman with a fellow officer named Sewell. Driving at top speed, the two men reached their destination about forty minutes later, pulling into town at approximately 6:45 P.M. Duncan Merlin was already there, waiting impatiently beside his Ford. Several minutes later, another car roared into town, carrying Leslie Morgan and several of his neighbors from Wakopa—John Whittingham, Jason Henderson, and Robert Gear.

With Merlin leading the way, the three cars raced back to where the stranger had last been seen, about a mile-and-a-half northwest of Bannerman. As they approached the spot, Gray caught sight of the suspect—a squat, thickset man in bib overalls and a white straw hat. He was moving along the edge of a wide, muddy ravine, as though trying to figure out a way across.

Gray ordered Sewell to stop, then leapt from the car. Keeping low behind some bushes, he made his way as stealthily as he could toward the suspect. When he was about twenty-five feet away, he drew his revolver and burst from the undergrowth.

At the sight of the constable, the suspect threw his hands in the air. "Honest to God, sir!" he cried. "I'm not trying to cross the line."

Revolver in hand, Gray strode up to the suspect. He could see that the man bore a close physical resemblance to the person described in the reward bulletin, though—except for the brown boots with bull-dog toes—he was dressed in different clothing. Gray asked him his name.

"Virgil Wilson," he answered.

To Gray's other questions, the man replied that he was a native of Vancouver who had been in Manitoba for the past three months, working on the ranch of a man named George Harrison, about a half-mile south of Wakopa. He had never been to Winnipeg or visited the United States. He was just taking a hike through the countryside and planned to return to Harrison's ranch later that day.

From both the man's accent and the fact that he used the term *ranchers,* not *farmers,* Gray could tell he was no Canadian. By then, his partner, Constable Sewell, had come trotting up, as had Albert Dingwall and George Dickson, who had been trailing the suspect from a distance. Dingwall, who knew every farmer around Wakopa, confirmed what Gray had already guessed, that the suspect's ostensible employer, "George Harrison," was a fabrication.

Confronted with this fact, the man confessed that he had lied about being a farmhand because he was afraid of being arrested for vagrancy.

While Gray kept his gun trained on the suspect, Sewell searched the man's pockets and found a cheap watch and chain, a fine-tooth comb, a white cotton handkerchief, a map of Manitoba, and the items purchased at Morgan's general store—the paper-wrapped cheese, Millbanks cigarettes, and wooden matches.

Placing the suspect under arrest, Gray and Sewell led him back to their car. The time was 7:35 P.M., Wednesday, June 15.

Word travelled fast. When Roy Armstrong and Joe Young drove into Wakopa twenty minutes later—having finally extricated their car from the mud—they saw a crowd gathered outside Morgan's general store. Still dreaming of splitting the reward down the middle, the two men could feel their hearts sink as soon as they stepped from the car and heard the news: the "Gorilla" had been captured and was on his way to the Killarney jail.

37

✝

A flapper who wants to force her boyfriend into marrying her decides to have sex with him. As they lay in bed after making love, she tells him that since she is sure to get pregnant they will have to get married before the baby is born.

"What do you think we should name him?" asks the flapper.

"Well," says the boyfriend, tossing a condom out the window, "if he gets out of that, let's call him Houdini."

Old joke (circa 1927)

Sewell drove, while Gray sat in the back beside the prisoner. The squat, dark-skinned man, who continued to maintain that his name was "Virgil Wilson," seemed as unconcerned as if he had been picked up for a minor violation. As the car sped towards Killarney, he chatted and joked and gave easy replies to all of Gray's questions.

He was a native of Britain, he claimed, born in Lancashire to an English mother and Spanish father. He had moved to Vancouver as a child. For the past few months, he had been travelling by foot around Manitoba, seeing the countryside and supporting himself with odd jobs, mostly as a "ranch hand." Unfortunately, work had been scarce for the past few weeks. He was completely out of money—a fact that Gray had already ascertained during his search of the man's possessions. Stroking his stubbled jaw, "Wilson" explained that he hadn't had a shave since Saskatoon, or a decent meal in days. As if on cue, his stomach rumbled so noisily that Sewell, seated up front behind the wheel, could clearly hear the sound.

By the time the car reached Killarney, Gray was beset by doubts. True, the prisoner's height, build, and physical appearance tallied with the description of the wanted man. But he seemed so ordinary and affable that it was hard to conceive of him as the monstrous "Gorilla" who had slain nearly two dozen women across the continent. Besides, he was dressed in completely different clothes from the ones itemized in the circular Gray had received a few days earlier.

Word of the arrest had already reached Killarney when the patrol car pulled into town. A cheering crowd greeted Sewell and Gray as they hustled the prisoner out of the car and into a little restaurant not far from the town hall. "Wilson" had prevailed on the officers to give him a solid meal before locking him up.

Scores of townspeople crowded around the restaurant's front window, jostling for a peek at the captive as he bolted down his dinner—steak, potatoes, carrots and peas, topped off with a dish of vanilla ice cream. Between mouthfuls, "Wilson" chatted and laughed, joking about the excellent service he was receiving.

After a cup of coffee and a cigarette, he was led off to the Killarney jail, located in the basement of the town hall.

While Town Constable William Dunn unlocked the cell, a cramped steel cage with grillwork walls, Gray ordered the prisoner to remove his shoes, socks, and belt. "Wilson" was his usual compliant self, obeying without a murmur of protest. Stepping barefoot into the cell, he stretched out on the narrow bunk, hands cradling his head.

Gray himself made sure the cell door was completely fastened, sliding the heavy steel bolt into place and securing it with double padlocks. Then, after instructing Town Constable Dunn to keep an eye on the prisoner, Gray headed up to the street accompanied by Sewell.

"Wilson," meanwhile, lay silently on his bunk, staring up through the heavy meshwork of his cell as though deeply immersed in thought.

Though Gray didn't say anything to his partner, his doubts about the prisoner had only deepened. Having spent a couple of hours in the fellow's company, he was finding it harder than ever to believe that "Wilson"—"the easiest-going, simplest sort of chap you ever saw in your life" (as Gray would later put it)—could be the notorious "Gorilla." And the disparity between "Wilson's" wardrobe and the clothing worn by the Winnipeg fugitive continued to nag at Gray.

Hoping to find an updated description of the suspect in the evening *Tribune*, Gray headed for the local drugstore to purchase a paper. It was already almost 10:30 P.M., however, and the drugstore was closed.

Proceeding to the telegraph office, Gray sent a message to his divisional officer, Inspector James Browne at Brandon, requesting the most recent information on the fugitive. Within minutes, Brandon wired back that the suspect had last been seen wearing blue bib overalls, a khaki shirt, and brown boots with bull-dog shoes.

That clinched it. Crossing the street to his room in Detachment Headquarters, Gray spent a few minutes refreshing himself—washing up, brushing the dust from his uniform. He unbuckled his holstered revolver and slipped a lightweight semiautomatic into his pocket. For the first time, he allowed himself a few minutes of self-congratulation. He had captured the most dangerous criminal on the North American continent, the notorious woman-killer known as the "Gorilla."

Years before that tabloid tag was applied to him, however, Earle Leonard Nelson had been given another nickname that Constable Wilton Gray knew nothing about: *Houdini*. And even at that moment, while Gray savored his moment of triumph, Nelson was living up to it.

At approximately 11:15 P.M.—twenty minutes after he was told to keep an eye on the prisoner—William Dunn, the sixty-year-old town constable, burst into Gray's room, so breathless that he could barely speak.

He didn't have to. Gray could see from the look on his face that something dreadful had happened.

Dashing back to the town hall, Gray tore down the basement steps, then stopped in his tracks, so stunned by what he saw that his mouth actually dropped open.

The two padlocks he had personally snapped into place lay on the concrete floor. The steel door of the cagelike cell stood wide open. And the "Gorilla" was gone.

38

†

In custody but out again. Such is the most recent episode in the hunt for the Strangler—the Gorilla—who has left a trail of death and fear across the continent.

Manitoba Free Press, June 16, 1927

When he'd told William Dunn "to keep an eye" on the captive, Constable Gray wasn't thinking about a jailbreak. He knew the cell was secure, having fastened the padlocks himself. It was suicide he was worried about—the possibility (as he later testified) that "the prisoner might do bodily harm to himself."

As for Dunn, it never crossed his mind that anyone could escape from the double-locked cage. And so, when he settled back for a smoke and discovered that he was out of matches, he didn't think twice about wandering upstairs in search of a light. He wasn't gone for more than a few minutes. But when he returned, the cell door was open and the prisoner nowhere in sight.

The marks of the fugitive's bare feet were clearly visible on the dusty floor of the cell. Gray and Dunn followed the trail to the furnace room, where the footprints led across the dirt floor to an open back door. Dashing to the doorway, the two men peered outside. Even in the darkness they could make out a pathway of tramped-down grass that cut across the rear yard and disappeared into the blackness of the surrounding woods.

Racing to the fire hall, Gray sounded the alarm, rousing the entire town. Within minutes, hundreds of people, most of them men, were assembled at the fire hall. Quieting the clamoring mob, Gray explained what had happened and organized a massive hunt. While a fleet of automobiles circled the town, a posse of several hundred men—equipped with lanterns and flashlights and armed with shotguns, revolvers, pitchforks, and ax handles—combed the surrounding woods and lake shore, searched through empty buildings, and patrolled every road within a five-mile radius of Killarney.

Gray, meanwhile, was busy on the telephone. After putting in a call to the electric department—which agreed to keep the street lights burning all night—he notified the Provincial Police Detachments in Crystal City, Deloraine, and Morden, alerted the U.S. border patrol, and got in touch with the constabularies of every town from Portage La Prairie to Hansboro, North Dakota. By midnight—with reinforcements from several neighboring towns aiding in the search—Killarney was (as one witness put it) "an armed camp."

Gray also telephoned Provincial Police Headquarters in Winnipeg. Hearing the news, Commissioner H. J. Martin immediately set about assembling a contingent of men for an expedition to Killarney. A hard rain had started to fall by then, and Martin—fearing that a convoy of automobiles might get bogged down in the mud—contacted officials of the Canadian Pacific Railway, who promptly made all the necessary arrangements.

At 2:30 A.M. a special train departed from Winnipeg. On board were Colonel Martin himself, six Provincial and four Canadian Pacific Railway constables, seven Winnipeg city officers, and a pair of bloodhounds. To expedite the trip, railway officials had dispatched emergency signals, instructing all other trains to make way.

The special train had a clear line to Killarney, with an anticipated arrival time of approximately 8:30 A.M.

There was a little wooden shelf bracketed to the basement wall, about a foot from the cell. Nelson had spotted it as soon as the steel door slammed shut behind him. Stretching himself out on the narrow bunk, he laced his fingers behind his head and waited for his chance.

It came sooner than he expected. Just a few minutes after Gray and his partner left, the old man named Dunn rolled himself a cigarette and stuck it in his mouth. After checking his pockets for a match and coming up empty, he rose from his chair and made for the stairway.

The instant he was gone, Nelson had leapt to his feet, shoved a hand through the grillwork, and groped around the shelf. Almost immediately, his fingers closed around a small, slender object that felt like rusty metal. Even *he* couldn't believe his good luck when he saw what he was holding— an old nail file. The Lord was surely with him.

It took him less than two minutes to pick both locks. Swinging open the cell door, he hurried barefoot through the basement, crossed the furnace room, and slipped out the unlocked back door. A cold drizzle had begun to fall, soaking the grass. By the time he reached the woods, just twenty yards away, he felt as if he'd been wading in ice water.

In the cloudy, moonless night, he couldn't see more than a few feet ahead of him. He knew the Canadian Pacific Railroad stopped in Killarney (he had caught a glimpse of the station when the police car brought him into town). If he could manage to hide out until daybreak, he might be able to slip onto a southbound freight car and make it safely across the border.

The trick would be to keep from getting caught. He knew the whole town would be after him before long. Sure enough, he was still standing near the edge of the woods, trying to decide which way to go, when an alarm bell began to clang. A few minutes later, he could hear the sound of muffled voices and see the sweep of flashlight beams as a search party rounded the rear of the town hall and moved in his direction.

There was an ancient tree at his back, with big, solid branches sprouting from its trunk. With a little jump, he grabbed hold of the bottommost branch and pulled himself upward. Then, just like the monkey-man they said he was, he clambered up the tree as high as he could go.

Straddling a branch about twenty feet above the ground, arms hugging the massive trunk, he remained as still as possible until the searchers were gone. Then he made his way down the tree and cautiously emerged from the woods. Moving in a crouch, he headed in the general direction of the railway station, ducking into an empty shed or outbuilding whenever he saw an approaching light.

Eventually, he came to a vacant barn not far from the railroad tracks. Slipping inside, he made his way carefully across the hay-littered floor to the opposite end. By now, his eyes had adjusted themselves to the darkness, and he could make out a heap of discarded clothing in one corner of the barn.

Again, the Lord seemed to be smiling on him. Rummaging through the pile, he came upon an old pair of hockey skates. Grunting with the effort, he managed to tear the blades off the leather soles, then shoved his bare feet into the boots. He also found a moth-eaten wool cardigan, large enough to fit him.

Crawling into an empty stall, he huddled in a corner, keeping his ears open for the sounds of the manhunters. He managed to remain awake for most of the night, though he fell into a doze towards daybreak.

It was already after 8:00 A.M. when something roused him from his sleep. He listened hard, then heard it again, a sound that made him scramble to his feet in excitement—the piercing whistle of an approaching train.

A local handyman named Alfred Wood was out early Thursday morning, doing some yard work for a neighbor, Herbert Monteith. At around 8:10 A.M., Wood had just started mowing the front lawn when he looked up and saw a stranger leaning over the waist-high picket fence.

"Can I bum a cigarette?" said the man.

Leaving his mower upright, Wood walked over and, after fishing a little pouch and a roll of papers from his hip pocket, handed them over to the man.

As the fellow rolled his smoke, Wood took a closer look at him. He was squat and swarthy and dressed in a raggedy green sweater with little bits of dried hay stuck all over it. His hair was dishevelled, his face unshaved, and his feet were shod in a most peculiar fashion—in what looked to be old hockey skates with the blades removed.

"You been out searching for that fellow who broke out of jail?" Wood asked.

The man—who was fumbling with the paper, as though unaccustomed to rolling his own—nodded. "Yeah. Been up all night. Tore my clothes in the bushes." Here he gave a little grunt of admiration. "Must be a damn smart man to escape the way he did."

Wood noticed that, beneath the old cardigan sweater, the man was wearing a khaki shirt and a pair of bib overalls.

While Wood was staring at him, the dark-skinned man, who had completely mangled the cigarette, tossed it away in disgust. "Mind giving me the makings of another?" he asked with a sheepish look. "I kind of messed that one up."

Wood obliged. After succeeding with his second try, the fellow stuck the clumsily rolled cigarette between his lips, accepted a light from Wood, then strode down the road in the direction of the railway tracks.

Staring after him, Wood felt convinced that the dark-skinned stranger was none other than the "Gorilla" himself. The way he had come right up to Wood, as bold as day, and asked for a smoke was completely consistent with the published reports of the man's almost incredible audacity.

Glancing around, Wood spotted Kevin and Brian Best, the teenage sons of the neighborhood physician, as they emerged from their house just across the road. They had their schoolbooks in hand and were heading for the family car, a Chevrolet Coach. Hurrying over to the boys, Wood quickly filled them in on his encounter with the stranger and urged them to drive downtown and alert the police.

As the Best brothers jumped into the car and sped away, Wood ran back to the road and hurried after the stranger, determined to keep him in sight.

As it turned out, the barn Nelson had taken refuge in belonged to a family named Allen that had vacated their premises the previous night. Mr. Allen had joined the searchers after ensconcing his wife and children at a neighbor's. As a result, Nelson had no problem leaving the barn undetected after awakening to the sound of the approaching train.

By sticking close to the bushes that grew alongside the

railway embankment—and ducking for cover whenever he felt in danger of discovery—he had managed to make it within a half-mile or so of the train depot by 8:25 A.M. In a few more minutes, he would be on his way to the border. Nelson was an old hand at riding the rails, having relied on the method many times during his journeys, whenever he couldn't hitch a ride or steal a car.

By the time he reached the house where the workman was mowing, Nelson—who was starving for a smoke, having gone without one since the previous afternoon—was so full of confidence that he felt no hesitation about approaching the man for a cigarette. Indeed, what he felt was even stronger than confidence. It was more like omnipotence, the sense that he could get away with anything, that nothing could touch him—as though he were the chosen instrument of an irresistible power that was using him for its own unimaginable ends.

Immediately after receiving the urgent midnight call from Wilton Gray, Constable W. A. Renton of the Crystal City Detachment had set off by car with a colleague named Lett. Upon their arrival, they were assigned to patrol the eastern section of Killarney. A local man named Maxwell volunteered to be their guide.

Sometime around 5:00 A.M., as he was negotiating a bumpy dirt road, Renton drove the car over a rock and tore the guard off the flywheel. Returning to town, he pulled into the police garage for repairs.

While the mechanic worked on the car, Renton joined Constable M. Maclean of the Morden Detachment and about twenty local men, who were setting off to search the heavy undergrowth on the north side of Killarney Lake. The group spent several hours combing the area. At one point, Renton thought he saw a burly man dash into a thick clump of bushes and spent nearly an hour searching for him before giving up.

By the time he returned to check on his car, it was already after 8:00 A.M. He was just about to enter the garage when a Chevrolet Coach roared up and a teenage boy leapt from the passenger side and began going on about someone named Wood, who had just been approached by a suspicious-looking stranger. Renton, who was having trouble following the boy, asked him to slow down.

Pausing for a breath, the boy exclaimed, "Mr. Wood thinks he's the man everyone's hunting for!"

"Come on!" Renton said, grabbing the boy by the arm and pulling him into the car. As the Chevrolet sped westward, Renton got the full story from the driver, who gave his name as Kevin Best. "We have to hurry," said Kevin. "We have to be at school by nine for examinations."

They hadn't travelled more than a quarter-mile when Renton spotted a dark-skinned man emerging from a thicket and making for the railroad tracks. Shouting for Kevin to stop, Renton jumped from the car and sprinted toward the man.

Spotting his pursuer, the dark-skinned man quickly scaled the railway fence and leapt onto the tracks. Before he could flee, however, Renton had dashed up to the fence with his revolver drawn and ordered him to stop.

The man froze, his hands raised. Quickly, Renton climbed the fence and dropped to the ground, his gun levelled at the suspect.

"Who are you?" asked Renton.

"A farmer," said the man.

"Where do you farm?"

The man glanced around, then pointed to a big wooden structure not far from the tracks. Renton saw immediately that the building was no barn—though he wouldn't learn until later that it was the city slaughterhouse.

"Let's go," said Renton, motioning with his gun.

As Renton marched his prisoner towards the station, Alfred Wood came running up, followed by a large crowd of Killarney residents, most of them armed. "We've got him!" Wood shouted as the others let out a triumphant roar.

For a moment, Renton feared that there might be a lynching. Just then, however, a patrol car swept up. Bundling the prisoner on board, Renton jumped in after him. As the crowd surged towards them, the driver—a provincial constable named George Whitfield—spun the car around, sped toward the station, and drove directly up onto the platform just as the special train was coming to a stop. Flinging open the car door, Renton leapt out, dragged the prisoner after him, and hustled him onto the coach, where the Winnipeg contingent was getting ready to disembark.

At that moment, it would have been impossible to say who was more startled: Earle Leonard Nelson, who suddenly discovered that the "freight" he'd intended to hop was packed with a large force of armed policemen; or the officers themselves, who had ridden all night from Winnipeg, only to have the fugitive delivered into their hands before they'd even stepped from the train.

39

On the whole, the temper of the mob was more exultant than ugly. They were there to see a marauding jungle beast safely in the net, his claws trimmed and fangs pulled. School children wriggled ecstatically when the distant hoot of the locomotive whistle announced the approach of the train. To them it appeared to be merely another chapter in a thrilling movie serial. The adults crowded around did so from sheer curiosity, and to taste the pleasure of seeing a maniac trapped.

Manitoba Free Press, June 17, 1927

Colonel Martin himself snapped a pair of handcuffs on the captive's wrists. It took Nelson less than thirty seconds to slip out of them. "These aren't much good," he said with a smirk, handing the cuffs back to Martin.

The colonel wasn't amused. He barked a command to one of his men, who immediately produced two sets of manacles. Two brawny constables shoved Nelson into a seat, while a third shackled his ankles and wrists.

As the rest of the officers looked on, Nelson struggled briefly with the restraints, then gave up with a shrug. "Much better," he said. "It would be damn hard to get out of these."

"Not like that rinky-dink jail," he added with a snort.

In answer to Martin's questions, Nelson described how he had jiggled open the locks with the old nail file, then hidden from his pursuers for the rest of the night, first in the woods behind the town hall, then in the empty barn. He leaned back in his seat as he spoke, his manner as relaxed and expansive as if he were regaling a bunch of cronies at a neighborhood saloon.

Meanwhile, a riotous mood prevailed in Killarney, undampened by the drizzling rain. Thousands of citizens poured into the streets and surrounded the station, shouting for a glimpse of the captive. "Bring him out! Bring him out!" they cried, pounding on the walls of the car and pressing their faces to the windows. Colonel Martin had the shades drawn and posted guards at every doorway. But the people continued to clamor.

Finally, Martin stepped out onto the end of the car and, after quieting the crowd, announced that he had no intention of exhibiting the suspect. "It would not be proper procedure to do so," he declared. Thanking the citizens of Killarney for their assistance, he urged them to disperse—a request that, with only a few exceptions, was completely ignored by the crowd.

After taking on some provisions, including (as one newspaper reported) "a large box of delicious sandwiches" prepared by "the kind ladies of Killarney," the train set off from the station at a few minutes past 10:00 A.M.

During the return trip to Winnipeg, the prisoner, who continued to give his name as "Virgil Wilson," seemed so relaxed and unconcerned that a number of the constables wondered aloud if they had captured the right man. For the most part, he alternated between breezy conversation and periods of silent contemplation. In the latter moods, he would turn his face to the glass and stare out at the flat, flowing countryside. In the former, he would chat about his favorite Wallace Beery movies or divert his captors with a dirty joke.

Continually grubbing cigarettes from his guards, he chain-smoked all the way to Winnipeg. His powerful hands lay manacled in his lap, except when he raised them to his mouth to remove a cigarette. He was under the most intense scrutiny during the trip, not from his guards—many of whom dozed for a good part of the journey—but from a newspaper correspondent named C. B. Pyper, who had wheedled his way onto the train just before it departed.

Pyper spent the whole trip studying Nelson. His observations—headlined "A Word Sketch of the Accused"—were published in the June 17 issue of the *Winnipeg Tribune* and offered the public its first extended look at the infamous "Gorilla Man."

Though remarkably detailed, Pyper's portrait, like all subsequent descriptions of Nelson, was hardly objective. However bizarre his behavior, Nelson was such an ordinary-looking man that his victims had never thought twice about welcoming him into their homes. In Pyper's article, however, he emerges as a hulking brute, an apish throwback with all the physical hallmarks of the Lombrosian "born criminal"—narrow forehead, oversized jaw, prominent teeth, powerful hands, dark skin, and thick, "negroid" lips:

He is heavily built, with broad, rounded shoulders, and an exceptionally deep chest. . . . His forehead is high, narrow and sloping. From the hair to the tip of the nose, the whole face slopes forward.

The lips are red and full, giving him a strong negroid appearance. His teeth are perfect, white, and regular, and strong. His tongue is always in evidence when he talks, and when he smiles, it sticks forward, thick and red, against his upper teeth.

His chin, below the protruding mouth, also juts forward. It has a shallow cleft, and slopes back to two powerful jaws, the breadth of which adds to the impression of narrowness in the forehead.

The eyes are small, slitted, just a little close together. They seem to be grey, but at times the pupils dilate. At these times, they might almost be described as black. . . .

His throat is thick and powerful and covered to the Adam's apple with a three-days' growth of beard. When his head is thrown back, the great width of his throat and jaw is evident.

His hands are thick and extremely powerful, with gnarled knuckles and broad, flat fingers. . . . His complexion is not sallow, but a light chocolate, much like that of the ordinary sun-burned worker of foreign extraction. He is not good-looking but not immediately repulsive in appearance. It would be hard to place his nationality, except to say that he is not pure British or Canadian stock. The thick, sensual lips give a suspicion of negro blood somewhere.

He was an interesting study on the train. He showed absolutely no concern over his position. But as you looked at him, you knew that he was speculating, with the cunning that has served him so well in the past, on his present chances of escape—or thinking of the other terrible subject with which his mind is obsessed.

Hoping for their own first-hand glimpse of the monster, thousands of people—men, women, and children—gathered along the tracks that stretched between Killarney and Winnipeg. The train bearing Nelson wouldn't have drawn larger and more excited crowds if it had been carrying a visiting member of the British royal family.

To everyone's disappointment, the train didn't make any stops. Still, just seeing it was a thrill. At every platform and crossing, the crowds whistled and cheered as the train swept past—"electrified by the knowledge," wrote Pyper, "that inside the coach, passing within a few feet, was the man who had terrified a city and a countryside for a week, and who had a score of murders on his head."

The largest crowds congregated in Winnipeg. Hoping to avoid a mob scene, the police kept the train's precise destination a secret, from the press and the public alike. But the ploy proved remarkably ineffective. By 3:00 P.M., every possible disembarkation point in the city—the Academy Road crossing, the Cement Works at Fort Whyte, the Westside platform on Portage Avenue, and the Canadian Pacific Railway station—was thronged with curiosity seekers.

As it turned out, the ones who opted for Portage Avenue made the right choice. Not that it did them much good. When the train finally arrived at around 5:30 P.M., the platform and surrounding streets were so densely packed with people (as many as 4,000, according to one estimate) that almost no one managed to see the main attraction, who was hustled directly from his coach into a waiting police car. A cameraman for the *Free Press,* who was positioned just a few yards from the platform, was able to photograph nothing more than the back of the prisoner's head as a trio of detectives maneuvered their man through the ocean of gawkers.

From the Portage Avenue crossing, the captive was driven to the Central Police Station on Rupert Street, where another horde of people had assembled. Again, all but a handful of them came away disappointed. "Fearing that some sort of demonstration might be made by the mob," the *Free Press* reported, "officers threw open the wooden double-doors of the garage, situated at the rear of the police station. The crowd—which had waited expectantly for hours in order to get a glimpse of the much-wanted man—was nonplussed, only a dozen or so seeing the prisoner's car turn onto Louise Street, then swing sharply into the lane behind the police station, pull straight into the garage, and come to a squealing halt."

No sooner had it stopped than six officers sprang from the car. Before the prisoner could emerge from the car, the heavy garage doors were swung shut with a bang.

Hauling their captive from the car, the constables marched him up the stairway, through the parade room, and into the elevator that led to the cells. Before being locked up, he was fingerprinted, then handed a stubby pencil and a blank sheet of paper, and asked to print his true name. Without hesitation, he wrote, "Virgil Wilson, Vancouver," the identity he'd been claiming since his arrest in Killarney.

Then he did something interesting. After contemplating the paper for a moment, he took his pencil and put a heavy line through the words he'd just written. Then—as if to acknowledge that he was finally, irrevocably caught and that further subterfuge was futile—he revealed, for the first time, who he really was.

"Earle Nelson," he wrote. "Born in San Francisco, 1897."

Less than forty-five minutes after his arrival in Winnipeg, Nelson was picked from a lineup by two witnesses: W. E. Chandler, the motorist who had given him a lift from Warren, Minnesota, to the International Boundary Line on Wednesday, June 8; and Sam Waldman, the secondhand clothes dealer who had sold him a complete outfit two days later.

Though Nelson looked considerably grubbier than he had when they'd first seen him, neither witness had any trouble identifying him. "A peculiar thing happened when I picked him out in the police station," Chandler told reporters afterwards. "As I laid my hand on his shoulder to let the police know that he was the man, he flinched under the pressure of my touch." Chandler also offered a vivid description of Nelson's hitchhiking technique. As Chandler's Ford approached, "Nelson walked towards the center of the road and raised his hand until the car slowed down, then jumped onto the running board and asked for a ride. Almost without waiting for permission, he vaulted over the side of the car onto the seat. When we got to the border, he vaulted out again, landing on the ground. He never opened the door of the car either to enter it or leave it."

Two other witnesses were preparing to identify the prisoner: Mr. and Mrs. John Hill, the proprietors of the boardinghouse where Nelson had strangled Lola Cowan. Early Thursday evening, a reporter for the *Free Press* visited the elderly couple at their Smith Street home and interviewed them in their kitchen.

"Will I be able to identify him?" Mrs. Hill exclaimed in response to the reporter's question. "Why it'll be as easy as picking out that stove from the wash boiler. Me and Mr. Hill both got a good look at the brute. Those black eyes alone will give him away!"

As the old lady talked, she grew increasingly incensed—though Nelson's failure to come through with his rent seemed to bother her more than his rape-murder of the fourteen-year-old girl.

"Imagine," she clucked. "Taking a room for a week and never paying for it! And he has upset my home and probably injured my business. I've always kept a good clean home, and I always will. I've never kept any evil persons about. I tell them to leave the minute I get suspicious."

"Better watch out when you go identify him," her husband admonished as his wife continued to fume. "Keep your hands off him. Don't try to hit him."

"Hit him!" the old lady scoffed. "Why, I'd crucify him if I could."

"Now, now," said her husband, who seemed genuinely taken aback. "Don't talk that way."

"You're right," said Mrs. Hill, slightly abashed. "Tell you what I *will* do, though."

"What's that?"

"I'll ask him for the two dollars he owes me," said Mrs. Hill.

40

†

In the opinion of Dr. C. M. Hincks of Toronto, director of the Canadian Mental Hygiene Association who is a visitor in Winnipeg, the man who murdered Mrs. Patterson and Lola Cowan is a moral imbecile.

Manitoba Free Press, June 18, 1927

The capture of the infamous "Gorilla Man" was widely reported in American newspapers, including the *New York Times,* which ran a story about Nelson's arrest on Friday morning, June 17. Still, no U.S. city—not even San Francisco, birthplace of the strangler and the site of his earliest murders—devoted as much media coverage to the story as Winnipeg, where the fascination with Nelson remained at a fever pitch for another full week.

Shortly after 10:30 A.M. on Friday, Nelson—"The Greatest Murderer Since Jack the Ripper," as the *Winnipeg Tribune* branded him—appeared in the city police court, to be formally charged with the murders of Lola Cowan and Emily Patterson. Outside the building, Rupert Street was jammed with spectators, who had begun gathering hours earlier, hoping for a glimpse of the monster. But police guards posted at the entranceway made sure that only authorized personnel gained admission. As a result, the courtroom was half-empty when the "Gorilla" was escorted to the dock by four armed constables.

Though Nelson's jaw was still dark with stubble, his hair

had been clipped, and his ratty green sweater replaced with a gray suit jacket and blue, collarless shirt. Head bowed, shoulders slumped, hands manacled before him, he stood by the rail and listened in silence while the court clerk, George Richards, read the charge.

Since Nelson, docile and despondent, looked about as fearsome as a short-order cook, it was left to local reporters to spice up their stories with suitably diabolical details. In the account of the *Tribune*'s correspondent, Nelson's slate-gray eyes suddenly acquired a demonic "yellowish hue." And when, following the proceedings, the prisoner was surrounded by officers and ushered back to his cell, a reporter for the *Free Press* was on hand to testify that Nelson had "a walk like an ape."

One of the courtroom spectators that morning was John Cowan, Lola's father. Though newsmen pressed him for a quote about Nelson, Cowan had little to say, though he did thank his fellow Winnipeggers, who had begun raising money for the families of the two victims. Started with a contribution of four silver quarters sent in by a young reader of the *Free Press*, the fund had grown to $42.30 by Friday morning.

Several hours after Nelson's courtroom appearance, Catherine Hill got her chance to confront him. Shortly after 1:00 P.M., two detectives picked her up at her boardinghouse and drove her to the central police station. The elderly landlady, who suffered from severe rheumatism, was escorted to the lineup room, where thirty male prisoners were ranged against one wall, hands manacled behind their backs. Near the center of the long row stood Nelson, head thrown back, dark eyes burning (according to the *Winnipeg Tribune*) with a "phosphorescent" glow.

Leaning on the arm of a detective, Mrs. Hill laboriously made her way along the row of prisoners. By the time she reached the center, she was breathing hard with the effort. Taking one quick glance into Nelson's face, she raised her gnarled right hand and laid it on his sleeve.

"It was the face of him that I knew," she explained to reporters afterwards. "His hair was brushed different and he needed a shave. But I knew him." Seated in a little antechamber, the landlady seemed visibly relieved that she had "done her bit." She had been under constant strain for the past week, unable to sleep or to eat a proper meal.

"But what's the use of breaking down when you have a job to do?" she declared as the newsmen scribbled down her every word. "So long as I can do the right thing for my country, I can get along."

In the view of the *Tribune*'s reporter, the spunky old woman was the very model of "true British courage. Even when most harassed, her greatest thought is of the bereaved ones and not of herself."

Nevertheless, when asked if she had been tempted to say anything to the prisoner, Mrs. Hill reverted to the subject that seemed most genuinely pressing to her.

"I wanted to ask him when he was coming back to pay me the two dollars he owes me," she replied. "But the detective said I was not to speak to the man." She paused for an instant, then emitted a sigh. "I'd like fine to get my money from him, though."

Several more people were brought down to the central police station that afternoon to identify the suspect: John Hofer, the "clean-faced" fellow who had struck up a brief acquaintance with Nelson on the trolley ride from Winnipeg exactly one week earlier; James Phillips, the lodger who had chatted with Nelson out on Mrs. Hill's veranda on Thursday evening, June 9; and Grace Nelson, the boarder at Mary Rowe's house in Regina, who had been reading a magazine in bed on the morning of Sunday, June 12, when Nelson abruptly barged into her room. All of them picked him from the lineup without hesitation.

It was close to suppertime before the prisoner was finally led back to his cell. Though Nelson, according to several observers, had appeared "cowed and crushed" during his courtroom appearance that morning, he seemed remarkably carefree by the time he was locked up for the night, chatting lightly with his guards about some of his favorite topics: baseball, Buster Keaton movies, and religion. Indeed, he seemed so indifferent to his circumstances that he had yet to request a lawyer.

To at least one journalist covering the case, Nelson

seemed like a perfect prospect for the most celebrated attorney of the day: Clarence Darrow, savior of the Chicago thrill-killers, Leopold and Loeb, and the champion of Darwinism during the celebrated Dayton "Monkey Trial." When asked if he had any interest in defending the "Gorilla Man," however, Darrow demurred—though he took advantage of the interview to put in a word for two of his pet causes, the abolition of the death penalty and the treatment of criminals as maladjusted individuals who deserved enlightened psychiatric care instead of punishment.

"I couldn't take the case," he told the reporter for the *Chicago Tribune.* "I am not doing anything nowadays. I haven't read much about Nelson. Of course, I am against capital punishment. I don't think anyone should be legally killed by the state, regardless of the nature of the crime or crimes charged. I don't believe this man, Nelson, should be hanged.

"If we look carefully enough, we will find some mental taint or environmental defect which causes men to commit the crimes they do. Criminals should be confined and treated."

Though months would pass before Nelson underwent a psychiatric evaluation, his mental state was a matter of public speculation from the moment of his arrest. Like Clarence Darrow, Dr. C. M. Hincks of Toronto, director of the Canadian Mental Hygiene Association, believed that faulty parenting was at least partly to blame for creating killers like Nelson. Dr. Hincks, who was visiting Winnipeg on business at the time of the "Gorilla Man's" capture, offered his opinion in an interview with the *Manitoba Free Press.*

Hincks diagnosed the suspect as a "moral imbecile"—the term used to describe Theo Durrant, the "Demon of the Belfry," who had provoked such fierce outrage in San Francisco just a few years before Nelson's birth. "Not mental disease but lack of development in one part of his make-up is responsible for his horrible crimes," Hincks explained. Such criminals were psychologically stunted: grown men with the crude amorality of vicious boys, the kind who take pleasure from plucking the wings off flies.

"Many children like to kill things," said Hincks, "to dismember insects or stone birds. This is usually only a passing phase." In the case of certain individuals, however, these tendencies "become exaggerated and fixed." Such children grow up to be men unfettered by conscience, immune to remorse, "perverts" who kill not out of conventional motives—rage, jealousy, revenge—but to "gratify their abnormal lusts. To a man like this, what is repulsion to a normal human being is appetite. In all other respects, he may be quite plausible, with nothing to indicate the freak in his nature. He is able to talk over his crimes rationally and without a trace of emotion, then go right out and commit another."

In the course of his career, Hincks had encountered several of these deviants, though he hastened to assure his interviewer that "such cases" were "rare in the world." There was, for example, an "eight-year-old boy who seared his baby sister's face with a red-hot poker and killed pigeons without any feeling" and "a man who took delight in disembowelling cattle."

And what was the cause of such monstrously warped behavior? asked the interviewer.

Hincks was forced to concede that science had yet to provide an entirely satisfactory explanation for the phenomenon, though "faulty upbringing" was certainly a factor. Once a person became a "moral imbecile," the condition was incurable. But "had the Strangler been subjected to proper influences as a boy," Hincks maintained, "he might have developed normally."

From a present-day perspective, most of Hincks' comments still make a great deal of sense, though his language has a dated and distinctly unscientific ring. The phrase "moral imbecile," which sounds more like a Victorian slur than a clinical category, has long since been abandoned by psychologists. Nowadays, we call such people *sociopaths*. And Hincks' remarks about the frequency of the phenomenon are almost touchingly antique.

In an age when sadistic lust murder has become so prevalent that the run-of-the-mill sex slayer barely rates a mention in the press, the world that Hincks describes—one in which "such cases are rare"—seems like a faraway dream.

41

✝

I don't see how my husband could be this Dark Strangler.
I know he was mentally deranged, but he was not violently
insane and he was always good to me.

Mary Fuller

Any doubts that the burly little man locked up in the
Winnipeg jail was the transcontinental killer of twenty-two
victims were dispelled within days of his arrest. Nelson's
mug shots and fingerprints were distributed to police departments throughout the United States. By Saturday, June 18,
he had been positively identified by various witnesses.

In Portland, Mrs. Sophie Yates, the tenant at the rooming
house where Nelson had lodged for several days in November, confirmed that the face in the photographs belonged to
the man she had known as "Adrian Harris," who had be-
stowed such lavish gifts on herself and the landlady, Edna
Gaylord. Grocer Russell Gordon also identified Nelson as
the "nice-mannered fellow" who had purchased fourteen-
dollars' worth of provisions from him on Thanksgiving eve.

When Marie Kuhn of Philadelphia was shown Nelson's
photograph, she clutched both hands to her bosom and let
out a gasp. "That is the man," she told Detectives Peter
Sheller and Frank Cholinski. "I can never forget those eyes.
They seem to haunt me day and night."

The proprietress of a bake shop located not far from the
home of Mary McConnell, the fifty-three-year-old widow

killed by the "Dark Strangler" in late April, Mrs. Kuhn had been standing behind her counter on the afternoon of the murder when the swarthy stranger entered her shop. He had an odd, rolling walk, "as though he had on tight shoes and his feet were hurting him," Mrs. Kuhn recalled. Doffing his hat, he extracted a gold lady's wristwatch from a pocket and held it across the counter.

"Interested in buying this?" he asked. "You can have it for two bucks."

Taking the watch from his hand, Mrs. Kuhn examined it briefly before giving it back with a shake of her head. The watch (one of several valuables Nelson had stolen from Mary McConnell's bedroom) was a handsome object, clearly worth the asking price. But Mrs. Kuhn wanted nothing to do with the stranger, who—though freshly barbered and redolent of eau de cologne—struck her as a "bum."

(That Nelson looked and smelled as if he'd just come from the barber's was consistent with the m.o. he later used in Winnipeg. Police suspected that Nelson would typically wait until his hair was shaggy and his face covered with a heavy stubble before committing a crime. Then, after trading his clothes at a secondhand shop, he would hurry to a barbershop for a shave and a trim, thus altering his appearance.)

Three other Philadelphia women—Margaret Currie, Rose Egler, and Sarah Butler, neighbors of Mary McConnell who had seen Nelson on the day of the slaying—were brought down to police headquarters and asked to pick his photograph from a batch of mug shots. All three identified him without any trouble.

Mrs. Butler, who supported herself by taking in lodgers, let out a scream when she laid eyes on his picture. Nelson had shown up at her door on the morning of the murder, asking to see a room, but her boardinghouse was full. Mrs. Butler felt certain that, had there been any vacancies, she might well have ended up like poor Mary McConnell.

Throughout the country—in Burlingame and Buffalo, Seattle and Detroit—people who had encountered the "Strangler" confirmed that Nelson was the man. Fred Merritt—the young boarder (and surrogate son) of the Buffalo landlady, Jennie Randolph—took one look at the mug shots and announced, "That's him!" Mrs. H. C. Murray, the Burlingame mother-to-be who had managed to fight off the "Strangler" in November, was equally emphatic.

Sergeant J. A. Hoffmann of Detroit, who had travelled to Canada to interview the suspect, was able to link him to the "Strangler" murders through a key piece of evidence, discovered by Winnipeg detectives in the pants Nelson had sold to the secondhand clothes dealer, Sam Waldman. The incriminating object was a jackknife with a big nick in the blade. The steel surrounding the nick was burnt, as though the blade had been used to slice through a live electric wire.

One of the "Strangler's" Detroit victims, the landlady, Mrs. Fannie C. May, had been garrotted with an electric cord, cut from a plugged-in lamp. Following the discovery of the murders, Sergeant Hoffmann had predicted that, when the killer was caught, he would probably be carrying a jackknife with a singed nick in the blade—exactly like the knife that had been recovered from the pocket of Earle Nelson's old pants.

Unfortunately one of the star witnesses in the case—Merton Newman of San Francisco, whose sixty-year-old Aunt Clara had been murdered at the start of the Strangler's eighteen-month spree—was unable to provide a positive identification. Shown Nelson's mug shots, Newman, who had not only seen but spoken to the killer, didn't recognize the face in the photographs.

In spite of this disappointment, however, California authorities remained convinced that the Winnipeg prisoner was the "Strangler." Within twenty-four hours of his arrest, San Francisco police had not only discovered the suspect's real name, Earle Leonard Ferral, but had dug up his police, military, and psychiatric records. The picture that emerged from this material—of a violently unstable man who had been in and out of jails and mental institutions for years, was known to be an accomplished breakout artist, and had been incarcerated for a vicious sexual attack on a young girl—certainly matched the profile of the "Dark Strangler."

Much to the gratification of the gossip-hungry public, investigators had also discovered that the "Gorilla" was a married man. Meek, long-suffering Mary Fuller suddenly found herself identified on the front page of newspapers up and down the Pacific Coast as the wife of America's most monstrously perverted killer.

In spite of the mortification this exposure must have caused her, however, she remained her usual steadfast self, protesting that Earle could not possibly be the culprit. "I don't see how my husband could be this Dark Strangler," she told a reporter for the *San Francisco Chronicle*. "I know he was mentally deranged, but he was not violently insane and he was always good to me."

When she was interviewed by San Francisco detectives, however, she revealed information that only added to the weight of evidence against Earle. Speaking of their life together, she described his abrupt disappearances in early 1926, not long after she had taken him back into their Palo Alto home. He had vanished for the first time on February 19, saying that he was going to Halfmoon Bay in search of work, and had not returned until June 25. It was during this precise period that the "Strangler's" earliest confirmed murders took place, beginning with Clara Newman's death on February 20 and climaxing with the slaying of Mrs. George Russell of Santa Barbara on June 24.

Nelson had remained at home with Mary until August 15, when he suddenly departed again, explaining that he was going to Redwood City. Less than one week later, two more West Coast women were slain, Mrs. Mary Nisbet on August 20 and Mrs. Isabel Gallegos the following day.

Detectives also located Nelson's aunt, Lillian Fabian, interviewing her at her San Francisco home on Monday, June 20. Like Mary Fuller, Lillian refused to believe that Earle was the "Strangler." Though she acknowledged that her nephew was prone to "queer streaks," she insisted that he was a "very mild" person, incapable of murder.

When asked about Earle's wife, Lillian responded with nothing but praise. "Mrs. Fuller is, of course, greatly worried over this," she said, her voice full of sympathy. "She is just as loyal to Earle as possible but hates all the publicity. She's almost a mother to him, you know, as she's nearly twice his age. Often he would leave her flat, and she wouldn't see him for months at a time. But she understands Earle, and he is much better off married to her than to a flapper."

Before the week was out, Nelson would be identified by another forty-odd witnesses. On Monday evening, June 20, the inquest into the deaths of Lola Cowan and Emily Patterson was conducted at the police court on Rupert Street. For a little over two hours, the twelve-member coroner's jury listened intently to the testimony of twenty-six people, including Dr. W. P. McCowan, who performed the postmortems on the victims; Bernhardt Mortenson, the boarder who first glimpsed the Cowan girl's body under the bed in Mrs. Hill's rooming house; Lewis B. Foote, the photographer who shot pictures of the victims; the clothier, Sam Waldman; the barber, Nick Tabor; and—most dramatically—William Patterson, who kept the courtroom transfixed as he recalled the moment when, kneeling at his sleeping son's bedside, he discovered his wife's savaged corpse.

The only person who seemed indifferent to Patterson's testimony was Nelson himself, who sat through the entire proceedings with a look of supreme unconcern on his coarse, stubbled face. Wearing dark-blue trousers, a gray jacket, collarless shirt, and gaping, laceless boots, he sat unmanacled in the prisoner's dock, staring absently at the wooden railing and stifling an occasional yawn. When the jury foreman, E. R. Frayer, read the verdict, finding the suspect responsible for the two murders, Nelson displayed not the slightest trace of emotion.

He was equally impassive three days later, when the preliminary hearing was held in the same place, the police court in the Rupert Street station. By 8:00 A.M., hundreds of would-be spectators, most of them women, had already gathered outside the building. Police guards posted at the entranceway kept the crowd under control. By the time the hearing began at noon, every inch of seating-space was occupied, while the hallway outside the courtroom was packed to the point of impassability. Though denied admission, a hundred or so people continued to mill on the sidewalk until the hearing was over.

More than sixty witnesses testified during the proceedings:

everyone from W. E. Chandler, the motorist who had picked Nelson up near Warren, Minnesota, to William Haberman, the old man who had seen the suspect fiddling with the Pattersons' front door on the day of the murder. Thomas Carten—the clerk at Chevrier's haberdashery, who had sold Nelson the champagne-colored fedora—was there, as were the Regina landlady, Mary Rowe; her boarder, Grace Nelson (who had been reading in bed when Nelson barged into her room); Leslie Morgan, the Wakopa storekeeper who had alerted the Provincial police; and several dozen more. Under questioning by Crown Prosecutor R. B. Graham, witness after witness added links to the long evidentiary chain connecting Nelson to the corpses in Winnipeg.

Guarded by four armed police officers, Nelson sat through the proceedings with an expression (as one reporter put it) "of unusual calm." He looked a good deal more presentable than he had at the inquest. His face was freshly shaven, his hair was neatly combed into a pompadour, and his scruffy clothes had been replaced with a new, forest-green suit. But his manner was just as detached. "Not a quiver of an eyelid nor the slightest change of expression was shown by Nelson throughout the trial," the reporter observed.

His expression remained completely unruffled when—after the final witness, Chief Detective George Smith, testified—Magistrate R. M. Noble committed Earle Leonard Nelson for trial on two charges of murder.

The following morning, Friday, June 24, Nelson was transferred from his cell in the Rupert Street police station to the provincial jail.

From the moment of his arrival in Winnipeg one week earlier, the police had been inundated with calls from anxious citizens, worried that the "Gorilla"—who had broken out of the Killarney jail as though the locks were made of tin—might escape again. As a result, extraordinary precautions were taken when the transfer was made on Friday.

Shackled, handcuffed, and surrounded by ten heavily armed constables, he was loaded into a patrol wagon and whisked off to the provincial jail. Immediately upon his arrival he was hustled into the "death cell," a heavily fortified structure customarily reserved for the condemned.

"There is not the slightest chance that he will get out," Warden J. C. Downie declared, giving reporters a look at Nelson's new accommodations—a cramped, steel enclosure surrounded by solid cement. "It is a tightly locked cage within another tightly locked cage, and several constables will be on constant guard."

It was the first time in the prison's history, Downie pointed out, that a man not yet convicted of murder (or, indeed, even tried) had been kept in the cell.

Later that day, Nelson, who had said nothing at either the inquest or preliminary hearing, made his first public statement. Under the circumstances, it would have been reasonable for him to show some concern. After all, though his trial date hadn't even been set, he had already been consigned to death row.

Nelson, however, remained so completely unperturbed that he continued to shrug off the need for a lawyer. Interviewed by a reporter for the *Manitoba Free Press,* he flatly denied his guilt. Indeed, he insisted that a man like himself could never commit such heinous crimes.

"I'm charged with two murders," he declared. "But I'm not the one who done it."

But what about all the witnesses, asked the reporter—the sixty-plus people throughout the United States and western Canada who had positively identified him as the "Strangler"?

Nelson had a simple answer for that one. "All of 'em are wrong," he explained. "Murder just isn't possible for a man of my high Christian ideals."

42

✝

This man, by being caught in Canada, is as fortunate as any man charged with such crimes could be. The more desperate the crime, the more scrupulous and exacting will be the evidence demanded to convict him.

Manitoba Free Press, June 18, 1927

During the week of June 27, two important developments occurred in the Nelson case. The start of his trial was fixed at July 26. And the court finally appointed two defense lawyers, James H. Stitt and Chester Young, who immediately set about seeking a postponement.

The basis of their petition was twofold. Though Stitt, in particular, felt that he'd been saddled with a thankless task, he also believed that Nelson, like everyone else, was entitled to the best possible defense. A month, Stitt argued in his motion for postponement, "is not sufficient to prepare for trial of the accused."

An even more compelling reason was the unbridled behavior of the press, which had already done its best to convict Nelson in print. To prove his point, Stitt assembled a sheaf of clippings from the *Manitoba Free Press* and the *Winnipeg Tribune*—stories with such inflammatory headlines as FRISCO POLICE CERTAIN PRISONER "THE GORILLA," NELSON IDENTIFIED AS MAN WHO KILLED BUFFALO WOMAN, PHOTOGRAPH IDENTIFIED BY WOMAN. NELSON BELIEVED TO BE PHILADELPHIA STRANGLER, and PRISONER IS "HARRIS," HUNTED KILLER, CHIEF SMITH INSISTS.

These were just a few egregious examples of "trial by newspaper instead of trial by jury," Stitt maintained. Given the overheated atmosphere generated by such publicity, it would be "impossible to obtain a jury impartial to the accused." Delaying Nelson's trial until the fall assizes would, at the very least, allow public opinion to cool off a bit.

As it happened, other members of Winnipeg's legal establishment shared Stitt's concern, most notably Chief Justice T. H. Mathers. At a meeting with a colleague on Monday, June 27, Mathers voiced his opinion in the most vehement terms. "I was astounded when I heard that it was fixed for the twenty-sixth of July," he exclaimed. "You cannot get a jury to give him a fair trial now. No jury would dare acquit him, even if he is innocent."

Firing off a letter to Attorney General W. J. Majors, Mathers blamed the Winnipeg press for having worked "the public mind into a state of excitement and indignation which renders a calm consideration of the evidence against him impossible. The newspapers have conducted a campaign during which he has been condemned over and over again. . . . The trial of a man for his life is a most solemn event and should be conducted in an atmosphere freed from all emotional prejudice, so far as that can be done. The trial should begin with a presumption in favor of innocence, but if Nelson is placed on trial before the press excitement has time to subside, his trial will begin with the presumption in fact that he is guilty."

In response to this communication, Attorney General Majors composed a letter of his own, mailing copies to both J. W. Dafoe and W. L. MacTavish, editors-in-chief of the *Manitoba Free Press* and the *Winnipeg Tribune*:

Dear Sir:

Re Rex vs. Nelson

As you are aware, much publicity has been given to this particular case and the public mind is still very much inflamed.

The prisoner is now committed for trial. The date of trial has been fixed for July 26th.

The comments and news items which are now constantly appearing in the two leading newspapers of our City, if continued, may constitute a ground for postponement of the trial, which you will understand is undesirable. Hence, it is essential in the interests of justice that all further unnecessary publicity should cease until the trial is over.

I take it that the general public is now reasonably well informed about the case and that no interests will suffer if, until the trial is over, the press refrains as far as possible from publishing anything about the matter.

I shall, therefore, be glad if you will give the necessary instructions so that your good paper may, until the trial is over, refrain from publishing anything more than such as is absolutely necessary about this Nelson case.

This appeal worked—at least to an extent. The kind of shrill banner headlines that had run for two solid weeks quickly disappeared from the front pages.

Still, both newspapers continued to feature regular items on the case—no surprise, given the public's insatiable hunger for any tidbits about Nelson. The very day after Majors sent his letter, the *Tribune* printed a titillating piece headlined MAN SLEPT IN ROOM WHERE SLAIN GIRL'S BODY LAY.

The story recounted the macabre experience of a railroad conductor named Joe Boner, who had taken a room in Mrs. Hill's boardinghouse on Saturday afternoon, June 10, the day after Nelson absconded from Winnipeg. As it happened, his room adjoined the one Nelson had occupied.

Several hours after his arrival, Boner went off to the Garrick movie theater to see the new George Jessel comedy, *Private Izzy Murphy*. Returning after midnight, the bleary-eyed boarder mistakenly entered the room adjacent to his own, tumbled into bed, and immediately fell into a profound slumber. It wasn't until the following evening—when his fellow tenant, Bernhardt Mortenson, caught sight of Lola Cowan's hidden corpse—that Boner realized he had spent the night "with the girl's naked body huddled under his bed" (as the *Tribune* wrote).

The press also lavished a good deal of attention on the nasty dispute over the $1,500 reward, whose claimants included just about everyone with a connection to the case, from John T. Hanna, the motorist who had given Nelson a lift from Emerson to Winnipeg on Wednesday, June 8, to the Regina landlady, Mary Rowe, to J. W. Whittingham, a section foreman for the Canadian National Railways who had exchanged a few words with Nelson at the Wakopa depot on the day of the latter's arrest.

The most controversial claimant of all, however, was Roy Armstrong, the Boissevain farmer who, along with Constable Joe Young, had conducted a day-long search for Nelson until his Ford got stuck in a mud hole. Armstrong insisted that he was entitled to a share because he had "trailed the 'Strangler' from twelve o'clock noon until almost dark, arousing the countryside to his aid and asking them to telephone in all directions and have the people be on the lookout."

Armstrong's claim, however, was bitterly refuted by various witnesses, including several dozen residents of Wakopa, who signed a petition to "protest in the most emphatic manner the rumor or statement that any telephone warning whatsoever was received by them to be on the lookout for the supposed strangler Nelson." As the precise details of the manhunt were reconstructed in the weeks following Nelson's capture, it became increasingly clear that, far from having sounded a general alarm, Armstrong and Young had deliberately refrained from "arousing the countryside" in the hope of capturing the suspect themselves and splitting the reward down the middle.

At least two witnesses testified that, when the pair finally showed up in Wakopa and discovered that the "Strangler" was already in custody, Armstrong had bitterly muttered that "$1,500 had slipped through his fingers that day." In the opinion of an editorial writer for the *Killarney Guide*, Armstrong's conduct was "more worthy of censure than reward."

This opinion was ultimately shared by Attorney General Majors, who, concluding that "the reward was the main object of Armstrong's search," dismissed the Boissevain man's claim. In the end, the money was divided eight ways, with varying amounts dispensed to the four Wakopa residents most instrumental in Nelson's initial arrest, Leslie Morgan, Albert Dingwall, George Dickson, and Duncan Merlin; two

Killarney men, Alfred Wood and Guy Ramsay, who had given "valuable help in the subsequent recapture"; and the Winnipeg clothiers, Jake Garber and Sam Waldman, who had provided the police with vital leads.

The suggestion that Nelson might not receive a fair trial in Winnipeg provoked a good deal of wounded protest in the press. Editorial writers insisted that, in wending his way into Canada, the "Gorilla" had found himself in the hands of the most civilized judicial system in the world. Several of these editorials drove home their points by contrasting Canadian justice with American vigilantism.

The most compelling of these was a piece in the *Manitoba Free Press,* written by someone identified only by the initials "T.B.R." In language whose understated tone only amplified his outrage and contempt, the writer recounted a visit he had recently received from "a quiet-looking, pleasant, elderly gentleman" who had lived for a time in the American Deep South. When the talk turned to race relations, this "twinkling-eyed, cheery old caller" began regaling his listener with a description of the "various lynching parties at which he had been a guest; and what he had seen with his own eyes on several fetid, blood-splashed nights in little towns south of the Mason and Dixie [*sic*] line":

> One pretty summer evening, he told us, a negro was arrested in a southern village on a serious charge and put in jail. . . . When the news got around that a "nigro" had been caught, the villagers, in a body, turned out and crowded around the jail. . . . This "nigro" apparently had been "identified" as the culprit. He, the crowd was convinced, was the offender. An elderly gentleman, standing near our friend, had a parcel, and he opened it, and there was "Oh, a fine, beautiful new rope." Great stuff for "nigroes."
>
> A new telephone line was being put up through the village, and the long, enormous poles were lying by the roadside. One of these poles was lifted by about a hundred men. They carried it into the prison yard . . . and pushed the pole through the door, and went in and brought out the "nigro". . . .

And then the old gentleman's beautiful, clean new rope was looped over the "nigro's" head, and the other end tied to a saddle-horn, and a mounted rider galloped off with the "nigro" leaping behind, flailed and pounded and ground and broken at the end of the taut rope— over rough road and bush and brier to a tall tree, and there our old friend saw the "nigro"—dead and pulp by now—hanged from a branch—"and about a thousand bullets shot into him as he swung."

And then they all went home to bed.

After relating this appalling tale, the editorialist compared the behavior of the Southern lynch mob to the comportment of the crowd that had gathered at the Winnipeg train station to catch a glimpse of the "Gorilla" upon his arrival from Killarney. "The arrested man is charged with being the most abominable character that ever injured this community. . . . What our old friend's 'nigro' did was mild compared to what this man is accused of doing." And yet, wrote "T.B.R.," when you look at the published newspaper photographs of "the crowd through which he is being led, you see it is the calmest, least excited, least revengeful-looking crowd in the world. They are standing in almost frozen calm, watching him being taken off. There is no lynching-instinct in our people: which is something to be very proud of. . . . Our people do not go insane with revenge and excitement and tear in pieces the prisoner whom the police arrest. . . . And we are saved, in consequence, the horrors of such scenes as those in that village in the Southern States."

This same note was sounded again and again by commentators who praised "the steady temper of the Canadian people," the "absolute fairness" of the "British system of justice," and the "becoming dignity, impressiveness, and strict impartiality" with which "all Canadian murder trials" were conducted.

Even as the papers were offering these paeans to Canadian justice, however, an exchange was taking place behind the scenes which suggested that, at least in the view of certain officials, Nelson's fate had already been sealed. On June 21—just a few days after the "Gorilla" was brought in chains to Winnipeg—John Allen, Deputy Attorney-General of

Manitoba, sent a letter to M. McGregor, Sheriff of the Western Judicial District.

"It is expected that the trial of Nelson, the alleged double murderer, will take place in July at Winnipeg," Allen wrote. "If he is sentenced to be hanged, the question arises as to where the execution should take place. The Winnipeg Gaol is unfortunately situated for executions, and it has been suggested that the execution might take place at Portage la Prairie or at Brandon Gaol. Can you advise me as to what facilities you have for taking care of a dangerous criminal such as this man Nelson?"

Sheriff McGregor's response was not very encouraging. "In respect to the situation of the Gaol for executions," he wrote, "I do not think it is more fortunately situated than the Winnipeg Gaol, as a public school is over-looking the Gaol, a City Park is immediately North of the Gaol, and residential houses are immediately East of the Gaol. There are no residences on the block immediately West, but on the next block it is fairly well built up and the General Hospital is situated two blocks West and one block South."

With Brandon ruled out, Attorney General Majors himself sent an inquiry to the Deputy Minister of Justice in Ottawa, W. Stuart Edwards. Dated June 23 (just one week after Nelson's recapture in Killarney), the letter explained precisely why the Winnipeg Gaol was so "unfortunately situated" for executions. "It adjoins the University buildings," wrote Major. "The University authorities have complained bitterly in the past because executions have taken place so close to the University buildings. As you can understand, the sight of the gallows being erected, etc., is not a pleasant one for the University students."

Edwards' reply was as disappointing as Sheriff McGregor's. "It seems to me," he wrote, "that the considerations hereinafter set out preclude the possibility of having the execution, if one takes place, carried out upon the penitentiary property. By section 1065 of the Criminal Code, judgment of death to be executed on any prisoner shall be carried into effect within the walls of the prison in which the offender is confined at the time of execution. So far as I am aware, the Court would have no power to commit the prisoner to the penitentiary, so that he could not be lawfully detained therein."

There is something grimly ironic about these letters, particularly in light of the self-congratulatory editorials running simultaneously in the Winnipeg press. Publicly, the media was busy proclaiming Nelson's good fortune in having been arrested in Canada, where he was certain to receive a fair, impartial trial, based on the presumption of innocence.

In private, meanwhile, the Attorney General and other high officials were already trying to decide where to hang him.

PART 5

†

BY THE NECK

43

✝

One of the striking characteristics of the era of Coolidge
Prosperity was the unparalleled rapidity and unanimity with
which millions of men and women turned their attention,
their talk, and their emotional interest upon a series of tremendous trifles—a heavyweight boxing match, a murder
trial, a new automobile model, a transatlantic flight. Most
of the *causes célèbres* which thus stirred the country from end
to end were quite unimportant from the traditional point of
view of the historian. The future destinies of few people
were affected by the testimony of the "pig woman" at the
Hall-Mills trial or the attempt to rescue Floyd Collins from
his Kentucky cave. Yet the fact that such things could engage
the hopes and fears of unprecedented numbers of people was
anything but unimportant.

Frederick Lewis Allen, *Only Yesterday*

By the end of June, Nelson had been indicted for first-
degree murder in five U.S. cities—Buffalo, Detroit, Philadelphia, Portland, and San Francisco. But Winnipeg prosecutors
were determined to win a conviction in Canada.

As to when the trial would take place, that issue was
finally settled in early July, when Nelson's lawyer, James
Stitt, appeared before Mr. Justice MacDonald to request a
delay. Stitt based his motion on two considerations, the same
ones he had raised at the time of his appointment: that public opinion, inflamed by the media, would militate against a

fair trial, and that the defense did not have sufficient time to prepare its case.

After listening to opposing arguments by Deputy Attorney-General John Allen, MacDonald offered his ruling. Stitt's first point carried little weight with the judge, who saw no reason why the public's mood, "aroused by the savagery of the crimes and intensified by the sensationalism of the press," should be any different in three months' time. "Criminal trials in our courts are not governed by public feeling or the excitement created by the public press," MacDonald proclaimed, "and I have no fear of the danger to the accused or any trouble in the selection of twelve fair, honest men into whose judgment his case will be cast."

Furthermore, MacDonald believed that there were compelling reasons to try Nelson "without delay, because if he is not the man, then the human tiger is still at large and should be run to earth. So long as this trial is delayed, so long will police vigilance lie dormant and the lives of our womenkind be in a state of unrest."

Still, there was no denying that Stitt and his co-counsel hadn't been given much time to mount a defense. To ensure that the accused was "surrounded by all the safeguards of a British court of justice," MacDonald had no choice but to rule in Stitt's favor, adjourning Nelson's trial until the fall assizes, scheduled to convene in early November.

The postponement was the last major news story about Nelson to appear for a while. From time to time in the succeeding weeks, the papers would print an item related to the case. In late September, Emily Patterson's father-in-law, a Belfast factory foreman who had never missed a day of work in sixty-three years, retired from his job. When he suffered a fatal heart attack less than forty-eight hours later, the *Free Press* ran a notice headlined FATHER-IN-LAW OF ONE OF "STRANGLER'S" VICTIMS DIES.

A few weeks later—in an episode that revealed just how far-flung Nelson's notoriety had become—the same paper published a squib headlined "Queerest of Letters Reaches Winnipeg Police." According to the story, Chief Constable Christopher Newton had recently received "the strangest letter ever delivered in Winnipeg": a query from a young man in Rotterdam, Holland, eager to know whether Nelson was "of Dutch, Spanish, or Italian nationality." What made this communication so bizarre, however, wasn't the letter itself but the envelope it came sealed in, which was addressed, "Chief Officer of Justice in Winnipeg, United States of America, State of Utah, Ohio." Somehow, the letter actually made it to Winnipeg, where a postal employee forwarded it to the Chief of Police.

For the most part, however, coverage of the "Strangler" case dwindled away, as the Canadian public, having gorged on the story for weeks, finally turned its attention to other matters: an election campaign in Manitoba; a gold strike in the northeast corner of the province, up around Hudson Bay; a visit from the Prince of Wales, accompanied by his brother, Prince George, and British Prime Minister Stanley Baldwin.

In the United States, a host of matters, large and small, diverted the newspaper-reading public: the furor over Sacco and Vanzetti's execution; President Coolidge's stunning decision not to run for reelection in 1928; Babe Ruth's record-shattering sixtieth home run of the season; the premiere of Al Jolson's *Jazz Singer,* the first motion picture "talkie"; Gene Tunney's controversial win over Jack Dempsey in their historical heavyweight rematch. Even in those cities most affected by the "Strangler's" crimes—San Francisco, Portland, Seattle, Buffalo, Philadelphia, Detroit—the story vanished from the papers.

And then, in the last week of October, the "Gorilla" roared back into the headlines.

Throughout the world, stories of nubile maidens beloved by and mated to ravening beasts are so common that folklorists have a special name for them—tales of the "Monster Bridegroom." In our own era, when oral folklore has largely been replaced by mass entertainment, this fantasy has been the stuff of countless movies, from grade-Z horror films like *Bride of the Gorilla* to certified masterpieces like the original *King Kong.* Clearly, there is something about the idea of a beautiful young woman embraced by a beast that captivates—and titillates—the popular imagination.

So it is no surprise that Earle Nelson's wife, a real-life

"bride of the Gorilla," was the object of intense curiosity in Winnipeg. Though Mary Fuller had been tracked down and interviewed by San Francisco reporters, no information about her, beyond her existence, had appeared in the Canadian press. The public—its dormant interest in the Nelson case revived by the approach of the trial—was burning to get a look at the monster's bride, who was slated to testify on her husband's behalf. According to published reports, she was scheduled to arrive on Saturday, October 29, three days before the start of the trial.

The story that ran in the October 28 edition of the *Manitoba Free Press,* therefore, came as a blow—and not just to the average sensation-loving citizen. WIFE IS NOT ABLE TO COME, read the headline. MRS. NELSON WILL NOT BE WITNESS AT WINNIPEG MURDER TRIAL.

The article cited an Associated Press dispatch from San Francisco, where the prisoner's uncle, Willis Nelson, was quoted as stating that Mary Fuller was too ill to travel. "She is suffering from shock and is under the care of a physician," he told reporters. "The only way she could go to Winnipeg would be on a stretcher."

Nelson's attorneys, James Stitt and Chester Young—who were completely unaware of this development until they read about it in the papers—were especially dismayed by the news. After firing off a telegram to the San Francisco police, requesting an immediate investigation of the report, Stitt announced that, should the story prove true, he would seek a postponement of the trial, since Mrs. Fuller's testimony was so central to the defense.

As it turned out, the whole story appeared to be a deliberate ruse on the part of Nelson's family to divert attention from Mary Fuller's arrival—to permit the excruciatingly shy woman to slip into Winnipeg without being besieged by the press. Even as Willis Nelson's announcement was travelling over the telegraph wires, the prisoner's wife—accompanied by his aunt, Lillian Fabian, and her fourteen-year-old daughter, Rose—was on her way to Winnipeg. Arriving at the railway station on Thursday morning, October 27, the trio hurried into a taxi and proceeded directly to the McLaren Hotel, where they took a room under an assumed name.

In spite of these efforts at secrecy, it wasn't long before

the press got wind of their arrival. Early Saturday morning, a reporter for the *Free Press* knocked on their hotel-room door. It was opened a crack by a tall, handsome woman in her mid-thirties, who peered out nervously at the newsman.

When he asked if she was Nelson's wife, the woman shook her head. "I am his aunt," she said. "Mrs. Lillian Fabian. And who might you be?"

As soon as he identified himself, Mrs. Fabian became highly agitated. "We don't want to talk about it!" she half-shouted at the reporter.

"But perhaps," he prodded, "if you could just bring yourself to tell something about your nephew's earlier life under normal home conditions, it might help create a better impression of him."

Mrs. Fabian seemed to detect something accusatory in this suggestion. "You can't blame us for what has happened," she cried. "We had nothing to do with it! We are in a terrible position!"

"Are you going to testify in favor of the accused?" asked the reporter, trying to peer over Mrs. Fabian's shoulder in the hope of catching a glimpse of Nelson's wife.

"I have nothing to say about that!"

"Have you any new evidence to introduce?" he persisted.

"It's no use," she exclaimed. "We have been told by our attorney not to talk, and we don't intend to." Then, without another word, she stepped back from the door, shut it slowly but decisively in the reporter's face, and threw the inside lock.

Undeterred, the newsman headed downstairs and repaired to his automobile, parked directly across from the hotel. Climbing into the front seat, he kept his eyes on the main entrance, like a cop on a stakeout. His patience was rewarded. About forty-five minutes later, Mrs. Fabian emerged from the hotel, accompanied by a pretty adolescent girl and a frail-looking, white-haired woman with thick-lensed spectacles and pinched, if kindly, face.

As the reporter jumped from his car and hurried toward the trio (who had decided to leave their room for a bit of sightseeing), he called out, "Mrs. Fuller!"

Reflexively, the white-haired old woman jerked her head in his direction, a bewildered look on her face. Seeing the newsman approach, she gave a little gasp and ducked behind Mrs. Fabian, like a toddler taking refuge behind its mother's skirt.

"Go away!" shouted Mrs. Fabian. "She won't talk to you."

Even as Mrs. Fabian spoke, the old lady turned and, with a determination that belied her fragile appearance, strode back into the hotel lobby.

The reporter never did manage to speak to Mary Fuller that day. But he had gotten his story anyway.

In folklore, film, and pulp fiction, women who find themselves in the grasp of dark, hulking creatures are invariably young and lovely. But Winnipeg's true-life beast-man—in a twist that seemed entirely in keeping with the grotesque nature of the case—wasn't wed to a beauty.

He was married to a crone.

44

✝

Of beasts, it is confess'd the ape
Comes nearest us in human shape;
Like man he imitates each fashion
And malice is his ruling passion.
        Jonathan Swift, *The Logicians Refuted*

On Friday morning, October 28, the day after Nelson's family members reached Winnipeg, a medical specialist arrived at the provincial jail to X-ray the "Gorilla Man's" brain. Nelson's attorneys, who were planning an insanity plea, were hoping to find some physical basis for their argument: evidence either of the dire head injury he had sustained as a child or of a syphilitic brain lesion, the morbid legacy of the disease both his parents had died from.

Admitted into the cagelike "condemned cell," the physician set up his apparatus in the center of the floor and proceeded to take several plates of the prisoner's head. Nelson—with his crude, omnivorous curiosity—submitted willingly, even eagerly, to the procedure, asking a steady stream of questions about the technique. When the physician was interviewed by reporters later that day, he confessed that he had rarely dealt with a more cooperative patient.

That cooperation was typical of Nelson's behavior in captivity. For the past five months, he had been the most carefully guarded prisoner in the history of the provincial jail. Locked inside the steel-and-concrete cell, he was under round-the-clock surveillance. Six guards shared sentinel duty, working two at a time in eight-hour shifts. One guard sat inside the cell, while the second remained posted just outside the door.

But in spite of the "Gorilla's" fearsome reputation, he had proved to be a model prisoner. Indeed, captivity seemed to agree with him. Supplied (at a cost of twenty-four dollars per day) with the standard jailhouse amenities, "three hots and a cot," he had put on a little weight and seemed quietly content, passing much of his time in casual conversation with his guards or immersed in his favorite reading matter: sensational novels, pseudoscientific tracts, and Scripture.

There was only one area in which he remained utterly intransigent. He refused to say a word about his alleged crimes. Virtually from the day of his arrest, a steady stream of American detectives had travelled to Winnipeg, seeking to clear up various unsolved killings in their jurisdictions. In the minds of police officials throughout the United States and Canada, there was not a shred of doubt that Nelson was the homicidal maniac who had strangled (and in most cases sexually assaulted) twenty-two victims in a sixteen-month span:

1. Clara Newman, San Francisco, February 20, 1926
2. Laura Beal, San Jose, March 2, 1926
3. Lillian St. Mary, San Francisco, June 10, 1926
4. Ollie Russell, Santa Barbara, June 24, 1926
5. Mary Nisbet, Oakland, August 16, 1926
6. Beata Withers, Portland, October 19, 1926
7. Virginia Grant, Portland, October 20, 1926
8. Mabel Fluke, Portland, October 21, 1926
9. Mrs. William Anna Edmonds, San Francisco, November 18, 1926
10. Florence Monks, Seattle, November 23, 1926
11. Blanche Myers, Portland, November 29, 1926
12. Mrs. John Brerard, Council Bluffs, Iowa, December 2, 1926
13. Bonnie Pace, Kansas City, Missouri, December 27, 1926
14. Germania Harpin, Kansas City, Missouri, December 28, 1926

15. Robert Harpin, Kansas City, Missouri, December 28, 1926
16. Mary McConnell, Philadelphia, April 27, 1927
17. Jennie Randolph, Buffalo, May 30, 1927
18. Fannie May, Detroit, June 1, 1927
19. Maureen Oswald Atorthy, Detroit, June 1, 1927
20. Mary Sietsma, Chicago, June 4, 1927
21. Lola Cowan, Winnipeg, June 9, 1927
22. Emily Patterson, Winnipeg, June 10, 1927

But during this same period, there were other brutal murders that bore a striking resemblance to the nearly two dozen atrocities attributed to the "Dark Strangler/Gorilla Man." On the evening of August 23, 1925 (not long after Nelson was discharged from Napa State Hospital), a sixty-year-old widow named Elizabeth Jones was found strangled to death in the bedroom of her home at 3565 Market Street in San Francisco. According to several witnesses, Mrs. Jones, who had recently put her house up for sale, had been visited on the day of her death by a stocky, dark-skinned man who professed an interest in buying the property.

Several weeks later, on October 1, another San Francisco woman was strangled and raped after death—a strikingly attractive, thirty-two-year-old divorcée named Elma Wells. Her naked, outraged corpse was found jammed into the clothes closet of a vacant apartment at 628 Guerrero Street, one of several buildings she managed.

The most sensational unsolved cases of all occurred in Philadelphia in early November—a string of killings that set off a wave of panic among the female population of the city. On Saturday, November 7, 1925, a waitress named Mary Murray was strangled in the kitchen of her house at 1811 Judson Street by an unknown fiend, who carried her lifeless body up to a second-floor room, carefully deposited it on a bed, then sexually violated the corpse. Just four days later, a thirty-three-year-old housewife named Lena Weiner of 2421 Napa Street was murdered and outraged in precisely the same way. An overcoat and two suits belonging to Mrs. Weiner's husband, Hyman, were stolen from the home.

A third Philadelphia victim (whose death received significantly less attention in the press) was a young woman dismissively identified in the papers as "Ola McCoy, colored," who was strangled to death in the parlor of her Montgomery Avenue house, just a few blocks away from the Murray home. As in the other cases, Mrs. McCoy's body was carried to an upstairs bedroom and subjected to postmortem rape.

A swarthy, thickset stranger—described as either "a dark-skinned white man or a light-skinned Negro"—was seen lurking in the vicinity of Lena Weiner's house on the day of her murder. But though several dozen suspects (nearly all of them black) were rounded up and questioned, the perpetrator of the three atrocities managed to escape.

There were other strangulation victims during this period, too: a fifty-year-old wardrobe mistress named Mae Price, slain in a Boston hotel room while touring with a show called *The Brown Derby;* a sixty-nine-year-old landlady named Rose Valentino, murdered in her apartment at 195 Norfolk Street in Newark, New Jersey; another elderly Newark woman named Lena Tidar, garrotted with a man's necktie in the bedroom of her Bergen Street house.

Hoping to close the books on these and other killings, detectives from around the United States made the trip to Winnipeg to interview Nelson and urge him to confess. But their appeals were always answered with the same disdainful response: "Why should I get myself hung to help *you?*" He had never even *been* to Newark, he would declare. Or to Philadelphia. Or Buffalo. Or Detroit.

He was innocent of every accusation. Others might be capable of murder. But not a man of his devout religious beliefs.

Copious as they are, the existing documents on the Nelson case contain very little psychiatric information. Still, it is possible to draw certain inferences about the workings of his deeply disordered mind.

Shortly before the start of his trial, one of his guards was struck by the intensity with which Nelson was poring over a certain passage in the Bible. When the guard asked what he was reading, Nelson glanced up and said, "Proverbs, Chapter 23, Verse 26."

"What's it about?" asked the guard.

Nelson, who normally welcomed any opportunity to hold

forth about religion, began to reply. Suddenly, he clamped his mouth shut, as though struck by second thoughts. He looked at the guard with a strange little smile, then returned to his reading.

Back home that evening, the guard, out of curiosity, consulted his own family Bible. This is what he read:

> My son, give me thine heart,
> and let thine eyes observe my ways.
> For a whore *is* a deep ditch;
> and a strange woman *is* a narrow pit.
> She also lieth in wait as *for* a prey,
> and increaseth the transgressors among men.

That Nelson was so taken with these lines suggests that he fell into an all-too-familiar criminal category: the type of sex-killer that sees his victims as "whores," filthy man-traps who get exactly what they deserve. Even in the face of overwhelmingly incriminating evidence, he vehemently denied his guilt. And after all, if every "strange woman" was a "deep ditch," a "narrow pit," a foul creature waiting to prey on unwary males and turn them into "transgressors," then how could *he* be held to blame?

At no point would Nelson display the faintest glimmer of remorse. As far as he was concerned, there was only one real victim in the case. He was certainly capable of feeling sorry—but (like other sociopathic killers before and since) only for himself.

45

A very real difficulty at the Nelson trial was to connect
Nelson, in the mind's eye, with the murder for which he
was being tried. . . . Nelson is a small, young man, smooth-
skinned and without a single indication in his appearance
that would warn the ordinary observer against him as a dangerous person. The effort which had to be made to see this
inoffensive-looking youth engaged in the furious violence of
a bestial murder strained the imagination heavily.

Editorial, *Manitoba Free Press,* November 9, 1927

Courtroom Number One of the Manitoba Law Courts
Building on Kennedy Street had enough seating space for
175 spectators. But the Nelson trial was shaping up to be
the hottest show in town, with thousands of people clamoring for admission. By Monday, October 31, the day before
the scheduled start of the proceedings, officials had been
swamped with requests. Every applicant received the same
response: apart from the bench space set aside for represen-
tatives of the press and assorted local dignitaries, reserved
seats were unavailable. The general public would be admitted strictly on a first-come first-served basis.

The sun had barely risen when the crowd began to gather
at the Law Courts Building on Tuesday morning, November
1. By noon, nearly 2,000 people had shown up—more than
ten times the number that the courtroom could accommodate. The majority of them were women, many teenage girls,

who packed the corridors and spilled out onto the streets, buzzing with anticipation. To more than one observer, they seemed less like a bunch of courtroom spectators than a mob of movie fans at a gala premiere. If Barrymore himself were about to appear, they couldn't have been more excited.

A reporter from the *Winnipeg Tribune* was on hand to describe the tumultuous scene when the courtroom doors were finally opened at 1:30 P.M.: "A great shout went up, and the mob lunged forward like a tidal wave. It was like a river trying to pass through a bottle-neck, and policemen on guard at the door were forced to use all their strength to prevent injury to members of the throng." Within minutes, the room was filled to capacity—every seat taken, every inch of standing space occupied. The doors were shut and locked, with no one permitted to enter or leave until court was adjourned for the day.

The remainder of the crowd continued to jam the hallways and mill in the street, still hoping for a glimpse of the notorious figure whose alleged crimes had (as the *Free Press* put it in in that morning's edition) "staggered and terrified the civilized world."

When Nelson was finally led to the prisoner's dock shortly after 2:00 P.M., an excited rumble filled the courtroom, as the spectators half-rose from their seats, craning their necks for a look at the main attraction. But if they were expecting some sort of sideshow monstrosity—a hulking human gorilla, led in chains by his captors—they were gravely disappointed.

In spite of his wrist manacles and the two burly guards at his side, Nelson—who was enjoying his first exposure to the outside world after nearly five months in solitary—seemed relaxed, even cheerful. Passing the witness area, he recognized two of the provincial police officers, Constables Sampson and Outerson, who had accompanied him on the train ride from Killarney to Winnipeg.

"Glad to see you again, boys," Nelson said with a big grin. "You were awfully good to me when we first got acquainted."

As the guards led the prisoner to his place and undid his manacles, one pretty young woman exclaimed to her companion, "Why, he's the best-looking man here!"

"He certainly doesn't look like a bad man to me," her friend agreed.

And indeed, freshly groomed and decked out in a gray suit, beige shirt, and polka-dot tie, Nelson looked not merely presentable but downright distinguished. In a photographic portrait taken at the time of his trial, he sits with his chin up, his expression calm and thoughtful, looking less like America's most notorious killer than a business executive posing for the frontispiece of his company's annual report.

As the jury selection got underway, Nelson appeared to take a keen interest in matters. But it wasn't long before he was stifling yawns. For the rest of the day—and indeed, for most of the trial—he seemed thoroughly disengaged, staring off into space when he wasn't shutting his eyes, tilting his head back against the marble wall behind him, and dozing off. He stirred to life only once on Tuesday, barking out a laugh when one of the spectators dropped a jar of peanut butter she had smuggled in for lunch and its contents spattered the legs of her neighbors.

And in truth—though the trial would dominate the news and keep the public transfixed for the remainder of the week—it offered very little in the way of drama or suspense. The flat, almost perfunctory, tone of the proceedings was set by the opening statement of prosecutor R. B. Graham, delivered on Wednesday, November 2, following the full empanelment of the jury. The courtroom was absolutely silent as Graham addressed the twelve jurymen: seven farmers, a machinist, a steel worker, a warehouse superintendent, a fireman, and a chauffeur.

Speaking in a brisk, businesslike voice—as though to suggest that the facts were so clear he could dispense with eloquence—Graham laid out a plain, step-by-step chronology of Nelson's movements from the time he arrived in Winnipeg until his recapture in Killarney.

After a brief examination of Lewis B. Foote—the professional photographer who had taken pictures of Emily Patterson's body—Graham began to build his case with painstaking care. Over the next day and a half, he called nearly forty witnesses to the stand, beginning with William Chandler and John T. Hanna, the motorists who had driven Nelson from the United States to Winnipeg, and finishing up with Detective Sergeant James H. Hoskins, who had been on board the special train dispatched to Killarney following the "Gorilla Man"'s escape. The obvious intention of the prosecutor, as one commentator noted, was to present a straightforward "statement of facts, each one a link which, when connected one with the other, would furnish a chain so finished and complete as to render [Nelson's] guilt unassailable."

The nearest thing to drama during this part of the trial occurred on Wednesday afternoon when William Patterson took the stand. As the entire roomful of spectators strained forward to catch every word, Patterson repeated the same wrenching tale he had related at the inquest in June. In a choked, barely audible voice, he described the devastating moment when, moments after begging God for the strength and guidance to find his missing wife, he found her violated corpse shoved beneath the bed he was praying beside.

When Graham asked him to identify a photograph of his murdered wife, Patterson nearly broke down. The poor man's suffering was so painful to see that several female spectators broke into sobs, and when Patterson was finally excused from the stand, the audience let out a collective sigh of relief.

In his cross-examination of the witnesses, Nelson's defense counsel, James Stitt, did his best to raise doubts about their testimony. He tried to discredit Sam Waldman by suggesting that the clothier, who had already applied for his share of the reward money, had a vested interest in seeing Nelson convicted. He brought out inconsistencies between the testimony of various witnesses. (Catherine Hill, for example, insisted that Nelson had arrived at her rooming house shortly before 5:00 P.M., wearing a shabby blue coat, baggy brown trousers, and floppy gray cap—clothes that the secondhand dealer Jake Garber testified he had sold to Nelson at 5:30 P.M.) But Stitt, who had absolutely no evidence to offer in rebuttal, was obviously grasping at straws.

By Thursday afternoon, the prosecution rested what was clearly an impregnable case.

46

Q. "Now then, Mrs. Fuller, doesn't it just come down to this: he was jealous, and he was eccentric?"

A. "He was what?"

Q. "Eccentric—odd."

A. "He was absolutely insane."

From the cross-examination of Mary Fuller

Since the verdict appeared to be a foregone conclusion, the most suspenseful issue at the trial had to do with the defense strategy. From the start of the proceedings, observers had been wondering if the "Gorilla" would be put on the stand.

As soon as the defense opened its case, however, it became clear that attorney Stitt had no intention of having Nelson testify. Beyond a stubborn assertion of innocence, Nelson simply had nothing to offer in the way of an alibi. Stitt's only recourse, therefore, was an insanity plea, and this tactic provided some of the most dramatic moments of the trial.

Everyone in the courtroom, with a single exception, was riveted by the sight of the witness who made her way up to the stand on Thursday morning, November 3—a small, white-haired old woman wearing a black dress with white-lace cuffs and collar. Though Nelson hadn't laid eyes on his wife for over a year, he was the only person there who seemed utterly indifferent to her presence. Throughout her emotional testimony, he yawned, dozed, or let out an occasional, low-throated chuckle—vivid proof of the bizarre affect and behavior Mary Fuller had come to bear witness to.

Stitt lost no time in showing that Nelson had already been deemed insane by experts. "I believe," he began, "that you once gave evidence in court concerning a matter in which your husband was involved?"

In a hushed, tremulous voice, Mary confirmed that she had indeed been a witness once before, in May 1921, when her husband—under his birth name, Earle Ferral—had been arrested for attacking a young girl in San Francisco and was subsequently committed to Napa State Hospital.

"What is the hospital used for?" asked Stitt.

"For mental cases," Mary replied. "It is the state hospital for the insane."

When Stitt inquired if Mary had seen her husband following his arrest, she told of visiting him at the Detention Hospital in San Francisco, where she found him strapped into a straitjacket and babbling "about seeing faces on the wall." At a later point in her testimony, she recounted her visits to Napa and described the other patients on Earle's ward: the young man who had cut out his tongue because "he imagined that his father and mother despised him," the former attorney who delivered strange impassioned speeches, as though he were addressing a jury.

Having established the defendant's long history as a mental patient—and offered both his commitment papers and psychiatric records as evidence—Stitt proceeded to ask Mary about her day-to-day life with Nelson.

"Well," she sighed, "he always seemed to me to be of a type having no moral responsibility whatever." Then, guided by Stitt's queries, she offered example after example of the outlandish, bewildering, and occasionally terrifying behavior her husband had displayed from the earliest days of their marriage.

She began by giving instances of his "insane jealousy"— the times he would accuse her of making eyes at everyone from passing pedestrians to streetcar conductors, or berate her for caring more about her female friends than she did for him. She described her fury at him when he destroyed her prized photograph of the British politician John Dillon and her utter mortification when, during her stay at St. Mary's Hospital, he loudly accused her of flirting with her doctor. And she repeated her brother's assessment of Nelson: "That man is crazy!"

She recounted other humiliations she had suffered at Earle's hands: the time they had gone househunting in Oakland and Earle had offered the real-estate agent a two-dollar down payment; the occasion when he had shown up at Miss Harker's school at midday, wearing a tux, a pleated dress shirt, and a safety pin instead of a tie; his appalling manners at restaurants, where, after drenching his food in olive oil, he would stick his face in the plate and slurp up his dinner, much to the disgust of the other customers.

And then there were his other weird and disturbing tendencies: his taste for "freakish clothes"; his "childlike" behavior; his bizarre bathing method (which consisted of pouring a glass of water over his toes); his periodic and protracted disappearances; his religious delusions; his morose, even suicidal moods; his devastating headaches; his vicious threats and violent outbursts.

Mary remained on the stand for over an hour. When Stitt concluded his questioning at around 3:00 P.M., Graham offered a cursory cross-examination, in which he tried to suggest that Nelson's erratic behavior amounted to little more than "eccentricity."

But Mary was adamant. "He was absolutely insane."

Fifteen minutes later, she climbed down from the stand and returned to her seat. She had managed to paint a vivid picture of a seriously unbalanced personality. But as Stitt well knew, her looks were just as telling as her words. That the sturdy young man seated in the prisoner's dock had chosen such a grizzled wife was, perhaps even more than anything Mary had said, eloquent testimony to his aberrant mind.

Following Mary Fuller's testimony, court was recessed for the day. When the trial resumed at ten the next morning, Friday, November 4, the defense called its second—and final—witness: Nelson's unfailingly loyal aunt, Lillian Fabian.

Fighting back tears throughout much of her testimony, Lillian confirmed Mary's account of Earle's bizarre fashion sense, table manners, and work habits. She also supplied additional details, largely about her nephew's childhood.

Earle had been a "morbidlike" little boy, she declared, who "never cared to play with other children" and whose behavior grew even more disturbed after he injured his head in a bike accident. She described Earle's disconcerting effect on her friends, who were so unsettled by the young boy's behavior that, after a while, they found excuses to avoid the Nelson home.

"He had a habit with all my friends," Lillian recalled. "He would sit there and he would never speak to them. He would sit looking up at the wall with his eyes turned up, just like he was looking in space all the time, and he wouldn't speak to my friends and say good day or hello or anything, which used to cause me to feel humiliated a great deal." And then there were the times when "without anybody asking him, he would get up and walk on his hands and pick very big chairs up with his teeth. He would pick them up and hold them up straight in his teeth."

As Earle grew into manhood, his "crazy disposition" became even more extreme. There was something endearingly childlike about some of his habits: his fondness for outlandish clothes and "dinky trinkets," his pleasure in playing hide-and-seek and ring-a-levio with her own little ones, his bursts of boyish enthusiasm (like his offer to build a three-story apartment building for his Uncle Willis—"with plumbing and everything"—all by himself). But his darker tendencies—his morbid moodiness, religious ramblings, sullen withdrawals, and outbursts of profanity—became increasingly dismaying even to the ever-devoted Lillian, particularly after Earle's first confinement to Napa.

In one of her most extended bits of testimony, Lillian described her relationship with Earle following his discharge from Napa in 1919. "He was with me a great deal off and on, a great deal for days at a time, and he was painting the interior of our home. We thought it would be good work for him to do to keep his mind off his condition and keep him around us. And he would paint quite hard for a few days, and all of a sudden he would walk out of the house and be away for three weeks at a time. And he would walk in on me, and we would say, 'Where have you been?' And he would say, 'Well, I have been looking for work.' I thought it was foolish. And he would then start right in, and he would smile about it, as if nothing had happened at all, and I understood how he was and kept quiet, because I wouldn't say anything to aggravate him, as I always lived in constant fear of him. And I was always careful, as I had two children and would have him sleep away from home. I would give him money to sleep in the hotels, and he would come the next day. But I was always in fear of him, on account of him being in the hospital, in Napa State Asylum for the Insane."

By the time Lillian was dismissed at around 11:00 A.M., she was unable to contain her emotions. "He is my own flesh and blood, and I love him," she sobbed as she stepped from the witness box. "I have known him all the days of his life, and I will continue to love him."

So geniune and moving was this outburst that it provoked sympathetic tears in more than one female spectator. Meanwhile, the object of Lillian's affection reclined in his chair—arms folded, head tilted back, snoozing peacefully.

47

✝

Q. "A person is killed—that is killed by strangulation or by a blow by a knife. That is murder; that is criminal. But when you add to that murder an anti-social repulsive act of such enormity as we have evidence of in this case, what would you say?"

A. "I say I would be willing to believe, if no more evidence than you have given, that that kind of conduct was the act of a mind that was certainly not an average mind."

Q. "It is way below the normal mind, isn't it?"

A. "Well, it is different."

From the testimony of Dr. Alvin Mathers

Mrs. Fabian was followed to the stand by the prosecution's main rebuttal witness, Dr. Alvin T. Mathers, head of the psychopathic ward of the Winnipeg General Hospital.

Though Mathers had a mild, almost self-effacing manner, he was a person of formidable energy and determination. As a young man, he had planned to pursue a career in internal medicine. In 1918, however, when Mathers was thirty and already regarded as one of the foremost physicians in western Canada, he agreed to take charge of the Psychopathic Hospital and spearhead the modernization of mental health services in Manitoba.

After an intensive course of psychiatric study at Harvard, Johns Hopkins, and the University of Michigan, he returned to Winnipeg and took up the post of Provincial Psychiatrist. Besides his private practice (the only one of its kind in Manitoba), he helped effect a number of sweeping changes, from the passage of a pioneering Mental Diseases Act to the improvement of psychiatric facilities in hospitals throughout the province. He also provided psychological evaluations of criminals, offering his services, gratis, to both the defense and prosecution.

At the time of Nelson's trial, Dr. Mathers was thirty-nine—a soft-spoken, scholarly, distinguished-looking man who radiated an air of quiet authority and was viewed as the most gifted medicolegal expert in western Canada. His opinion carried so much weight that, when he took the stand on Friday, Crown Prosecutor Graham felt the need to solicit only a single assertion from him.

After establishing that Mathers had examined Nelson five times between July 27 and October 24, Graham simply asked, "And what was the result of your examinations?"

"I did not find any evidence that to me would constitute insanity," Mathers declared.

"No further questions, my Lord," said Graham, reseating himself at the prosecution table.

Since lunchtime was approaching, James Stitt, who clearly intended to keep Mathers on the stand for a while, asked permission to put off his cross-examination until the afternoon session. Judge Dysart granted the request. At 2:00 P.M., following the recess, Mathers was back in the witness box, this time facing an interrogator with a reputation for tenacity that matched his own.

For more than an hour, Stitt hammered away at the witness. But Mathers was unflappable, calmly insisting that, though Nelson's actions were certainly symptomatic of a disordered personality, they did not add up to insanity.

"And what *is* the supreme test of insanity?" asked Stitt.

"The supreme test of insanity is the social test," Mathers explained. "The ability or not of a person to live in conformity with the rules and regulations of life. We ordinarily consider insanity as an entirely social concept. It is not a disease."

"Is disordered conduct a sign of insanity?" Stitt asked.

"Well, not any disorder of conduct."

"Well now," said Stitt, folding his arms, "such conduct as this: if an individual was rather inclined to be melancholy, and would sit in a chair and look for hours at the wall, and not speak to people coming in or people going out, and stay in that staring condition, what would you say?"

Mathers lifted his eyebrows. "I would want a lot more information than that before I would say he was insane."

Stitt's tone grew more challenging. "And if he would do *these* things: if he was inclined to disappear without any notice to his relatives and reappear and make no explanation; if he lacked, for instance, a sense of the social fitness of things; if he would eat gluttonously in company; if he would mix up his food and pour lavish amounts of olive oil on it; if he would, for instance, appear at a public school in the afternoon in a full dress suit without any collar on, or without any tie, and with just an ordinary steel pin in his collar; if he was a man who was insanely jealous of his wife to the point that it aroused his anger when she paid her fare to a streetcar conductor; if this individual had never held a job for any considerable time; if he was filthy and dirty in his habits; and if all this followed after concussion of the brain, and a sufficient concussion at ten or eleven years of age to render him unconscious for four or five days with the frequent reoccurrence of tremendous headaches, what would you say? And also with a very decided nomadic tendency and extremely melancholic episodes, sometimes punctuated with what you might call exalted moods and sickly piety?"

Mathers took a moment to absorb this lengthy hypothetical question before responding. "I don't think anybody could say as to that particular man just what the influence of that accident or that concussion was," he said in the same mild tone that had characterized his entire testimony. "Symptoms such as you have mentioned, or at least modes of life such as you have mentioned might readily occur, and do occur in people who have no concussion whatever.

"As to the number of different episodes that you have mentioned," he continued, "not any of those would to my mind constitute or make me willing to declare that such a person was insane. I think I know people who have done every one of those things and who would be horribly incensed, and their families and everybody else would be highly incensed, if they were considered insane. They are willing enough to have them considered perhaps a little queer and eccentric—unstable. But as to having them declared insane, which carries with it the presumption that their liberty must be curtailed, I doubt very much if that could be done."

The remainder of Stitt's cross-examination proceeded in much the same way, with Mathers maintaining that—in spite of Nelson's "viciously anti-social conduct," his extreme "sexual abnormalities," and his weird beliefs (including his conviction that the guards at the Provincial Jail had been using some sort of sinister "electrical device" on him)—there was no justification for regarding him as legally insane.

"But, Doctor," Stitt protested, waving Nelson's medical records from Napa. "As he has been previously found to be a constitutional psychopath with psychosis, you would agree, wouldn't you?"

Mathers shook his head. "I agree with the first part, not the second."

"Not with psychosis?"

"Not with psychosis," Mathers confirmed. As for the phrase "constitutional psychopath," Mathers explained that it was a vague and ill-defined catchall, used to describe "a person who does not lack in intelligence but whose willpower is defective and who is likely to act very often, in fact most often, with his own ends in view, with not a great deal of regard for other people." Such individuals were "likely to have unstable feelings" but could not be considered insane.

"But you admit that this man is not normal," Stitt persisted.

"What do you mean by normal?"

"Well, you agree that he is a constitutional psychopath."

Mathers shrugged. "Yes—and there are thousands of them walking around the streets of Winnipeg today."

48

†

My learned friend made a stirring appeal for the tempering
of justice with mercy, but that is far outside your
province. . . . Mercy is no part of a jury's deliberations.

R. C. Graham

Except for the sobs of Lillian Fabian, who had wept
throughout much of Mathers' testimony, there was absolute
silence in the overpacked courtroom as the psychiatrist
stepped from the witness stand. Moments later, James Stitt
rose from the defense table and approached the jury box to
deliver his final summation.

His speech lasted just twenty-five minutes. Looking earnestly from one juror to the next, he began by reminding
them of their obligation—as the upholders of "British justice"—to rid their minds of prejudice and render a verdict
purely on the basis of the evidence.

"What *is* the evidence?" he asked, raising his hands for a
moment, then letting them drop to his sides. "It is entirely
circumstantial. Circumstantial evidence may look strong. But
remember this—that any chain of evidence is no stronger
than its weakest link."

Stitt then proceeded to discuss the ostensible "weak links"
in the evidentiary chain. But his argument only underscored
the weakness of the defense, since he could come up with
little more than Sam Waldman's poor eyesight and a minor
discrepancy between Jake Garber's and Mrs. Hill's sense
of chronology.

As if to acknowledge the flimsiness of this approach, Stitt quickly switched to another tack. In a voice charged with emotion, he beseeched the jury not to condemn a man who was so clearly insane.

"Can you say, after looking at the evidence, that the accused has any moral responsibility whatsoever?" he entreated. "Does he know the difference between right and wrong? The man's whole life has been a life of aberration, the life of a man whose mind is disordered.

"Gentlemen," he said, with an incredulous shake of his head. "It is rather extraordinary that you have to determine upon the guilt or otherwise of a man who has escaped from a lunatic asylum. The evidence is that the man has escaped. It is all there in the documentary evidence! It was agreed to by the Crown. He has been in an asylum twice, and he has escaped several times. There is no doubt that this man has a mind diseased and that he was irresponsible."

As Stitt continued, he seemed to concede that, based on the evidence, Nelson was undoubtedly the perpetrator. But the very nature of the crime—brutal strangulation followed by postmortem rape—was flagrant proof of insanity. "If you find him guilty, you *must* find that he is a maniac," he exclaimed. "It could not be done by a man with an ordered mind. It is absolutely impossible."

He paused, as though to bring his emotions in check. When he resumed again, his voice was tinged with sorrow.

"Gentlemen," he said softly. "Some of you have sons. Some of you have little boys around the farm or around the home. If your little boy was struck by a streetcar and suffered concussion of the brain and grew up in your home abnormal, unfit, without any responsibility whatsoever, what kind of justice would you expect to be meted out to your son?"

Bringing his summation to a close, Stitt made a heartfelt appeal to the jurors' sense of Christian mercy and national pride, striking the first notes of genuine eloquence that had been heard at the trial.

"I do not know the justice that can be rendered without the element of mercy," he proclaimed. "There is no man or woman under heaven who does not need to pray for mercy. What was the whole spirit of our civilization in the war that we have just gone through? It was against the ruthless exercise of power. It was to show that there was something in life besides power. That there was a spiritual element and that man does not live by bread alone but by the finer things of thought and being.

"I trust it shall never be said that in this case a Canadian jury found a lunatic responsible and sent him to doom without a full consideration of that fact. It would be a terrible thing to tell the people of the United States of America that, because of publicity and vengeance, we held a lunatic responsible and placed him on the gallows. As I speak, I have visions of people with disordered minds. Some of them pluck my gown, and they say, 'Mercy!' Others howl in their maniacal way. Others can say nothing. They have only got staring eyes."

Stitt paused for an instant before offering a final, humble appeal that was meant to convey the awesome responsibility that rested on all their shoulders, his own no less than the jury's.

"I may not be sufficient advocate for this man," he said. "I may not have demonstrated to you in the way the case should have been demonstrated. It may not have been brought home to you in the way it should have been done. But I have tried to do my duty. I have tried to handle the case as a member of an honorable profession.

"I want you to remember that principle of everlasting mercy in our law. If I am not a sufficiently great advocate to put this before you, then I ask you to remember the words of the greatest of all advocates, uttered nearly two thousand years ago: 'Father, forgive them, for they know not what they do.' "

Nelson, who had looked supremely bored throughout his attorney's oration, perked up a bit at Stitt's closing words. He straightened up in his seat and nodded vigorously, as though in emphatic agreement with the implied comparison between himself and the crucified Christ.

As soon as Stitt returned to the defense table, his opponent rose and strode towards the jury box. Though Graham began with a disclaimer—insisting that his speech would be devoid of eloquence—his thirty-minute summation was every bit as forceful as Stitt's.

"It is not the part of the Crown counsel to be too strong an advocate," he began, addressing the jury in a measured, solemn voice. "It is not the part of the Crown counsel to indulge in oratory or flights of beautiful language in order to influence your verdict. It is the part of the Crown counsel to put before you cold-bloodedly, carefully, and scrupulously the evidence placed before you, for and against the accused."

He paused for an instant, gesturing towards the defense table. "My learned friend, Mr. Stitt, in opening his magnificent address, used those words, 'The chain of circumstantial evidence is no stronger than its weakest link.'" Here, Graham rested a hand on the railing and swept his gaze around the jury box. "I must ask you to wipe that part out of your minds. Circumstantial evidence is not a chain. It is a *rope,* not as strong as its weakest strand only, but having the strength of all its strands combined.

"I outlined to you in my opening address the story of this crime," he continued, "and all the movements of the accused from two days before the crime to the moment of his arrest. That leaves little to say to you, except to point out how clearly, how *thoroughly,* the evidence given here in the last three days is borne out and amplified by the story, weaving it all together.

"That has been done in such a way," he declared, "that every strand has been spun and bound and twisted with its fellow strands into a cord that is almost perfect."

Graham had only spoken for a few minutes, but he had already performed a clever rhetorical feat. By shifting metaphors—from a chain to a rope—he had evoked an image not only of the ligatures Nelson had used on his victims but of the punishment that justice demanded.

Graham had no trouble showing that the "weak links" Stitt had cited were trivialities, "little discrepancies" that did nothing to undermine the enormous mountain of evidence against the accused. He reminded the jurors, first, that there was direct evidence linking Nelson to the crime: William Haberman's sworn testimony that he had seen Nelson lurking around the Patterson home on the day of the murder.

Beyond that, the evidence against Nelson was admittedly

circumstantial. But such evidence, Graham insisted, "must be carefully considered. When it leads to your irresistible belief that the accused is guilty, it must be followed, because circumstances very often speak more plainly than words."

In this case, as he proceeded to demonstrate, the circumstantial evidence offered irrefutable proof that "the accused, within an hour or more of the commission of the crime, was in possession of shoes and personal articles" taken from the Patterson home. "Are you to be asked to assume," he said, allowing a note of sarcasm to enter his voice, "that he merely stole the articles, and somebody else killed Mrs. Patterson?"

As for the issue of Nelson's sanity, Graham was insistent that the defense had merely provided "evidence of eccentricity and evidence of insane jealousy. Nothing more. Unless you can say with a clear conscience that the evidence shows that this man has crossed the borderland to the region where the mind does not function, you cannot find him insane."

Responding point-by-point to Stitt's summation, Graham brought his own speech to a close by addressing the issue of mercy. "My learned friend made a stirring appeal for the tempering of justice with mercy," Stitt said gravely. "But that is far outside your province. You have no power to consider mercy. To find a verdict of guilty or not guilty according to the evidence, that is all you have to do. Mercy is no part of a jury's deliberation. Mercy is for the executive power.

"That," he concluded, "is a serious and cruel task to fall upon the shoulders of twelve men whose hearts are kind. But it is a duty that they must perform without fear, without favor, without affection, without thought of what the other person may possibly lose."

When Graham walked slowly back to the prosecution table, it was already after 4:00 P.M., too late for Judge Dysart to deliver his charge. After commending all the participants in the trial, including the counsel, for their citizenship, Dysart adjourned court until the following morning, Saturday, November 5, assuring the jurors that their wearying task was nearly at an end.

"In the morning," he said, "I will give you the facts as briefly as I can, as I see them; and I will state the law to you. I will not be very long."

By eleven o'clock the next morning, according to the judge's estimate, the fate of Earle Leonard Nelson would be in the jury's hands.

49

✝

Woe unto the wicked! it shall be ill with him:
for the reward of his hands shall be given him.

Isaiah 3:11

As crowded as it had been since the start of the trial, the courtroom was even more packed on Saturday morning, November 5. By one estimate, nearly 300 people had somehow managed to squeeze inside the room. Hundreds more milled in the corridors, while a buzzing mob, numbering at least 1,000, jammed the streets around the building.

Two regular members of the audience, however, were conspicuously absent when the trial reconvened at 10:00 A.M., Lillian Fabian and Mary Fuller. Knowing full well what the outcome would be, they could not bring themselves to attend. They passed an agonized morning locked in their hotel room, offering each other whatever comfort they could.

In spite of his promise to keep his charge brief, Judge Andrew Dysart spoke for over an hour. The papers would tout his summing up as a model of impartiality. Some observers, however, formed a different opinion.

Dysart began with a step-by-step recap of the evidence, placing particular emphasis on the articles removed from the Patterson house—the old whipcord suit, the victim's gold wedding ring, the $70 in $10 bills—that had later turned up in Nelson's possession.

"Now, if those things were believed," Dysart summed up, "the accused is the man who was there, and being there, in the absence of all other evidence, the woman being found dead after his departure, the only reasonable inference is that he is the man who murdered her."

Having made it clear that the defendant's guilt could hardly be doubted, the judge proceeded to address the question of sanity. It was here, according to at least one commentator, that Dysart's remarks "bore most heavily to the side of the prosecution."

After reviewing the facts supplied by Nelson's wife and aunt—their detailed history of Nelson's erratic behavior—Dysart saw fit to inform the jury that the two women were obviously biased in favor of the accused. They "came here, I have no doubt, with fidelity, loyalty, to help out one who was near them." Their testimony "must therefore be viewed as the evidence of persons who are very, very closely associated with him and who are fond of him, and it must be weighed in that light. It is not scientific evidence."

Furthermore, while there was documented proof that Nelson had been confined to an insane asylum, the crucial fact—according to Dysart—was that he had been discharged in 1925. "He returned to the wife and aunt, or to one of them—I have forgotten which—about a year ago. They did not have him recommitted. A man may be insane for a period at some time in his life and get over it. I think the evidence would warrant you in coming to that conclusion. So that the real point is whether or not on the tenth of June, the accused—if he is the man who killed Emily Patterson—that he understood that by strangling her, he was committing an act that would cause her death, that he knew the nature and quality of the act, and that he knew that his act was wrong."

As he brought his charge to a close, Dysart homed in on the issue that makes insanity such a difficult defense. A strictly legal concept, "insanity" is commonly defined as an inability to distinguish right from wrong. In a case like Nelson's—where there is overwhelming evidence of concealment, of a calculated effort to cover his tracks—it is hard to persuade a jury that the defendant didn't know he had committed a crime.

"In coming to your conclusion on this question of insanity," Dysart said, "keep in mind what I have mentioned about his change of clothing after the murder, his movements, his change of name, and all these things. And if you find that these things indicate a sense of guilt, then from that finding you may infer that he knew the act was wrong, or he would not attempt to escape the consequences of it. Read those acts, and try to discover from them whether they are the acts of an insane, irresponsible man—irresponsible in the eyes of the law—or the acts of a man who realized that he had done some wrong and was trying to elude pursuit and capture."

At precisely 11:16 A.M. the judge completed his charge, and the jury filed into the deliberation room. They emerged less than forty minutes later. It required just one glance at their taut, ashen faces to know what decision they had reached.

"Gentlemen," asked the clerk, "have you agreed upon your verdict? If so, who speaks for you?"

When the foreman, William Wiedman, rose and announced the anticipated verdict—"Guilty, my Lord"—a murmer of excitement rippled through the courtroom, and there was a smattering of applause.

"Oyez! Oyez! Oyez!" cried he clerk. "All manner of persons are strictly required to keep silence on pain of imprisonment while the sentence of death is passed on the prisoner."

At Dysart's order, Nelson rose. He stood erect, hands clasped lightly behind his back, feet slightly parted. He wore his usual expression of utter indifference.

"Prisoner," intoned the judge, "have you anything to say why the sentence of the Court should not be passed upon you?"

"Only by reason that I am not guilty," Nelson said casually.

"Nothing further? You have nothing further to say?"

Nelson gave a little shrug. "Not that I know of."

With that, Judge Dysart pronounced his sentence: Nelson would be taken from his "place of confinement to the place of execution" and hanged on the second Friday of January 1928—Friday the thirteenth.

It was a Winnipeg social worker named Lucille Davies who broke the news to Lillian and Mary in their hotel room. Though the two women had expected nothing less, the finality of the verdict hit them like a physical blow. As Mrs. Davies looked on, blinking back tears, Nelson's aged wife and youthful aunt fell into each other's arms and abandoned themselves to their grief.

Later that evening, they received permission to visit Nelson in his cell. It was an emotional meeting—at least for Lillian and Mary. They wept over Earle, stroked his hands, called him their "poor, unfortunate boy." They were still tearfully professing their faith in his innocence when their allotted time ran out, and—with a final embrace—they bid goodbye to him forever.

Earle was as unmoved by their departure as he had been by their visit. Indeed, he seemed blithely unconcerned with everything but his food. Now that he had only two months to live, he told his guards, he fully expected a more varied menu. And he was already worried about the upcoming holiday.

Thanksgiving, he reminded his captors, was less than three weeks away. As an American citizen, he felt entitled to a turkey dinner—complete with all the trimmings.

50

AUDIENCE OF MONKEYS
IGNORES APE IN MOVIE

Pittsburgh Scientists Find Simians
in Zoo Don't React to Picture,
"The Gorilla"
New York Times, November 23, 1927

On Thursday, November 17, 1927, exactly one week before Thanksgiving—the silent-movie version of Ralph Spence's hit play *The Gorilla* opened at the Mark Strand Theatre in Manhattan. Directed by Alfred Santell, the film was praised by the *New York Times* as a delightful combination of humor and thrills—"very much as if Mack Sennett . . . had turned to Edgar Allan Poe's 'The Murders in the Rue Morgue' and decided to adapt it to the screen in his inimitable manner." In spite of its occasional descent into "crude horseplay and silly stunts," wrote the reviewer, this cinematic version of *The Gorilla* offered moments of genuine suspense, along with some "excruciatingly funny bits that evoked roars and shrieks of laughter in the audience."

To drum up publicity for the movie, exhibitors concocted a stunt whose outright silliness was thoroughly in keeping with the nonsensical tone of Spence's farce. Special performances were arranged at the monkey houses of several big-city zoos, and well-known scientists were invited to observe the reactions of the simian spectators. As scientific experiments, these screenings were of dubious value, to say the least. But they were a smashing success from a p.r. point of view, eagerly attended by various eminent zoologists and prominently reported in papers throughout the United States, including the *New York Times.*

In Pittsburgh, where *The Gorilla* was shown at the Darwinian Hall of the Highland Zoo, a cageful of South American ring-tailed monkeys let out a howl when the film began to roll, then quickly settled down and returned to their normal routine. "Scientists, keepers at the zoo, and officials of the film company," wrote the *Times,* "admitted that, in so far as the monkey audience was concerned, the show was a 'flop.'"

The primate reaction was slightly more positive in New York City, where *The Gorilla* had its official premiere at the monkey house of the Central Park Zoo. Among the scientific luminaries in attendance were Dr. Raymond Ditmars, curator of the Bronx Zoo, and Dr. J. H. McGregor, head of the Zoology Department at Columbia University. Both men were particularly intrigued by the reactions of a chimpanzee named Bessie, who "raised a racket" whenever the projectionist stopped to change reels, then fell into a rapt silence as soon as the film started up again.

As to the exact significance of this response, there was a difference of scholarly opinion. Dr. Ditmars, according to the *Times,* believed that Bessie's behavior "indicated a real curiosity about the figures on the screen." Dr. McGregor, on the other hand, "was not prepared to say whether [the chimp's] attention was held by figures recognized as human or merely by the changing lights and shadows on the screen." Both experts agreed, however, that—at least in one respect—the monkeys "were superior as an audience to some spectators in the movie houses."

They didn't read the title cards out loud.

Meanwhile, locked in his own cage up in Winnipeg, the real-life "Gorilla" continued to generate news. On November 18, the *Winnipeg Tribune* ran a page-one story headlined EARLE NELSON TALKS FROM PRISON DEATH CELL. After six months of steadfast silence on his case, the convicted "Strangler" had finally decided to go public with his own version of events.

Interviewed in his cell, Nelson looked even pudgier than he had at his trial—no surprise, given his torpid existence and caloric intake. The warden of the provincial jail had acceded to Nelson's request for more varied and plenteous meals. At the start of the interview, a guard arrived with a typical lunch—ham, tomatoes, French-fried potatoes, cheese, bread, and coffee—which Nelson wolfed down with his usual, noisy voracity.

Besides eating, his main activity seemed to consist of lounging on his cot and knotting strands of silk floss into miniature pouches—"quaint little knick-knacks," wrote the reporter, "that might well grace a lady's dressing table." Nelson proudly showed off a dozen of these trifles to his visitor, explaining that each of them required more than 10,000 knots. The reporter did his best to picture the "Gorilla" at this "fancy work"—the blunt, powerful fingers busily weaving delicate filaments into dainty little gewgaws. But he simply couldn't envision it; the whole concept seemed almost dizzyingly incongruous.

Noisily sucking the last shreds of ham from his teeth, Nelson leaned back on his cot and laced his hands behind his head. "Go ahead and ask me what you want to."

Prompted by a question about his travels in the months preceding the Winnipeg murders, Nelson launched into a long, disjointed speech that alternated between hazy, highly selective recollections and bitter tirades against the authorities who had ostensibly framed him. According to his story, he had set out from San Francisco, where he'd been working as a carpenter, in March 1927.

"I left in one of those kind of spells I had, sort of a dream, not knowing where I was going. I got to Sacramento, from there to different towns, reached Truckee, California. From there I went to Nevada, then to Idaho, then to Wyoming—quite a ways I wandered into Wyoming. Then to Montana, into Butte and Helena. And I was at Great Falls, I think."

He paused, so that the reporter, who was writing furiously in his notepad, could get down every word. "Go on," said the latter after a moment.

"Let me see," said Nelson, tugging on his lower lip. "I

went through South Dakota, over east as far as Sioux Falls, and up to Bismarck. Then I came up past Bismarck through a lot of small places much west of here."

"Were you ever in the state of Illinois?" asked the reporter.

Nelson shook his head emphatically. "No. I have been in just seven states—California, Nevada, Idaho, Montana, Wyoming, South Dakota, and North Dakota." He thought for a moment, then added, "Oh yes—I have been in Salt Lake, Utah."

"That makes eight," said the reporter.

"Eight, that's right."

"And when did you reach Winnipeg?"

Nelson, who had been perched on his cot with his back against the wall, suddenly leaned forward and jabbed a finger at his visitor. "I never was here at all!" he exclaimed. "I admit that I am subject to spells of lunacy in which I function the same as in a dream and sometimes find myself in strange places. But I never hurt *anyone* in these spells. And I was certainly not even *near* Winnipeg before the police brought me up here. That's all there is to that."

"I see," said the reporter as he rapidly transcribed Nelson's remarks. "But what about the witnesses?"

Nelson snorted. "The Crown's witnesses are mistaken, wrong, and prejudiced," he declared. "It seems to me, they have been pretty well-coached in their parts. An investigation would reveal this. Their testimonies made me look unfavorable, and the jury was probably swayed by some force—some influence unfair but strong. They were so prejudiced that they could give me no benefit of the doubt. If they would have brought in insanity, just for doubt's sake, there would have been no blood on their hands."

Suddenly agitated, he sprang to his feet and began pacing in front of the reporter. "My innocent blood is on the hands of those who have done me up or who were instrumental in the identification parade!"

"What do you mean by that?" asked his interviewer.

"Whenever I was called out for identification, they dressed me up in clothes similar to those found in the secondhand clothes store, like those that belonged to the man who was supposed to have done the crime. And they made me comb my hair back, even though I generally wear it parted. That blond detective, Smith, was managing it. I dreamed one night that he was telling witnesses when bringing them in for identification, 'He's the fourth man or the sixth man in line. Pick him out.'"

"But why," asked the reporter, "would the police behave so unscrupulously?"

Nelson gave him an incredulous look. "Because by getting me done up quickly, they have a chance to make themselves look like the captors of a real desperado. *Me*—a proven subject to lunacy. What better material did they need to work on, being that they didn't have the real culprit?"

"These are serious charges," said the reporter.

"That's right," said Nelson in indignant tones. "And I demand an investigation of the whole case. I am a native American citizen and have been promised a square deal like a man gets in America. If I was treated square from the start, I never would have been arrested at all."

"What you are describing is not consistent with British justice," said the reporter, whose patriotic sensibilities had evidently been piqued by Nelson's imputations.

"Well, I'm glad of that," Nelson replied as he reseated himself on the edge of his cot. "Anyway, I have nothing against the country. But the police up here want to get a feather in their hat, see. Anything that Smith and his aides could do to make me look like the 'Gorilla Man,' it means a lot to them. I think they will go as far as they can."

"So you still hope to win a reprieve?"

"Of course!" Nelson exclaimed. "Why shouldn't I? I am innocent. Lots of people know it, too."

To support the latter assertion, Nelson dug under his mattress and extracted a fat bundle of letters tied together with string. "I get mail all the time," he explained, undoing the knot and flipping through the envelopes. "Mostly from women." Locating the envelope he was looking for, he passed it to the reporter.

Inside was a note from a woman named Martingale, asserting her faith in Nelson's innocence—a belief based not only on his "gentlemanly demeanor" but on well-known astrological principles. After all, wrote Mrs. Martingale, Nelson was born in May 1897, and "the zodiacal signs for May are conclusive that a man born in that month is incapable of murder."

"And what do you believe are your chances?" asked the reporter, handing the letter back to Nelson.

"I have some hope," Nelson allowed. "But I am not betting on it." Leaning forward, palms pressed together between his knees, he fixed the reporter with an earnest look. "Do you know what I would do if my sentence was commuted?"

The reporter raised his eyebrows inquiringly.

"I would devote the rest of my life," Nelson said with a little catch in his voice, "to an exhaustive study of religion."

51

✝

We see in the criminal a savage man and, at the same time,
a sick man.

Cesare Lombroso, *Criminal Man*

Nelson wasn't the only one incensed over his impending
execution. True, most people heartily endorsed his sentence.
The prevailing attitude was summed up by one Winnipegger
who, interviewed outside the courthouse shortly before the
trial ended, declared that Nelson should be put to death
"whether sane or insane. Why all the fuss? Why don't they
just get through and hang him?"

Not everyone, however, shared that feeling. In the weeks
following the trial, some highly articulate people spoke out
against the verdict. To these dissenters, it was a matter of
outrage and sorrow that, in a nation dedicated to the tradi-
tions of "British justice," a criminal so clearly deranged had
been condemned to the gallows.

In mid-November, for example, a man named Fred Robinson, an avid follower of the Nelson case, wrote a letter to
the *Free Press,* taking Judge Dysart to task for using the
phrase "moral imbecility" in his charge to the jury. "What
has imbecility got to do with insanity?" Robinson asked.
The first was a form of "feeblemindedness . . . a mental
deficiency caused by arrested mental development." By contrast, the latter was a "*disorder* of the mental faculties."

"There is quite a difference between a disordered mind

and a deficient mind," Robinson pointed out. Among other things, imbecility was a constant condition, whereas the symptoms of insanity were, in certain cases, intermittent or "cyclic."

That Nelson was capable of rational moments didn't mean that he was sane. "Does the fact that the accused knows right from wrong at the present moment, or at any previous time, prove conclusively that he is and always was sane?" Robinson wrote. "Is not cyclic insanity attended with similar lucid intervals as the accused may now have? The twelve good men and true had to bring in a verdict—but did they comprehend what insane or not insane meant?"

Like other observers, Robinson was forced to conclude that—if not exactly a travesty—Nelson's trial was hardly a shining example of "British justice." "While the evidence proving the identity and crimes committed by the accused may have been perfect," he allowed, "the plea of insanity, in my estimation, was not treated as seriously as it should have been, the enormity of the crimes and maybe public opinion taking first consideration."

Similar sentiments were voiced by an anonymous editorial writer for a Winnipeg weekly, who summed up his view of the Nelson affair in the title of his essay, "A Double Tragedy." Like Robinson, this writer recognized that "the evidence against Nelson was overwhelming. Seldom has such a web of circumstantial evidence been woven around a prisoner. Well might the jury say to Nelson as Nathan said to David: 'Thou art the man.'"

The question of sanity, however, was far more complicated. While acknowledging that "there were attempts to give this ogre a fair trial," the writer could only conclude that the verdict was largely determined by emotional factors: "fear as to what Nelson might do if he escaped from custody . . . profound horror at his frightful deeds . . . a primitive desire for revenge."

"Was it humanly possible for this general attitude to be kept out of the courthouse?" he asked. "Probably not. There is no reason why it should be. Administration of justice, like all other human institutions, is approximate and imperfect. It cannot possibly, in the long run, be better than the people themselves. Passion and prejudice penetrate the walls of a courthouse almost as easily as waves from a wireless station."

It was "passion and prejudice," suggested the writer, that accounted for the jury's decision. After all—in spite of Dr. Mathers' testimony—it seemed glaringly evident that no sane, no "morally responsible" man could have committed such atrocities.

"Consider what this man Nelson did," the writer exclaimed. "He comes to Canada on June 8 after, it is alleged, strangling two women in Detroit on June 1 and another in Chicago on June 3. If that is true, he must have come up to Winnipeg, a strange city in a strange country, like a flaming fiend. He arrives here on June 8, and on June 9 strangles an innocent and defenseless child and ravishes it.

"The following day, June 10, he starts off for Elmwood. It is June, the time of year when everything is suggestive of life, of new life. Longfellow has a line: 'A morning of June with all its music and sunshine.' On such a morning, Nelson goes to the humble home of a young couple, finds a young mother alone, a young mother who has done him no manner or shadow of wrong. He strangles her and outrages her.

"If this is the act, the procedure, of a sane man, of a man knowing right from wrong, accountable and responsible, then what must we think of those who hold up their hands in horror at the thought of being descended from monkeys?"

To be sure, it was hard to blame the jury for its decision, given the enormity of Nelson's crimes. The writer himself conceded that there was "an argument for doing away with beings like Nelson, even if insane." Still, he added dryly, "this is not yet a recognized procedure."

From the writer's point of view, the whole case was shaping up to be a "double tragedy." By executing Nelson, society was throwing away the chance to learn something invaluable. "It would seem highly desirable," he maintained, "that the last bit of knowledge to be derived from this fearful affair should be obtained. The whole history of Nelson should be studied as thoroughly as possible by the best alienists on the continent and every fact securable secured. How did this man come to be what he is today? What produced this monstrosity? Are the same causes at work and to what extent? Could anything have been changed or prevented?"

Such scientific study of the maniac's mind might prove to be of immeasurable social benefit. For, while "cases like Nelson's" were "happily rare" at the moment, there was reason to fear that they might become more common in the future.

Whoever this editorialist was, his words weren't heeded. And for a perfectly understandable reason: he was fifty years ahead of his time. His vision of a future filled with "cases like Nelson's" must have seemed impossibly grim in 1927. A systematic study of sociopathic killers wouldn't be undertaken until the late 1970s, when agents of the FBI's Behaviorial Science Unit would begin visiting prisons throughout the United States to interview the likes of Charles Manson, David Berkowitz, Ted Bundy, and John Wayne Gacy—the beings who would (as the unknown editorialist foresaw) follow in the "Gorilla Man's" wake.

Needless to say, the anonymous author of "A Double Tragedy" was not articulating a widely popular attitude. If anything, the average Winnipegger regarded the coming execution as a cause for celebration. But James Stitt, Nelson's attorney, certainly shared the editorialist's viewpoint.

Stitt (who would go on to have a distinguished legal and political career, winning election to the Dominion Parliament in 1930) was a man of notable integrity and compassion. Another lawyer, assigned to represent such a despised (and foredoomed) defendant, might have contented himself with a perfunctory job. But Stitt—who had grown convinced that Nelson was, in fact, the victim of a severe mental disorder—believed that the verdict was a tragic miscarriage of justice. From the moment the trial ended, he had focussed his energies on saving Nelson's life, applying himself to this task with an ardor that (in the view of many observers) the "Strangler" scarcely deserved.

No sooner had the verdict been returned than Stitt announced his intention to "make representations to the Justice Department at Ottawa for remission of the death sentence, based on the plea of insanity." Over the next few weeks, he collected a batch of affidavits from Nelson's relatives and acquaintances, all of them testifying to Earle's life-long peculiarities.

According to the deposition of Arthur Edward West, who grew up "two doors from the Nelson residence" and had known Earle for eighteen years, "I . . . was forbidden as a child to associate with him for reason that he was mentally deranged, was confined to a reform school and would boast to boys of the neighborhood how easy he could steal. He was branded by neighbors as 'crazy' and no good would ever come of him, which proves that he was and continues to be of unsound mind."

Nelson's Uncle Willis testified that his nephew "showed freakish tendencies as a small child. The U.S. Navy officers were the first to officially pronounce him insane. There is no doubt about his insanity. His father died of syphilis when he was about a year old. Blood tests made in Napa State Asylum showed this same condition [in Nelson]."

A friend of the Nelson family named George Miller—who had once let Earle "live in my home with my wife and two children for a period of three weeks"—declared that "I came to realize at that time, from his way of talking about large sums of money and building contracts in such a child-ish manner, that he must be of unsound mind. He was also a religious fanatic, always quoting the Bible in the course of his conversations. He is, in my mind, insane and does not realize right from wrong, though he was always playful and gentle with my two little kiddies."

Caroline Wellman, one of Mary Fuller's co-workers at Miss Harker's School for Girls, described the time that Nelson "entered the kitchen door without permission, chased his wife into the pantry and then into the school office, his eyes in a staring condition, looking wild and excited, without apparent reasons for his actions. It was necessary to call the police to make him leave the premises. On another occasion, I found him in the pantry, holding his wife and talking in an excited, unreasonable manner."

A brief but vivid portrait of Nelson's weird behavior was provided by Mrs. L. J. Casey, Jr., who had observed Nelson in the spring of 1926, when he had worked as Frank J. Arnold's groundskeeper. According to Mrs. Casey, "I told my friends I would not have that man around. He is surely crazy. I hear him laughing and talking to himself all the time. One day while I happened to be there, he sat right outside in the drenching rain, looking at the sky, without a coat, until he was soaked through. But my friends said 'he is only a simple fool, he likes it here and works hard,' so we let him stay."

Altogether, Stitt assembled affidavits from twenty individuals, all of whom swore that they were "in a position to know full well the character and mentality of the said Earle Nelson and that [they] verily believed without exaggeration or mental reservation that the said Earle Nelson has been for a long period of time a person of unsound mind and has been and is irresponsible for his conduct and that if he did commit the act of murder for which he has been convicted that such act was the act of an unfortunate man who did not know the difference between right and wrong and who was so far insane as not to know the nature and quality of his act."

At the end of December, Stitt forwarded these documents to the Minister of Justice, Ernest Lapointe, along with his own appeal for clemency—an eloquent, even moving, document that ran nearly thirty pages. Though the appeal was filed in strict accordance with the judicial calendar, the timing—just a few days after Christmas—couldn't have been more symbolic, since Stitt's plea was based, not only on a scrupulous review of the facts, but on the principles of Christian mercy.

"I desire to say," he began, "that I do not approach this issue from any sentimental basis, or from any desire to save the life of a client of mine merely because he happens to be my client, but I do feel that the taking of a human life is an act far better left to the Giver of All Life Himself, especially when the question of responsibility is in grave doubt as it must be in this case, for in the first instance the accused has been proven to have been at one time absolutely insane, and the only rebutting evidence offered by the Crown now is that he is not insane at present."

Stitt got right to the nub of his argument, pointing out that, in response to the overwhelming evidence of insanity, all the Crown had to offer was the opinion of a single alienist, Dr. Mathers, whose testimony was, at best, equivocal.

"May it not truly be said," Stitt wrote, "that the evidence of Mary Fuller is that the accused is insane; the evidence of Mrs. Fabian, who brought up Nelson, is that he is insane; the evidence of the documents is that he is insane, was found so by a court of competent jurisdiction, and was ordered confined to an asylum; and all the Crown has to offer in rebuttal is—'well, he is mentally inferior, a constitutional psychopath, a borderline case, not with psychosis now, but he might have psychosis of any degree at times?' And I ask you what ought the verdict of the jury to have been, surely nothing less than 'Not guilty on account of insanity'?"

Stitt acknowledged that Mary Fuller and Lillian Fabian might have had reason to lie. After all, they were Nelson's closest and most loyal relations. But "I maintain there is nothing fantastic or far-fetched in their story. The first instruction I gave to these women was to tell the truth and nothing but the truth, and to tell it without exaggeration. This counsel was, I believe, absolutely adhered to. What a story could they not have told had they been willing to lie, for who was there to contradict them? But such a story was not told, was never considered for a moment. . . . The question of the integrity of these women was never raised at the trial."

If anything, the two women had withheld some information that would have painted an even more disturbing picture of Nelson. It was not until after the trial, for example, that a red-faced Mrs. Fuller revealed to Stitt "that the accused was an exhibitionist and . . . that he even masturbated in bed with his own wife. These were among the reasons she left him."

There was one other fact relating to Mary Fuller that, as far as Stitt was concerned, proved something significant about Nelson's mental status: "The wife of the accused is 64 years of age—66 years of age!—whereas Nelson is 30 years of age at the present moment. They were married in 1919, eight years ago, which would leave the condemned man at that time 22 years of age and his bride 58. That certainly appeals to me as being evidence of insanity."

Stitt then addressed another question which might arise "in the mind of the reader" (and which certainly didn't reflect well on the reputation of the U.S. legal system): "Must you not pay little attention to American court records, for does not wealth often subvert justice there?"

Stitt's response was that—though "American court records may not be very reliable"—the "order declaring Nelson insane by the Superior Court of San Francisco was not the only or the first declaration of Nelson's insanity." Nelson had been declared insane by naval authorities as early as 1918, when he was confined to the Mare Island Naval Hospital.

"Now there can be no question of money or influence affecting the commitment by the naval authorities," Stitt argued. "My experience of military life—and I had three years of it—is that precious little malingering was successful there, and I presume that what applies to the army is true of the navy in this regard. Moreover, my experience was that if a man was unfit for service, he was discharged. But not so with Nelson. He was not only unfit for service but unfit for life, and the authorities could not take a chance and discharge an insane person. Therefore, he was committed to the asylum."

After spending about ten pages dissecting the flaws in Mathers' testimony, Stitt advanced the same argument that had been made by the writer of "A Double Tragedy": that the outrageously vicious nature of Nelson's crimes was *"itself evidence of insanity."*

"What other hypothesis can the mind conjure up explanatory of the facts?" Stitt asked. "You can hardly dismiss the crime and say it is simply a case of utter degradation; for it is more than that, it is disordered conduct, abnormal emotion—or the complete and utter lack of it—coupled with the annihilation of the moral faculty. And, in fact, it does seem to me that this case illustrates above all else a creature made in the image of God but lacking altogether moral consciousness.

"It is true that defenseless women have been throttled to death to cover up the traces of crime, in cases of robbery, for example," Stitt allowed. "But what criminal rapes the body of his helpless victim at the same time, or afterward when life has vanished? Then, when the act is completed, calmly dresses in the room where his victim lies dead, without hurry, and then shows no immediate anxiety to escape detection, but wanders around from secondhand store to clothing store, from barbershop to restaurant, irresponsibly garrulous, acting like a child? Whilst all the time another victim, a helpless child, lies cold in death, waiting for discovery to break the awful silence and proclaim him a double murderer.

"There's only one explanation under Heaven—insanity, mania, madness itself shrieks its name in our ears!"

Stitt proceeded to discuss other, physiological factors— Nelson's head injury, the evidence of syphilis, the possibility of "masked epilepsy"—before turning to the issue of prejudicial publicity. "Everybody was biased," he exclaimed. "Do you know that over 50,000 extra papers of the *Free Press* were sold on the day of his capture. Fear stalked in every unprotected home in Winnipeg during the week of the manhunt, and from not a few vicinities there was a general emigration of womanhood. . . . At the trial, all the jurors were challenged for cause; some openly stated that they could not give him a fair trial. Those who said they could admitted they had read the papers. What man of red blood, having read the news, could go in scorn of prejudice and seek justice in a quiet way? There is not a lawyer in Winnipeg who has not said words to me of this effect: 'The jury's verdict was written by the newspapers for them. There could be no other verdict under the circumstances.' "

After urging that Nelson be reprieved on the grounds of "moral imbecility" and "relegated to special treatment," Stitt (who composed both poetry and music in his spare time) concluded with a deeply impassioned plea whose soaring language stood in marked contrast to the dry, formal diction of most legal writings.

"It has been told to me that any effort to save the life of an accused such as Nelson is vain, and the reason advanced has been that his life is not worth saving in the first place; and in the second, no advisor of His Majesty would have the temerity to bring upon himself such public displeasure as would ensue from the grant of a reprieve.

"Let me conclude by saying such conceptions of justice are not mine and are, I know, utterly foreign and repugnant to the chief executives of my country. Ten years ago, I left the plains of France, where my countrymen engaged in an assault at arms to vindicate the message of the Prince of Peace to a world of men weary of injustice. Many of them now sleep among the lilies of that foreign land. But the principles for which they died are pure and eternal.

"It is therefore in the light of those principles that I pen this argument. In the light of that justice which has come by the road of the common law for upwards of a thousand years, I crave your careful consideration. May justice not be mocked by her own process in this, our beloved country, but may her healing and beneficent rays be extended unto every man—even unto the least of these my brethren."

Clearly, Earle Leonard Nelson couldn't have asked for a finer advocate. But all the eloquence in the world couldn't save him. On Tuesday, January 3, 1928, the *Manitoba Free Press* reassured its readers that (as the headline put it) "Clemency Is Not Expected for Nelson."

That prediction came true eight days later, when—after reviewing all the relevant material—the federal cabinet decided not to interfere. Official word reached Winnipeg on Wednesday afternoon, January 11, when Attorney General W. J. Major received a telegram from Thomas Mulvey, under secretary of state. The message read: LAW WILL TAKE ITS COURSE IN THE CAPITAL CASE OF EARLE NELSON ALIAS VIRGIL WILSON SENTENCED TO BE EXECUTED JANUARY 13.

Whether Nelson was insane, according to legal definitions, is a question that will never be conclusively resolved, but he certainly wasn't deluded about his chances for survival.

Hearing the news in his cell shortly after Mulvey's telegram arrived, he merely shrugged, gave a little sigh, and said, "That's what I expected."

52

✠

Whoso walketh uprightly shall be saved; but he that is
perverse in his ways shall fall at once.

Prov. 28:14

A few hours after Nelson received the bad news, a gray-
haired, birdlike little man checked into a downtown hotel in
Winnipeg, having just arrived from his home in Vancouver.
Peering through thick-lensed, gold-rimmed spectacles, he
signed the register under an assumed name—his standard
practice whenever he was engaged in official business. The
sixty-year-old gentleman preferred to remain anonymous,
since his presence, as he had learned over the course of his
long career, tended to make people extremely uneasy.

His true name was Arthur Ellis, and he was the official
executioner of the Dominion of Canada.

Ellis spent part of the following day, Thursday, January
12, inspecting the scaffold that stood in the jail yard. A
thoroughgoing professional, he also visited the condemned
man in his cell, to size up Nelson's stature and weight.

Afterwards, Ellis was interviewed by reporters from the
city's dailies. His precise words were never printed, but in
its evening edition, the *Free Press* summed up the gist of his
remarks. "Regarding Nelson's crimes as the most horrible
he has ever known," the paper reported, "the hangman expressed keener anticipation at carrying out this execution
than any other in his history."

*   *   *

Ellis wasn't the only one looking forward to Nelson's execution. For weeks, the sheriff's office had been swamped with requests from people eager to witness the hanging. The letters poured in from near and far. One particularly pressing appeal came from a woman in Minneapolis.

Regarding these applicants as little more than ghouls, the sheriff consigned all their letters to the trash bin. "Only those whose duty calls them there," he announced on Thursday afternoon, "will be present at the hanging."

Barred from the big event, a bunch of rubberneckers gathered outside the jail on Thursday morning, hoping to catch one last glimpse of the "Strangler" through his cell window. Guards were posted on the street to maintain order, but aside from their unabashed prurience, the gawkers were perfectly well-behaved. For the most part, they did nothing but mill on the sidewalk and peer eagerly up at the barred window.

One or two of the bolder women cupped their hands to their mouths and shouted Nelson's name, but their calls went unanswered. When it finally became clear that the condemned man had no intention of coming to the window, most of the crowd began drifting away, leaving only a few diehard curiosity seekers, who remained throughout the day.

There *was* one vantage point from which spectators could watch Nelson swing, even without an official invitation. As far back as June, right after Nelson's arrest, officials had expressed concern about the proximity of the jail to the University of Manitoba, whose main building directly overlooked the courtyard where hangings took place. These officials believed that the mere sight of the gallows would be intensely distressing to the students.

In point of fact, the students were so excited about the hanging that a bunch of them planned to sneak into the upper-floor rooms of the building and watch the execution through the windows. Much to their disappointment, the university president got wind of this scheme and issued an immediate warning:

"Swift and stern," he proclaimed on Thursday afternoon, "will be the end of the career of any university students who attempt to witness the execution of Earle Nelson tomorrow morning. Any students who attempt to reach rooms overlooking the jail yard at the time of the hanging will face instant expulsion."

While the city buzzed with excitement over his impending death, Nelson himself remained remarkably calm throughout Thursday. For much of the day, he was attended by his "spiritual advisor," a priest named J. A. Webb.

At the urging of his wife, Mary, who had written to him regularly since her return to California, Nelson had converted to Catholicism in early December, when he was baptized in his cell by Father Webb. Since then, he had continued to receive instruction in the fundamentals of his newly adopted faith.

Besides Father Webb (and, briefly, hangman Ellis), Nelson had a number of visitors throughout Thursday. In mid-afternoon, he agreed to see William McConnell, whose wife, Mary, was the sixteenth murder victim officially attributed to the "Dark Strangler." Desperate for what we now call "closure," McConnell had made the long trip from Philadelphia in the hope of securing a confession from Nelson.

But Nelson refused to oblige. "I have no confession to make," he insisted. "I did not do the deed." He had never been to Philadelphia in his life; indeed, he had never travelled "east of Nevada." The whole thing was a "frame-up," he told McConnell. "I just hope for your sake that the real guilty party will be caught one day and pay the penalty."

After nearly two futile hours, McConnell finally gave up. Though the Philadelphian had every reason to abominate Nelson, he somehow found it in his heart to forgive him. "I hope he's made his peace with God," he told reporters afterwards. "From the bottom of my heart I forgive him. I think he's insane. I have no malice whatever against the man."

Nelson displayed the same heartless obstinacy towards another bereaved visitor, Lola Cowan's mother, Randy. Like William McConnell, Mrs. Cowan was seeking whatever solace could be derived from the conclusive knowledge that Nelson was the killer. But she, too, came away empty-handed. "I never saw the child," Nelson maintained, insisting that he had never even been in Winnipeg before his arrest.

* * *

Nelson granted one more interview that afternoon, to a reporter from the *Free Press*. Once again he protested his innocence. Speaking in "the most solemn tones," he declared that "God in his own good time will disclose the guilty parties to the world." He appealed to the reporter to "proclaim to the people of Canada and the United States" that he was "the victim of circumstances.

"Before God and man I am innocent," he avowed. "I am ready to meet my God, who I'm sure will have pity on me for everything I've suffered."

When the reporter suggested to Nelson that he was "on the brink of eternity" and ought to avail himself of this final opportunity to unburden himself, Nelson became even more emphatic. "Why should I lie?" he exclaimed. "Tomorrow morning I'm going to hang. There's no hope of saving my body, and I'm certainly not going to do anything to hurt my soul. I swear to you, I'm telling the truth. I never murdered anybody—never, never, never!"

Seated on the edge of his cot, he gave a deep, self-pitying sigh. "I've been unfortunate from the day of my birth," he said. "I've been handicapped by the sins of my parents, who left a taint in my blood that's caused me all kinds of agony of body and mind. They blame me for attacking women in my earlier years. But that's untrue! I never did so. Women as such never even interested me. I was never anxious to be among them."

"Is it possible that you committed the crimes when your mind wasn't functioning normally," asked the reporter, "and that you've completely forgotten the facts?"

"No, sir," Nelson replied, shaking his head vehemently. "That's absolutely impossible. I am innocent—innocent!" Here, he gave the reporter an imploring look. "Don't you believe me?"

"Well," said the newsman. "The jury found you guilty. And the evidence against you looked pretty strong."

"I know that," Nelson admitted. "But I was wrongly identified by people who didn't realize what they were doing."

The reporter had just one more question to pose. "Are you afraid to die, Nelson?"

The condemned man took a moment to reply. "Life is sweet," he said earnestly. "Like everyone else, I prefer to live—but only long enough to clear my name. I've thought everything over and—you know what?—I think God is good to take me away. If I lived, the law would just send me away to the penitentiary for life. Or to an insane asylum. I don't want that. I'd rather die than be locked up with hardened criminals or madmen."

Here, his eyes took on a dreamy look. "Tomorrow morning, I expect to be in Heaven. There are no detectives or policemen up there—only the good. Maybe I'll finally find the peace and happiness that have been denied me here on earth."

Not long after the interview ended, a guard brought Neson his final supper, which he consumed with his usual gusto—grapefruit, liver and bacon, apple pie, and coffee.

At around 9:00 P.M., an unusual ceremony took place in his cell, when His Grace Archbishop Sinnott arrived to administer the sacrament of confirmation. Never before had this rite been conducted within the precincts of the provincial jail, and various guards and prison officials crowded around the open door of the death cell to watch as Nelson was confirmed.

Afterwards, the archbishop spent several moments quietly conferring with Nelson. When the cleric departed at around 9:45, Father Webb seated himself on the cot beside Nelson and opened his Bible.

The two men spent the rest of the night reading and discussing passages from Scripture. From Nelson's tranquil demeanor, an observer would never have guessed that his death was so near—that, within a few hours, on the morning of Friday the thirteenth, he would mount the thirteen steps of the scaffold and (as the newspapers never tired of pointing out) become "the thirteenth man to be hanged for murder on the gallows of the provincial jail."

At 5:00 A.M., Father Webb, assisted by another priest named Holloway, conducted a mass. Nelson received Holy Communion. Another mass was said at 5:30.

Shortly afterwards, a guard brought Nelson a tray holding a light breakfast of toast and tea. Nelson calmly consumed his last meal.

A crowd of people—some of whom were authorized witnesses, others who were there simply to satisfy their morbid curiosity—had gathered outside the jail at daybreak. At approximately 7:30 A.M. a prison official appeared to admit the former into the courtyard, where the scaffold, partly enclosed by a tentlike canvas shield, hulked against a grimy, far wall.

The spectators spoke in hushed whispers as they huddled at the foot of the gallows. Suddenly, their murmuring ceased. The hangman, Arthur Ellis, had materialized. Mounting the scaffold stairs, he made a last-minute inspection of the apparatus, then asked that the condemned man be brought out.

All eyes turned to the door through which Nelson would emerge. He appeared a moment later, arms strapped behind him, flanked by a pair of burly guards, and followed by the two chanting priests. He was dressed in a collarless shirt, blue serge trousers, tan shoes, and stockings. His face was pale, hair unbrushed, his face unshaven.

With Father Webb at his heels, he climbed to the top of the scaffold, took his place at the center of the trapdoor, then turned and faced the assembled crowd. After holding out a cross for him to kiss, Father Webb murmured a few final words to Nelson and descended the stairs, while the hangman adjusted the noose around the condemned man's neck.

Asked if he had any last words, Nelson—speaking in a clear, firm voice—said, "I declare my innocence before God and man. I forgive those who have injured me and I ask pardon from those I have injured. May the Lord have mercy on my soul."

No sooner were these words out of his mouth than Ellis slipped a black hood over the prisoner's head, stepped away from the trap, and drew the bolt. The trap crashed open, and Earle Leonard Nelson plunged through the hole.

The hooded, pinioned figure fell, bounced, dropped again. Neck broken, head cocked at a grotesque angle, he spun lazily in the shadows beneath the scaffold, his limbs giving an occasional spasmodic twitch.

Stepping up to the body, hangman Ellis removed the leather straps from Nelson's wrists. In spite of his long experience, he seemed strangely unsettled, his hands shaking visibly as he undid the restraints.

When the straps were off, the prison physician, Dr. J. A. McArthur, strode up to the body and felt Nelson's pulse. Though the evening papers would report that "death was instantaneous," it wasn't until 7:52 A.M., eleven full minutes after Nelson took the plunge, that Dr. McArthur turned to the witnesses and said, "It's over." A black flag was promptly hoisted on the prison tower to signal that the execution had been carried out.

Minutes after the corpse was cut down and transported to the prison morgue, the coroner's jury returned its verdict. The official cause of Earle Nelson's demise, fittingly enough, was "death by strangulation."

EPILOGUE

Less than nine hours before Nelson's execution, a pair of onetime lovebirds named Ruth Snyder and Judd Gray, the principal figures in one of the most sensational murder cases of the twentieth century, were put to death in the electric chair of New York's Sing Sing prison.

At the time of her arrest, Snyder—a voluptuous blonde with baby blue eyes and a lantern jaw—had been unhappily married for thirteen years to an overbearing art editor named Albert. A perennial "party girl" who looked much younger than her thirty-odd years, she had been seeking solace from her domestic misery in the arms of assorted lovers.

In 1925 she was introduced to a mousy, myopic, thirty-two-year-old mama's boy named Judd Gray, who made his living as a corset salesman. Before long, they were involved in a torrid affair—meeting clandestinely in Manhattan hotel rooms, exchanging love letters composed in cloying baby talk, addressing each other by saccharine nicknames. To Judd, the domineering, brazenly sexual Snyder was his "Momsie"; she called her Milquetoast paramour "Lover Boy."

One year after meeting Gray, Snyder resolved to do away with her detested husband. After tricking him into taking out a $48,000 life insurance policy with a double indemnity clause, she set about trying to kill him: spiking his whiskey with bichloride of mercury, sprinkling poison on his prune whip, piping gas into his bedroom while he slept. Snyder not only survived these attempts; in spite of his wife's barely disguised abhorrence, he apparently never suspected her.

Finally, the "Granite Woman" (as the tabloids would eventually dub her) decided to enlist her lover's help. Though Gray was genuinely appalled when his "Momsie" first broached the subject, he was helplessly in her thrall. (The tabloids would brand him the "Putty Man.") In the early hours of Sunday, March 20, 1927, they put their plan into effect.

Fortified with enough bootleg liquor to intoxicate a dray horse and armed with a heavy iron sash weight, Gray snuck into the Snyder home after dark, entering through a side door Ruth had left unlatched. When the victim was soundly asleep, Gray crept into the Snyders' bedroom and brought the bludgeon down on the sleeping man's head. The blow was so weak, however, that it only caused Albert Snyder to sit up with a roar and grab his assailant by the necktie.

"Momsie!" screamed Gray. "For God's sake, help!"

Rushing to the bedside, Ruth grabbed the sash weight from her "Lover Boy's" hand and delivered a crushing blow to her husband's skull. Albert Snyder subsided onto the bed with a shuddering moan. For good measure, the assassins garrotted him with a wire and stuffed chloroform-soaked rags up his nostrils.

Putting the second phase of their scheme into action, the pair proceeded to ransack the house to make it look as if Snyder had been killed in the course of a break-in. They upended furniture, opened drawers, even ripped the stuffing out of pillows. Ruth wanted Gray to make off with her jewels but, for unexplained reasons, he refused. They settled for hiding her valuables under her mattress and stashing her fur coat in a bag inside her closet. Their clever idea for disposing of the bloody murder weapon was to rub it with ashes and stick it in Albert Snyder's basement tool chest.

Though Ruth urged Gray to knock her unconscious, he couldn't bring himself to hurt her. Instead, he bound her wrists and ankles, gagged her with cheesecloth, and made off into the night.

A few hours later, at around 7:30 A.M., Ruth dragged herself to her sleeping daughter's bedroom and managed to rouse the eleven-year-old child, who immediately summoned help. Though Ruth stuck to her prerehearsed story, police were wise to her from the start. All the evidence was against her. Burglars are not known for knocking over armchairs and tearing open pillows in their search for booty. And Ruth's claim of being knocked unconscious by the intruder failed to persuade the medical examiner, who was unable to detect a single contusion on her scalp. Her cause wasn't helped when detectives turned up her "stolen" jewelry underneath her mattress, found the blood-stained murder weapon in her husband's tool chest, and discovered a tie tack with the initials "J.G." at the foot of Albert Snyder's bed. The bumbling conspirators were in custody within twenty-four hours.

The Snyder-Gray case, which broke just a few months after the conclusion of the Hall-Mills murder trial, became an immediate cause célèbre, not only in America but throughout the world. Ruth Snyder instantly became the most reviled woman of her time—the Whore of Babylon in the guise of a buxom Queens housewife. The Snyder-Gray trial—attended by such Jazz Age celebrities as David Belasco, D. W. Griffith, Sister Aimee Semple McPherson, the Rev. Billy Sunday, Damon Runyan, Will Durant, and others—received almost as much attention as the Lindbergh flight and was rich in both lurid melodrama and coarse comedy, particularly when Ruth was on the stand. (In one memorable exchange, Assistant District Attorney Charles W. Froessel—trying to establish Ruth's earlier affair with a man named Lesser—asked, "Did you know Mr. Lesser carnally?" "Yes," Ruth replied. "But only in a business way.")

Public sentiment was so inflamed against Ruth that after she and Gray were convicted and sentenced to death, every member of the Court of Appeals received a copy of the following postcard:

COURT OF APPEALS, QUEENS COUNTY
JUDGES:

We will shoot you if you let that Snyder woman go free. She must be electrocuted. The public demands it. If she is not done away with, other women would do the same thing. She must be made an example of. We are watching out.

THE PUBLIC

The public got its wish. Shortly after 11:00 P.M. on Thursday, January 12, 1928, Ruth went to the chair, followed eight minutes later by Gray. As it happened, one of the witnesses, a *New York Daily News* reporter named Thomas Howard, showed up at the execution with a small camera secretly strapped to his ankle. Casually crossing his leg, he waited until the executioner threw the switch, then released the shutter button with a cable that ran down his pants leg. The resulting photograph, a blurry shot of Ruth Snyder's body stiffening as the current coursed through it, was featured on the front page of the *Daily News,* becoming the most infamous picture in the history of tabloid journalism.

So all-consuming was the public's obsession with the "Granite Woman" and her hapless "Lover Boy" that, in spite of Earle Nelson's own notoriety, his death was barely noted by the U.S. news media. The "Gorilla Man's" hanging had been completely overshadowed by the two most highly publicized and eagerly anticipated executions of the twentieth century.

In Canada, however, the situation was different. Though the electrocution of Ruth Snyder and Judd Gray was front-page news even in Manitoba, the "Gorilla Man's" death was the main story of the day. Indeed, the Nelson case would continue to stir the passions of Winnipeggers for several weeks after his execution.

Immediately after the hanging, the Reverend Father Webb, acting on behalf of Lillian Fabian and Mary Fuller, claimed Nelson's corpse and arranged for its transportation to a funeral home called Barker's, where, after receiving the usual ministrations, it was laid in an open gray coffin and displayed in the parlor chapel. Affixed to the coffin, at Lillian Fabian's request, was a small brass plaque engraved with the dead man's real name, Earle L. Ferral.

Within a short time, word had spread throughout the city that the "Gorilla Man's" corpse was available for viewing.

By 6:00 P.M., more than 1,000 people had gathered at the funeral home. Special constables were dispatched to the scene to maintain order. It was almost midnight before the last of the curiosity seekers filed past the coffin.

By eight the next morning, Saturday, January 14, 1928, a fresh crowd had assembled at Barker's, eager to get a final glimpse of "the man whose crimes had repulsed the world" (as one reporter wrote). A front-page article about the viewing appeared in that morning's edition of the *Manitoba Free Press*. "Never before in the history of Winnipeg has such widespread curiosity been manifested by the public to view a criminal's body," the article stated.

Reading the newspaper at his desk that morning, Attorney General W. J. Major was deeply distressed by this report. Summoning Deputy Attorney John Allen to his office, Major vented his feelings in the most emphatic terms.

Allen immediately repaired to his office and telephoned Mr. Barker to convey the attorney general's displeasure at the "revolting practice."

"I am only giving the public what it wants," Barker protested.

"Surely you must understand that you have no such right," Allen said firmly. "The body does not belong to you. It belongs to Nelson's estate, and I feel certain that if his wife were here, she would not permit this ghoulish exhibition."

"That may well be the case," Barker acknowledged.

Allen's tone grew stern. "Are you, perchance, charging the public any money for an opportunity to view the body?"

"I resent that question," Barker huffed.

"I am sure you do. But you still haven't answered it."

Barker indignantly denied that he was charging an admission fee.

"Mr. Barker," said Allen, "the attorney general and I will expect you to prevent the public from viewing Nelson's body. Otherwise, the police will be sent to your premises at once."

After reporting this conversation to Attorney General Major, Allen telephoned Chief Constable Newton. Within minutes, a special contingent of constables was at Barker's. This time, however, the police were there not to keep the crowd under control, but to disperse it. By noon, the morbid show had been shut down for good.

The incident, however, continued to reverberate. For the next two weeks, the city's newspapers were swamped with letters from outraged citizens, decrying the "awful show that was made of the notorious Nelson." A typical example appeared in the January 18 issue of the *Winnipeg Tribune*:

To the Editor:

Sir,—Can it be possible that the authorities allowed the body of the notorious criminal who was hanged last week to be made a sordid show of here? Can this be allowed in Canada?

Of course, a lack of Christian feeling and fine breeding can do a great many unheard-of things. But that the body of a criminal should be treated rather as that of a hero is a blot on our city which should not be allowed to pass without protest.

The authorities should have seen to it that this man's remains were sent as speedily and quietly as possible to his relatives in the United States. It is to be hoped our mayor will prohibit any further copying of sordid, morbid fashions in this city in the future. I hope many protests will be sent by our citizens and societies so that such a blot can never besmirch our British city again.

"DISGUSTED CITIZEN"

Many other letters objected to the hanging itself, condemning the practice as a "relic of the Dark Ages" and urging that, as one citizen put it, "some other, less barbaric method be found. If a murderer resorts to the most terrible way of killing his victim or victims, is it becoming to the State to pay him back in savage kind? I do not think so. Kill the murderer, if the state so decrees, but electrocute him, or shoot him; almost any method, save the brutality of hanging with all its attendant gruesomeness."

By the time these letters were published, however, the corpse that had prompted them was long gone from Canada. Placed in a metal-lined box and loaded onto a train at the Union depot, the plain gray coffin had departed from Winnipeg late Saturday afternoon, one day after the execution. "Back over the long trail which he left strewn with death and misery" (in the words of one reporter), the "Gorilla Man's" body had been carried by rail to his birthplace, San Francisco.

There, in the early morning hours of Sunday, January 15, 1928, it was received by Lillian Fabian and Mary Fuller, Earle Leonard Ferral's only mourners.

SOURCES AND
ACKNOWLEDGMENTS

✝

The versions of Earle Nelson's life found in most histories of American crime aren't entirely trustworthy (they often have him born in Philadelphia, raised by an old, fanatical aunt, and married to a lovely young woman). The best brief account of his case appears in L. C. Douthwaite's classic study *Mass Murder* (New York: Henry Holt, 1929), published just one year after Nelson's execution.

To reconstruct the "Gorilla Man's" cross-country murder spree, I relied primarily on the following newspapers: the *San Francisco Chronicle*, the *Santa Barbara Daily News*, the *Portland Oregonian*, the *Seattle Times*, the *Kansas City Star*, the *Council Bluffs Nonpareil*, the *Chicago Tribune*, the *Detroit News*, the *Buffalo Courier Express*, the *Philadelphia Inquirer*, the *Manitoba Free Press*, the *Winnipeg Tribune*, and the *New York Times*.

My descriptions of the 1920s were likewise drawn from newspapers and periodicals of the era, as well as from assorted social histories, including the following: Frederick Lewis Allen, *Only Yesterday* (New York: Harper & Row, 1931); Ann Douglas, *Terrible Honesty* (New York: Farrar, Straus and Giroux, 1995); James H. Gray, *The Roar of the Twenties* (Toronto: Macmillan of Canada, 1978); and Paul Sann, *The Lawless Decade* (New York: Bonanza Books, 1957).

For information on specific subjects (such as the San Francisco earthquake, Harry Houdini, the Scopes "Monkey Trial," the horrors of the Great War, the quasiscientific theories of Cesare Lombroso, and the Snyder-Gray and Hall-Mills cases), I consulted the following: William Bronson, *The Earth Shook, the Sky Burned* (Garden City, N.Y.: Doubleday, 1959); Milbourne Christopher, *Houdini: The Untold Story* (New York: Thomas Y. Crowell, 1969); L. Sprague de Camp, *The Great Monkey Trial* (Garden City, N.Y.: Doubleday, 1968); Paul Fussell, *The Great War in Modern Memory* (New York: Oxford University Press, 1975); Martin Gilbert, *The First World War* (New York: Henry Holt, 1994); Stephen Jay Gould, *The Mismeasure of Man* (New York: Norton, 1981); John Kobler, *The Trial of Ruth Snyder and Judd Gray* (Garden City, N.Y.: Doubleday, Doran, 1938); and William Kunstler, *The Minister and the Choir Singer* (New York: William Morrow, 1964).

I owe special thanks to a number of people in Winnipeg and elsewhere in Canada for their help and generosity. Foremost among these is Larry Halcro, who graciously shared his own extensive knowledge of the case, gave me access to his private collection of Nelson papers, and assisted me in tracking down some obscure but vital information. I am also grateful to Professor Alvin Esau, Faculty of Law, University of Manitoba, who provided me with a mountain of material, including a complete trial transcript and other legal documents, that proved indispensable.

Others to whom I am indebted include: Cameron Harvey of the Archives of Western Canadian Legal History; Janet Murray of the National Archives of Canada; Gerry Berkowski, Peter Bower, and Nancy Stunden of the Provincial Archives of Manitoba; Annie Vialard of the Winnipeg Medical College; Ab Brereton; and Mary Shelton, daughter of Dr. Alvin Mathers.

As has been the case with every book in this series, I received significant support from my friend and researcher Catharine Ostlind. My thanks also to Mike Wilk for his usual, unhesitating generosity, to John E. Vetter, and to Nancy Ferrara.

the A to Z Encyclopedia of Serial Killers

Harold Schechter
and David Everitt

"Harold Schechter combines the graphic style of a horror novelist with a keen eye for bizarre material....One of the few names that guarantee quality."

—John Marr, *The Bay Guardian* (San Francisco)

Available
from Pocket Books Trade

POCKET
B O O K S

1231-01